The Death of
Right and Wrong

The Death of Right and Wrong

Exposing the Left's Assault on Our Culture and Values

TAMMY BRUCE

THREE RIVERS PRESS • NEW YORK

The author can be contacted at heytammybruce@yahoo.com.

Published by Three Rivers Press, New York, New York.
Member of the Crown Publishing Group, a division of Random House, Inc.
www.crownpublishing.com

THREE RIVERS PRESS and the Tugboat design are registered trademarks of Random House, Inc.

Originally published in hardcover by Prima Forum in 2003.

Design by Susan Sugnet

Library of Congress Cataloging-in-Publication Data
Bruce, Tammy.
    The death of right and wrong : exposing the left's assault on our culture and values / Tammy Bruce.
    Includes index.
    1. United States—Moral conditions. 2. Social values—United States.
3. Social ethics—United States. 4. Culture conflict—United States.
5. Liberalism—United States. I. Title.
HN90.M6 B78   2003
306'.0973—dc21   2002155837

ISBN 978-1-4000-5294-3

First Paperback Edition

For all Classical Liberals
who know the ideals of the American Dream
—including decency, freedom, and individual liberty—
are not contradictory and are absolutely worth fighting for.

Contents

Acknowledgments

When I first spoke with my publisher about this book, I made sure that I would have the same team with me that helped make my first book, *The New Thought Police*, not only a success, but a wonderful experience. I knew writing this book would not be easy because of the subject matter and how deeply I felt about the importance of the message. I also knew I needed a group of people who were not only the best in the business, but who were kind, decent, and as committed to making a difference as I.

First, David Richardson, my editor, who was adventurous enough to trust this lesbian feminist when I said I wanted to write a book about values and morality. He took a deep breath (I heard it) and then went to work so I could get this done. Thank you, David, for being such a wonderful, creative, and courageous man.

Special thanks to Linda Bridges, in all her brilliance, for helping me craft my ideas and the words that express them in just the right way. Linda kept me focused, challenged me, questioned me, and on more than a few occasions kept me down to Earth and from dizzying you with theory.

Libby Larson, my project manager, watched over all the commotion involved with writing this book, kept me on track, and knew when to push me. Libby was extraordinarily gracious when dealing with issues from the monumental to the seemingly not-so-big; she took every issue as seriously as I. Thank you, Libby.

Thank you, David Horowitz, president of the Center for the Study of Popular Culture and FrontPageMag.com, for helping to make work like mine possible, and for the pleasure of allowing me to be a FrontPageMag.com columnist.

The terrific people at NewsMax.com also deserve a special thank you for their ongoing support and encouragement of my work. Chris Ruddy, Sandy Frazier, and Rita Samols, thank you so much for your terrific work and for the honor of being a NewsMax.com pundit.

To my best friends, who, in the process of my writing this book, once again endured month after month of my being a hermit, hunched over my iMac and being less than a perfect friend. Broken dinner and lunch dates, and e-mails and phone calls from me at hours far too late for a normal person were among so many other irritations and intrusions. What they've endured has been, well, challenging. Thank you, Monty Warner, David Trulio, June Bundy Csida, Stephen Densmore, Max Reinhart, and Sadie Bruce, for being there no matter what (and there was plenty of 'what'). And especially thanks to my significant other, Maria, who has put up with the most, giving me the time and space to do this work. Thank you, my dear.

And thanks to Dr. Laura Schlessinger and her husband, Dr. Lew Bishop, for once again giving me the courage to do what was right. Their friendship has been an extraordinary gift. It is an honor and a pleasure to know them.

And finally to you, my readers, who continue to inspire me to make a difference and who, ultimately, make all this work possible. Thanks for being there.

Introduction

Dinner with Dr. Laura

I never really wanted to tell the story I'm about to tell in this introduction. I was urged to do so by Dr. Laura Schlessinger, the vastly popular radio talk show host and bestselling author. Laura and I first got to know each other when we hosted radio programs at the same station in Los Angeles. Against all odds, coming as we do from opposite ends of the political spectrum, she and I gradually became good friends. I admire her greatly, and I think I can say we add some spice to each other's lives!

One evening I was discussing the idea for this book with Laura and her husband, Lew, over dinner at their home. I was complaining about the increase of moral relativism in society and the Left's complicity in it, and the hypocrisy and double standards of people in power. Laura, not as cynical as I, was disappointed at how easy lying was for some people. I, however, had the answer. "Nothing is what it seems," I brazenly offered. One thing I knew, I said, was that "people lead one life in public and another in private." This, you see, is what I had learned from my life experience.

Laura, on the other hand, *is* who she is. There is no strange underworld in the life of Laura Schlessinger. What you see is what you get. She asked me why I believed what I did. She also asked me about my newly expressed interest in issues of morality. I then told her the story I'm about to share with you.

Shocked by this story—which I had never told before, although some reporters and others have guessed at it for over 20 years—Laura said I would need to be completely honest about my life if I was going to write a book calling the powerful on the carpet for being hypocrites and twisting issues of morality. If I didn't, she warned, I would be nothing more than a hypocrite myself. Laura appreciated the insight I had gained as I got older about the necessity of values, and she counseled me to make sure you knew how it came about.

The Convenience of Deception

Frankly, I never expected to reach my 36th birthday. Why? Thirty-six was an important milestone for me because it was the age of my first partner—ah, the euphemisms! my first lesbian lover—when she committed suicide. The start of that relationship changed my life, as did its end.

It was April 7, 1982. I was 19 years old and on my way to a lunch date with Brenda Benét, a featured actress on the NBC daytime soap opera *Days of Our Lives,* and the ex-wife of TV star and producer Bill Bixby. Brenda and I had become lovers when I was just 17. It was a clandestine, closeted relationship, to be shared, as she instructed me, with no one. Brenda wanted what she wanted, but she also needed to hide the relationship in order to maintain the image she had created for her friends and, most importantly, for her colleagues and fans.

I realize now that this was the message conveyed to my teenage mind: You must not let personal responsibility, let alone morality, get in the way of what you want. It was this duality with which I was conditioned to believe—as I parroted 20 years later to Laura—that nothing is what it seems, people lie about who they really are, and deception is a normal part of life.

I had been living with Brenda for nearly a year when, two weeks before that lunch date, I moved out of the house. Life with Brenda had simply become too difficult. Later I realized she was pushing me out with a pattern of behavior that included alcoholism, sexual promiscuity, and the entry into her life of a man who, she told me, regularly beat her.

Brenda was, to say the least, self-destructive. She was also an extraordinarily beautiful woman, charming, smart, and charismatic. Her stormy marriage to Bill Bixby had ended in divorce, and she remained tortured over the loss of her son, Christopher, who had died at age seven in a bizarre medical accident. Brenda never truly recovered from that shock, and at one point she told me I was her "last hope." A pretty heavy thing to say to a 17-year-old—although at the time I couldn't fathom exactly what she meant. Our lunch date was meant to help us forge a friendship after the ending of our relationship. At least, that's what I thought. For Brenda it was no lunch date.

Arriving at her house, I let myself in. I found the door to the downstairs bathroom (the one I most often used) closed and the house in silence. I called out and got no response, although I was sure she was in that bathroom. I tried the door, but it was locked. I begged her to come out. In my teenage mind I had sensed all along the possibility that Brenda would try suicide, but it was never discussed. In that moment as I stood in the foyer, I knew we were in trouble.

As I backed away from the door I told her nothing was so awful that it couldn't be handled. I said I would be calling the police. I was more scared than at any other time in my life.

I stepped out of the house and closed the front door, intending to go to a neighbor for help. As I went up the steps to the gate I heard the gunshot. Brenda had heard me, listened to my pleas, waited for me to leave, and then shot herself.

None of the neighbors were home, so, in terror, I went back into the house and called the police from there. I sat alone in the dining room, knowing Brenda was likely dead just behind the locked bathroom door. It couldn't have been more than a few minutes before the phone rang. It was syndicated newspaper entertainment columnist Marilyn Beck. Brenda had given Marilyn an interview the week before, and it was scheduled to run in a few days. Now Marilyn was laughing. "Tammy, I just got the oddest phone call from NBC asking me to not run my interview with Brenda. They said she had just killed herself! Can you believe that?!"

You may be wondering, as I was, how Marilyn Beck had heard of Brenda's death so quickly. This would become one of my enduring lessons about people, Hollywood, and the media. I found out later that when the call for a squad car and for an ambulance went out over the police radio, a local Santa Monica reporter who was routinely monitoring the dispatches recognized Brenda's address. The reporter thought to call NBC to see if they knew anything.

It was no secret that Brenda had not really dealt with Christopher's death, and so when the NBC press person received the call, she presumed Brenda had killed herself (go figure). In classic Hollywood fashion, the flack didn't bother to call the house to confirm but thought immediately of the interview she had to stop. She called Marilyn within five minutes of my calling the police, and seven minutes of Brenda's death. Welcome to Hollywood.

The police arrived soon after that, guns drawn. They asked me where Brenda was, and proceeded to kick down the bathroom door.

There was nothing much left to do. I answered the policemen's questions, the coroner came and took the body, and the house was sealed. It was over. Brenda was dead, at the age of 36.

Aftermath

Brenda's suicide made national news, but I kept the truth about our relationship secret. Even now, after all these years, I only feel somewhat comfortable telling about it because Brenda, Christopher, and Bill are all gone and I feel that I am exposing only myself.

There were acts of kindness during this indescribable time that stand out for me. In the weeks following Brenda's death, many of her friends literally came to my rescue and, to my surprise, so did Bill Bixby.

I stopped eating after Brenda's death, and after a week of that I ended up in the emergency room of a Los Angeles hospital. I was eventually admitted, although I was without insurance and certainly didn't have access to funds sufficient to cover a hospital stay. Weeks later, I found out that it was Bill who had picked up the cost of my care. It was something he did not have to do, and yet he did it without hesitation.

What Bill did was decent and kind. Unfortunately, I was so used to indecent things that the examples of kindness I received from Bill and some of Brenda's friends did not eclipse the impact Brenda had had on me.

In the years that followed, my entire focus was on *me*— what *I* wanted, what *I* was going to get, how much money *I* was going to make. There were no moral standards in my life. It was a world of self-indulgent narcissism. What was Tammy going to do today? What was Tammy going to buy today? What could people do for Tammy today?

I considered myself bisexual through my mid-20s—and boy, I sure acted on it! I was promiscuous and indiscriminate. I also experimented with a variety of drugs during my early 20s. If it felt good, I did it.

It was this self-absorption that facilitated a view of myself as Victim. With my narcissism running wild, everything bad that happened to me happened because I was a woman, or because I was gay. After all, if I wasn't responsible for the things that happened in my life (especially the bad things), then someone else had to be.

This mind-set, and the emotional and psychological damage I had suffered, made me a perfect foot soldier for the organized Left because of their romanticization of Victimhood and promises of empowerment. However, unlike many of my colleagues in feminist and gay activism, I sought psychological help. One way or another, I was seeing a psychologist throughout my time as president of the Los Angeles branch of NOW (National Organization for Women), and I began to make considerable progress in dealing with the aftermath of my childhood (which was no picnic) and young adulthood. It was that personal progress, I believe, that kept me from getting completely sucked into the relativism and hypocrisy I saw in the actions and agenda of other leaders in both the feminist and the gay movements.

Moral Clarity

For me the true lesson to be drawn from this experience became clearer as I approached the age Brenda was when she killed herself. At first, I was shocked that I had made it to my 36th birthday. (I then told myself that the real test would be making it to my 37th—which has now also come and gone!) But then the most fascinating thing happened to me: After years of living with what-ifs, I was finally able to look back on my experience as an *adult,* and not as a confused and guilt-ridden teenager.

Reaching 36, I asked myself, What could Brenda have seen in a 17-year-old? I was probably precocious, but obviously not the most stable of teens. Only at 36 could I look back and see, for the first time, how morally bankrupt that entire situation had been.

Brenda's pulling essentially a child (and I do view teenagers as children) into her world of lies, deception, booze, and sex was indeed morally corrupt. The ultimate indecency, though, was her arranging for a 19-year-old to find what she must have known would be the obscene result of a gunshot wound to the head.

So, there you have it. My relationship with Brenda, culminating in her death, is *the* crucial event in my life. It framed my young adulthood consciously and subconsciously, creating for me a worldview replete with moral relativism, paranoia, and cynicism. More than that, it kept me from looking at politics, the people I was dealing with, or other parts of my own life with any kind of a values-based perspective. When your life does not incorporate those things, you're less inclined to seek them out or expect them of others. It's that simple.

I had learned from my experience with Brenda how to *not* apply a value or make a judgment. Right and wrong were relative. That is how I reconciled myself to my past, while my left-wing activism—and indeed our entire culture in the 1980s—continued to reinforce that perspective. My life experience and damaged outlook made me a perfect candidate for the Left Elite in more ways than you can imagine, but primarily because of my skewed vision of right and wrong and my willingness to enter a world swirling around a moral vacuum.

It was no accident that my expanded personal awareness today is tied to my ability to see my own past for all that it is. Some may argue that I'm projecting my own issues onto the political landscape. Well, that's part of human nature. All our political views are wrapped up with our own histories, our personal experiences, with those we have loved, those who left us, our parents, our lovers. And what I also realized, after spending nearly 20 years immersed in the Left's agenda, is that Brenda wasn't the only one. There were thousands like her—except that, instead of committing suicide, they were trying to manipulate the culture to mirror their own damaged worldview, to impose their own agendas on the rest of society. As Brenda had done, however briefly, with me.

In the pages that follow I examine the Left Elite in this country, from the decision makers in entertainment and academia, to the leaders of the black, feminist, and gay civil-rights movements, to politicians and those in charge of the justice system. I will explain why a moral vacuum is engulfing the Left, and how it corrupts our culture and threatens our very liberty.

As we know, knowledge is power. The first step to releasing the grip the damaged Left Elite have on our culture and our future is to see them for what they truly are.

CHAPTER ONE

Through the Looking Glass

Freedom cannot exist without discipline, self-discipline, and rights cannot exist without duties. Those who do not observe their duties do not deserve their rights.

—*Oriana Fallaci*

On May 30, 1997, late in the afternoon, Jonathan Levin, a beloved English teacher at a Bronx high school, answered a phone call from Corey Arthur, a former student whose mentor he had been. Arthur pled with him: "I need to see you. It's important."[1] As court records and testimony show, Levin responded to Arthur's plea by inviting him to come to his apartment. When Levin opened his door, however, he found not only Arthur but also another young man, Montoun Hart. Jon Levin's tortured and partially decomposed body was found three days later.

According to Hart's 11-page confession, he and Arthur misled Levin in order to gain access to his apartment. They then tortured him to make him tell them the PIN for his ATM card.

According to Hart, Levin asked, in the final moments of his life, "Why are you doing this to me?"[2] The young men stabbed him in the chest and the back of the neck; they then pulled his head back and cut his throat three times before shooting him in the back of the head with a .22 caliber pistol.[3] They then went to an ATM near his home and withdrew $800.

Jon Levin was the son of Gerald Levin, then the chief executive officer of media conglomerate Time Warner. Jon had made a decision not to follow his father into corporate America. Instead, he had dedicated his life to helping the disadvantaged and had become a teacher at an inner-city school where most of the kids were poor and black. His payback was brutal.

The evidence was overwhelming against the two defendants. Corey Arthur's voice begging to see Levin was on the answering machine, his fingerprints were found on the duct tape used to bind Levin to a chair (which Arthur admitted doing),[4] and his girlfriend testified that he had confessed the killing to her. Even Arthur's lawyers admitted their client was present for the robbery, though he always denied pulling the trigger.[5] He insisted it was the older Hart, who had no history with the victim, who had committed the murder. Hart, in his own confession, gave details of the crime that only someone who had been present would know.[6] A witness identified Hart as the person who was making a withdrawal from the ATM at the relevant time.

It looked like an open-and-shut case of first-degree murder. For many years the homicide law in New York State had classified as first-degree murder only the killing of police officers and prison guards. However, in 1995 the law was amended to include killing "in the course of committing . . . and in furtherance of robbery," and also killing where "the defendant acted in an especially cruel and wanton manner pursuant to a course of conduct intended to inflict and inflicting torture upon the victim prior to the victim's death."[7] First-degree murder is a capital crime, punishable by death or by imprisonment with no possibility of parole. Corey Arthur's jury *acquitted* him of first-degree murder. Instead, he was convicted of second-degree murder and sentenced to 25 years in jail, with eligibility for parole.

The verdict for Montoun Hart is even more shocking and dangerous. In the face of overwhelming evidence, Hart was found *not guilty* and *freed*. What got Hart off? The jury said it was the fact that he looked "wasted" in a picture they saw of him after his six-hour interrogation by the police. In a Herculean intellectual epiphany, they determined he must have been drunk or high when he confessed and therefore—*voilà!*—his confession didn't count.[8]

Welcome to a culture where right and wrong have taken such a beating they're no longer recognizable. If you think this debasement of our culture can never really affect you, think again. Today's moral relativism and selfish agendas are moving through the body of society like a cancer, putting all of us at risk.

The Death of Right and Wrong

Carol Levin, Jon's mother, confessed to a reporter for the *New York Post* that she thought she was going to vomit in the courtroom as Hart, upon hearing "Not guilty," jumped up and shouted, "Ha! Yes! Thank you!" to the jury.[9]

Carol and Gerald Levin are condemned to never seeing Jon again. Each morning, in her longing for the son who will never come home, Carol dabs a drop of his Pierre Cardin cologne on her right wrist. She even hears his voice, she told the *Post* reporter, her eyes welling with tears as she imagined him telling her, "Mom, go on with your life. There's not much left. Live it."[10]

And Montoun Hart? Courtesy of a culture that is furiously erasing the concepts of right and wrong, he is free—not even on parole, where he would be watched. He is free among people many of whom are probably, like Jon Levin, willing to extend a helping hand to those in need. Many of them probably have ATM cards and remain ignorant of the killer who lives among them, placing them, and their children, at a risk they cannot even fathom.

The depravity of this story comes not only from Arthur and Hart, but also from a jury that could not, or would not, distinguish right from wrong. Where did this breakdown occur? How have our cultural mores and ethics deteriorated to the point where confessed murderers are allowed to go free? Certainly, injustices have existed for centuries in the United States, and millennia in the rest of the world. As a strict defender of the Constitution, I do not want to see our rights infringed upon by cruel and unusual punishments or by shoddy, deceptive police work. Nor am I one, believe me, to hark back to the days when "men were men" and women were in the kitchen. But I can't help thinking that there was an element in those days that created a certain trustworthiness, a certain stability. In recent decades, in all walks of life, it seems that our society has been hurtling down a slippery slope of selfishness, immorality, and cultural laziness. Enron, the Catholic Church, the Clinton White House—these are just grander instances of the kind of poor judgment and willful self-indulgence witnessed every day on the freeway, at the local diner, around the watercooler.

So how did we arrive at the state we're in? To help explain, let me offer another story.

Killer as Hero

In the early morning hours of December 9, 1981, Philadelphia police officer Daniel Faulkner[11] stopped one William Cook because he was driving the wrong way on a one-way street with his lights off. Before Faulkner got out of his patrol car, he called for a police wagon to back him up.

When the reinforcements arrived, they found Cook's brother, former Black Panther Mumia Abu-Jamal (born Wesley Cook), lying in the street, wounded, with his shoulder holster empty. A gun registered to him was a few feet away, with five empty chambers. Police would later learn that Abu-Jamal had not arrived on the scene with his brother; he was sitting in his cab across the street when Faulkner pulled Cook over.

Faulkner also lay on the street, dying from five bullet wounds,[12] one of which was to his back. Three witnesses specifically identified Abu-Jamal as the man who fired all the shots at Faulkner and testified that once Faulkner was down, Abu-Jamal stood over him and unloaded more shots directly into his groin and head.

At the hospital, Daniel Faulkner lay on a gurney in the emergency room as doctors and nurses worked in vain to revive him. Abu-Jamal was brought to the same hospital, kicking, screaming, and cursing. During his trial, hospital security guard Priscilla Durham testified that she was standing just a few inches from him and that as he struggled on the floor with hospital workers and police, he cursed Faulkner and said he hoped his victim would die.[13]

Abu-Jamal was eventually found guilty, after courtroom antics that included fighting with the judge and making political speeches. With overwhelming evidence against him and because of the special circumstance of killing a police officer on duty, during the penalty phase the jury of ten whites and two blacks deliberated for less than two hours and came back with a sentence of death.

So far, our justice system seemed to be working. Yes, we lost a good man that winter day in Philadelphia, but his murderer was where he belonged—on Death Row. But of course, in our world of growing moral relativism, that could not remain the case. Mumia Abu-Jamal, instead of being regarded as the criminal he is, has become a *cause célèbre* for the Left—a martyred idealist, if you will.

Years of the Beast

The drumbeat to "Free Mumia" began almost immediately after his sentencing. By 1994 it was a favorite slogan for fashionable leftists. With the assistance of international television, the Mumia craze swept the world. *Time* reported his supporters' contention that the "real killer" had been spotted running from the scene; National Public Radio signed Abu-Jamal to do reports on prison life from behind bars (although the network cancelled the contract in response to overwhelming public pressure); Leonard Weinglass, the leftist attorney who is handling Abu-Jamal's appeal (and who had entered the national spotlight by defending the Chicago Seven and Patty Hearst's kidnappers), rounded up a herd of celebrities for the cause, including Paul Newman, Susan Sarandon, Ed Asner, and Ossie Davis.[14]

In 2000, the city of Paris, France, in all its anti-American socialistic glory, made Abu-Jamal an honorary citizen (a status last accorded to Pablo Picasso in 1971). There have been protests supporting Abu-Jamal from Japan to South Africa; "benefit" rock concerts have even been held to raise money for him. Also in 2000, François Mitterrand's widow, Danielle, visited Abu-Jamal in prison. Norman Mailer and Nelson Mandela piped up, contending that Abu-Jamal's trial was a "miscarriage of justice."[15] Even Amnesty International joined the feast, citing "a pattern of events that compromised Abu-Jamal's right to a fair trial."[16]

Pattern of events? Spare me. The only pattern here was Abu-Jamal pulling the trigger of his .38 five times in order to murder Daniel Faulkner. As for any sign of repentance, after he heard his sentence, Abu-Jamal screamed, "Judge, you have just sentenced yourself to die."[17] With several deputies pulling him out of the chaotic courtroom, his final words were "You have just convicted yourself, and sentenced yourself to death. . . ."[18] Meet the Left's Ideal Man.

All this depends on the myth that somehow, some way, Mumia Abu-Jamal was railroaded. I know it seems absurd. Even Abu-Jamal's supporters know it's absurd. Consider Stuart Taylor, a journalist for both *National Journal* and *Newsweek*, who at least has the guts to weave the obviousness of Abu-Jamal's guilt into his support of him. How does he manage this? As the *New York Times* reported Taylor's artful but morally inane spin, he "speculates that some facts suggest the defendant, found wounded at the death scene with his legally registered gun lying nearby, might indeed have shot the policeman, but in an unplanned confrontation possibly involving elements of provocation and self-defense. He might, in other words, be neither guilty nor innocent."[19]

THROUGH THE LOOKING GLASS • 15

Wow! Neither guilty nor innocent! How's that for Through the Looking Glass? That's how the liberals would have our world be. No judgment, no conclusions, no reality, no rules, no personal responsibility. No guilt or innocence. The death of right and wrong.

I can't dismiss these liberals as simply confused or stupid. No, I believe the leaders of the Free Mumia campaign, and especially the Black Elite, know Abu-Jamal is guilty. In fact, that's *their* crime. They know this and they *embrace* it. They not only do not care, they *want* this type of man to be their people's heroes. For blacks, indeed for all of us, this is the ultimate betrayal of our communities.

The Drumbeat of Death

The drumbeat of support for Mumia Abu-Jamal began when the murderers of Jon Levin were little boys. They spent their lives being conditioned by the rhetoric that black men are so oppressed that even if you do the most heinous thing, you will be supported, you will be lied for, you will be celebrated. The message for Montoun Hart's jury was that, like Abu-Jamal, he was provoked, or perhaps he was even the victim. Certainly he was the victim of a racist, unforgiving society. Black men don't have a choice; they're defending themselves against the monster of White Amerikkka, they chant against the monster of the White Man's justice system.

The support for Abu-Jamal continued to gather steam throughout the 1990s. Wherever there were cameras, there were "Free Mumia" signs. During the 2000 Republican and Democratic national conventions, over 3,000 people marched in each convention city in support of Abu-Jamal. Gay-rights and animal-rights activists, feminists, and Hollywood celebrities all poured into the streets of Los Angeles and Philadelphia that year demanding that Abu-Jamal's death sentence be overturned and that he be given a new trial. [20]

Also in 2000, Antioch College in Ohio invited Abu-Jamal to deliver the commencement address. That's right. It was recorded over the phone and played for the graduates, faculty, and parents.[21] Besides being overwhelmingly offensive, this represents a much more serious problem. It demonstrates the Left's agenda of infecting young people specifically with a chaotic disregard for life and responsibility. After all, colleges invite people they want their students to *emulate* to deliver the commencement address. Abu-Jamal knows this. Here's part of what he, the Admired One, had to say to the graduating students of Antioch that day: "Think of the lives of those people you admire. Show your admiration for them by becoming them."[22]

Isn't that comforting? The Left is working to create a nation full of Mumia Abu-Jamals. The debacle of the Jon Levin murder trials is one sign of how we as a society are becoming complicit in this destructiveness.

And so Daniel Faulkner's widow, Maureen, has to face her husband's killer as he writes his Internet column and delivers college commencement speeches, as he is celebrated on T-shirts and in the media and is compared to Martin Luther King Jr. and Nelson Mandela. She and Danny were newlyweds when he was murdered. Now Maureen works to make sure that Mumia Abu-Jamal is indeed executed, as he was sentenced to be over 20 years ago.

Maureen Faulkner was also at Antioch on Commencement Day 2000, specifically to counter the myths that surround her husband's murderer. While Abu-Jamal was applauded and adored, his victim's widow was sequestered on another part of the campus and surrounded by police for her protection. Welcome to the World behind the Looking Glass.

A Struggle for the Soul

The death of right and wrong is finally serving its purpose for Mumia Abu-Jamal. In December 2001, three years after the acquittal of Montoun Hart, Abu-Jamal's death sentence was overturned by Federal District Court Judge William H. Yohn Jr. This lone federal judge accepted an argument based on a technicality, to the effect that the sentencing instructions to the jury were unclear,[23] a claim that has been unanimously rejected by the Pennsylvania Supreme Court.

Although Judge Yohn upheld the first-degree-murder conviction, the overturning of the sentence means more years of suffering for the Faulkner family. Upon hearing of the judge's decision, Maureen Faulkner asked, "When are we going to be able to live a normal life?"[24] Unless the appellate courts overrule Yohn, what this could mean for Maureen and for Danny's brothers, Pat, Larry, Tommy, and Kenny, is yet another sentencing hearing where they will have to relive the brutal murder and face the orgy of support for the murderer.

Just as Judge Yohn was no doubt affected by the benefit concerts, by the campaigning of clueless bleeding-heart celebrities, and by the decades of efforts in the press to transform murderer into hero, so the jury pool is far too likely to be drowning in the swamp of moral relativism.

At one of the many rallies for Abu-Jamal, Ed Asner made this pronouncement: "We must fight the establishment . . . This fight is for the nation's soul. Mumia must not die."[25] Asner is right: This is a fight for the nation's soul. The Left Elite, those who dream that the nation's soul will one day look like Mumia Abu-Jamal and Montoun Hart, are determined to win this fight. We must be as determined not to let them.

Welcome to the Bacchanal

The Left Elite has worked for years to brainwash us into a sort of values lobotomy. We are not to judge those who kill, if the guilty are people of color or women; we are to excuse those who destroy lives as victims of a racist, sexist, and homophobic world, or now, on the global scale, the unfair and oppressive "multinational corporate" world; we are to blame the innocent and lionize the guilty.

Ultimately, we have been encouraged to accept verdicts like Corey Arthur's and Montoun Hart's. And if you dare to say you don't believe injustice to be justice, then, as I demonstrated in *The New Thought Police,* you will be dismissed as sexist, racist, or homophobic. We have been led behind the Looking Glass, where everything is the opposite of what it should be.

How *does* the Left Elite indoctrinate decent, thoughtful people into accepting, as an example, that some killers are victims and deserve to be set free? Keep in mind, I speak of the Elite not necessarily as a cabal, but as a group of people who share certain basic assumptions, a certain worldview. One now-accomplished goal is the brainwashing of society into believing that because of the color of their skin, or their gender, or their sexual preference, some in our "multicultural society" can never be understood by others, making judgment and punishment inappropriate. The corollaries are that traditional concepts of personal responsibility are outdated, and that expecting others to behave with dignity, and expecting society to recognize the concepts of right and wrong, is contrary to the ideal of liberty. Every idea, every act, has the same value—none is more worthy than another. And judgment? That, of all intellectual actions, is heresy in this bacchanalian new world.

Of course, this effort has to start with convincing you that the standards by which you were raised were wrong. Your ideas about religion, family, and sex are wrong, perhaps even harmful. In the world as defined by the leaders of the Left Elite:

- Murdering your children isn't murder if you're a woman—it's post-partum depression.

- Sex addiction, compulsion, and promiscuity aren't problems if you're gay—they're part of an "alternative lifestyle."

- Vandalizing, degrading, or mocking the symbols of a religion is only a hate crime if the object is Islam or Judaism. If the target is Christianity, it's "art."

- Murdering a police officer isn't murder if you're black—it's self-defense or a heroic act.

- Murdering 3,000 Americans isn't terrorism if the murderers are Muslims—it's the Freedom Fighters' heroic last act against an oppressor.

- Cheating on and lying to your wife isn't a sin, it's a sport—after all, it happened in the Oval Office.

- Taking vows, claiming to represent God, and then molesting adolescent boys is the fault of "the Church," not of the reprehensible gay men who betray their vows, their church, and their community.

How best to change Americans' fundamental values? How best to indoctrinate you into a culture that grows sicker and more corrupt by the minute? As I will discuss in more detail in the chapters that follow, the Left Elite uses every medium at its disposal—television, film, music, and art; politics and the justice system; higher education; and the news media. One of its most important tools is constant special-interest-group rhetoric.

Keep in mind, the leftism I'm describing has nothing to do with the classical liberalism on which our country was founded—the political philosophy based on individual freedom. In fact, it's quite the opposite. The Left has had to restrict individual freedom of thought and deed in order to destroy the concept of judgment and undermine notions of right and wrong that have been held nearly universally for millennia. This is the result of the wrong people getting control of our culture at a time when we were vulnerable. It's that simple and that scary. It also can be reversed without having to diminish the benefits of liberty that flow naturally from our system and our hearts.

The Legacy of the Left

I'm an odd bird on today's Left—I actually believe that we can embrace individual liberty while also applying some standard of dignity to the way we lead our lives. As a gay woman, I live a life made possible by the tolerance of the average American.

The efforts of activists in the 1960s to bring about an environment that would be safer for homosexual adults, and freer for all those who are minorities in our society, have been generally recognized as a good thing. Now, on the contrary, I see the Left demonizing the very idea of decency in their determination to lobotomize Americans into a foggy silence about anything cultural. In truth, being gay and living with decency and dignity are not exclusive concepts. But the Left has dirtied those words to such a degree that when I've used them in conversation, they have elicited the same reaction as if I had suddenly uttered the word *nigger.* Friends have urged me not even to use the word *morality* because it was too "loaded." All the more reason to dust it off!

You don't, after all, need to be steeped in religious fundamentalism to realize things have gone terribly wrong. I personally refuse to be silent when a movement I've worked for, believing it was meant to expand tolerance and increase liberty, devolves into an effort to eliminate all value-based concepts.

> The Left has had to restrict individual freedom of thought and deed in order to destroy the concept of judgment and undermine notions of right and wrong.

For example, as a gay woman, I expect tolerance. But I understand that tolerance is not "acceptance" or "buy-in." I don't expect other women to run out and become lesbians just because they tolerate me, or even if they like me or admire the stands I have taken. A fundamentalist Christian may think my lifestyle is wrong, but it's not fundamentalist Christians that have attacked and demonized me over the last seven years.

A good example of the difference between today's Right and today's Left can be seen in their reaction to murder. People on the Right, no matter how strongly opposed to abortion they are, nearly all recognize that antiabortion activists who kill doctors are wrong. Contrast that with the Left's lionization of black men who kill whites, and especially white police officers.

The noble effort in the 1960s to encourage individuality apparently had no braking mechanism. It continued to a point where self-gratification became the goal, at the expense of values that could coexist with and even enhance our newfound sense of our individuality and sexual self-awareness. Faith, family, fidelity, truth, and honor all became casualties of America's Cultural Elite. *Tolerance,* once a genuine American ideal, has become a code word for moral relativism and all its side effects. Once it was realized that the American people were willing to accept diversity and even some challenge to the status quo, the Left's goal changed from extending the boundaries of what was considered right to having no boundaries at all. Moral relativism became the order of the day—a view that moral standards are entirely grounded in social custom, varying from culture to culture, moment to moment, circumstance to circumstance. It is this attitude that allows a jury to set Montoun Hart free because, after all, who are we to judge?

The death of right and wrong is most dramatic in cases like Montoun Hart's or Mumia Abu-Jamal's, but it may be more easily *seen* by taking a look at the core of our culture—the art world. The disintegration of our culture, and the conditioning of people into accepting it in silence, begins with legitimizing the depraved. This requires a trip to San Francisco.

"Art" and the Inhuman

Our institutions of higher learning are places where some sort of moral foundation and understanding of right and wrong are to be reinforced. Right? No longer. While this country's academic intelligentsia work themselves into a frenzy to squelch any kind of speech that challenges the left-wing status quo, they are also busily leading the next generation to embrace a perverse moral relativism that will take us further into a world devoid of right and wrong. I'll offer more details about the moral misadventures of the academic and art worlds later on, but consider this for now.

At the San Francisco Art Institute, the 24-year-old "scholar" Jonathan Yegge, after getting the go-ahead from his instructor, Tony Labat, presented a performance piece for a class in the school's New Genres department. The project involved himself and a student "volunteer." I don't enjoy giving accounts like the one that follows, but it is precisely the reluctance of the mainstream press to give graphic descriptions of disgusting acts that has kept the general public in ignorance of exactly what sort of "art" has been allowed to flourish—often with the support of our tax dollars. Here's how Yegge himself described his "art" to the *San Francisco Weekly:*

He [Yegge's student volunteer] was tied up. He had a blindfold and a gag, but he could see and talk through it. He had freedom of movement of his pelvis. I engaged in oral sex with him and he engaged in oral sex with me. I had given him an enema, and I had taken a shit and stuffed it in his ass. That goes on, he shits all over me, I shit in him. There was a security guard present. There was an instructor from the school present. It was videoed, and the piece was over. [26]

This depraved trash actually satisfied one of Yegge's course requirements at an institution entrusted with the cultivation and nurturing of our society's next generation of artists.

In *The New Thought Police,* I encouraged all of us to speak our minds and live as we choose; but what makes us great and our lives valuable is the fact that although we could do anything we please, *we don't.* The value of freedom is the recognition that the choices we make in the process of exercising that freedom are what is most important, and what makes us who we are.

Remember, too, that valuing freedom of expression does not mean remaining silent or withholding our opinion when it contradicts someone else's opinion. We have a *duty* to interact with those who are determined to change our culture, because our very liberty—the right to determine our future and make it worthy of our children—is at stake.

Unfun Pod?

Yegge's appalling, inhuman, and simply *wrong* behavior is fairly typical of what you'll see on performance-art stages today. One of the more famous alumnae of the San Francisco Art Institute is Karen Finley. Her "art" involves forcing candied yams into her anus, defecating into a bowl and having another "artist" eat the result, then inviting the audience to lick goo off her naked body.[27] You probably remember Finley. Quite a dust up was caused when it was revealed that she had received funding from the National Endowment for the Arts to create this garbage.

Even now, I sometimes fall into the trap of asking myself if something is wrong with *me* for thinking these actions are not just outrageous but *wrong*. My answer to myself, after asking if I have grown into some unfun Pod Person, is a resounding No! Our social conditioning to not question and not judge has been so complete, so successful, that it is now virtually *automatic* to retreat and wonder and even doubt. When that happens, all you have to do is ask yourself: Is this what I want for my children? For any child? For the next generation? Is this what I want my generation's cultural legacy to be? The answer to these questions is what you should trust.

Let's be honest. Most of us are concerned about not being aware enough, about being so stuck in our present paths that we automatically reject change, even when it might be for the better. These are legitimate concerns. Here, though, we are dealing with a dynamic that is inherently different. The Left Elite wants us to go blithely along, accepting Yegge and Finley as comparable to what the Beatles represented for modern music. Nothing could be further from the truth.

The Importance of Red Flags

We have to remind ourselves that we are generations of Americans who do get it. We have seen tremendous changes in the last 40 years, and we have adapted, where and when appropriate. Which means that when a red flag goes up, we should trust it with all our hearts. We're not facing the sort of dilemma presented in the 1960s, where, for example, many people who supported equal rights for blacks worried about the effects of an expansion of the federal government's power. No, this goes beyond the pale, at every level of moral consciousness. These are the no-brainers.

Of course, the other tactic is to place assaults on our culture in a special-interest-group perspective. Yegge, the moment his so-called art was challenged, started waving the gay banner: "It's about pushing the notion of gay sex, pushing the notion of consent, pushing the notion of what's legal. We are living in the era of AIDS. This is about his responsibility, my responsibility."[28]

This is when your red flag should *immediately* go up. The moment someone on the Left waves the banner of "gay rights" or invokes AIDS and "responsibility," it is intended to render your perspective moot.

> The disintegration of our culture, and the conditioning of people into accepting it in silence, begins with legitimizing the depraved.

The tactic, once again, is to tell you that this is a culture of which you know nothing, and therefore you are not to come to judgment about it. I've seen that tactic succeed over and over again in my feminist work and in the gay community. It is the primary offensive defense, designed to shut objectors up while the obliteration of our culture rolls merrily along. It works because we *want* to be understanding, we *want* to be compassionate. That goodness is what is so easy for the Left Elite to manipulate and so easy for them to use against us. But only if we let them.

A Contradiction in Terms

The Left Elite's "values" are a contradiction in terms. Their values are that they have no values. Theirs is the standard of no standard. My friends on the Left even ask, What's the danger of a morally relative culture? After all, they argue, everything *is* relative. "What makes me happy doesn't necessarily make you happy—and so it's none of your business." Our world (of gays and feminists), they claim, *relies* on people not coming to judgment about what we choose to do.

In some ways this is true, but this is the stage where respect for others should be a factor in our decision making about how we live our lives. Ironically, my friends' arguments, if seriously applied, would also make it impossible to intervene in some of the more heinous "cultural" practices that they strenuously oppose, including apartheid, female genital mutilation, Islamic "honor" killings of women, and bride burnings. It is the Left, with their multiculturalism and accompanying moral vacuum, that condemns women first, here at home and all around the world. And despite all the rhetoric you hear about the Left being the protectors of American liberty, it is the Left's moral failure that has kept America from being able to protect itself and others from the scourge of "cultures" that are not, thank you very much, on a par with the American way of life.

The isolated, multicultural, ghettoized world of the Left refuses to consider the fact that everything we do as individuals affects everyone else. Instead, theirs is a world of self-gratification that *requires* an end to personal responsibility. Values, decency, and knowing right from wrong—*and* having the courage to act on that knowledge—are all verboten.

While the religious are marginalized as "right-wing fanatics," "extremists," or "intolerant neoconservatives," the conditioning of the general public into moral relativism continues. We are told that gay men need to be "understood," yet the gay community is full of men who are sexual compulsives, having hundreds of sex partners a year while spreading an incurable disease or two. Men and women who commit crimes are victims of "society"—a society that expects too much and gives them no other choice. Radical Islamist terrorists are agents of the "oppressed," who, of course, have been victimized repeatedly over the last 50 years by the Ugly American. In truth, Radical Islamists are bitter men who are jealous of what others (America and Israel) have achieved and resentful at seeing what they will never accomplish on their own.

Women's independence and liberty have come to mean freedom to be promiscuous and to be the sex objects that, ironically, we were demanding *not* to be at the beginning of the modern feminist movement. Courtesy of that effort, women are now free to live without dignity or the "burden" of self-respect. That's not my type of feminism, but it is what you and your daughter are being fed daily by today's Cultural Elite.

Why does the Left in particular, as gatekeeper of our culture, seem bent on twisting it out of shape? It's not that *you* are out of touch with progressive new thinking—it's the fact that those who are the most determined to change your world are not acting with your best interests, values, or virtues at heart. They act with only themselves in mind.

Damage and the Left's Malignant Narcissism

From where does this madness spring? Why this compulsion to change our society's culture to mirror the Left Elite's own worldview? This pattern of the Left Elite's projecting their issues onto society isn't as odd as you may think. It makes perfect sense, according to the most respected psychoanalysts of our age. Childhood trauma, stress disorders, and the resulting malignant narcissism all play a part in the Left's victim mentality and in their effort, mostly subconscious, to shape our world to mirror their own damaged psyches.[29]

Pathological narcissism was first described in detail by Freud. The onset of narcissism may occur in infancy, childhood, or early adolescence. It is commonly attributed to childhood abuse and trauma inflicted by parents, authority figures, or even peers.[30] What is narcissism? "A pattern of traits and behaviors which signify infatuation and obsession with one's self to the exclusion of all others and the egotistic and ruthless pursuit of one's gratification, dominance and ambition."[31]

While narcissism takes root early, it is possible to manage one's narcissism, especially with professional help, and at least keep it from moving into the aggressively destructive stage of malignant narcissism.

The syndrome of malignant narcissism, originally described by psychoanalyst Otto Kernberg, has been widely referred to by political psychologists in characterizing leaders who pose a threat to civil society, political stability, and world order.[32] I know some of this is a little technical, but stay with me. It's worth it, because it helps make sense of so much of what is going on in the world. In an interview with the semi-annual journal *What Is Enlightenment?*, Kernberg put it this way:

> This pathological idealization of the self as an aggressive self clinically is called "malignant narcissism." And this is very much connected with evil and with a number of clinical forms that evil takes, such as the pleasure and enjoyment in controlling others, in making them suffer, in destroying them, or the casual pleasure in using others'

trust and confidence and love to exploit them and to destroy them.[33]

The core components of this syndrome are pathological narcissism, antisocial features, paranoid traits, and aggression. Self-preservation, self-promotion, and maintaining power are all traits that prevail in the malignant narcissist. The people and issues they supposedly serve exist only to be exploited for their own benefit.[34]

I have participated at both the local and national levels of NOW; I have spent time with other feminist and gay special-interest groups and their leaders; I have worked in the entertainment industry and closely with all

> The isolated, multicultural, ghettoized world of the Left refuses to consider the fact that everything we do as individuals affects everyone else.

forms of news media; and I have worked with political campaigns for Democratic candidates (can you imagine NOW endorsing a Republican?!). I have also spent a fair amount of time around universities. I can say with full confidence that what I have seen driving and controlling the actions and agenda of the Left Elite in all those venues—culturally, politically, and socially—is malignant narcissism. Issues are used and people exploited for the sake of power. Malignant narcissism is the god of the Left Elite.

Trauma and No Recovery

What I am seeing today in the activist ranks of NOW and in the gay-power elite is something of which I have firsthand knowledge. You see, as I related in the introduction, I was a perfect candidate for leadership in the Left Elite specifically because of the trauma I experienced in my youth. I was subconsciously attracted to the political spectrum that feeds on, exploits, and ultimately projects its demons onto the culture.

Dr. Judith Herman, an associate clinical professor of psychiatry at the Harvard Medical School, notes in her seminal book, *Trauma and Recovery:*

Trauma isolates; the group re-creates a sense of belonging. Trauma shames and stigmatizes; the group bears witness and affirms. Trauma degrades the victim; the group exalts her. Trauma dehumanizes the victim; the group restores her humanity.[35]

Dr. Herman actually makes note of the similarity between the emergence of the modern feminist movement and "consciousness-raising," which is really a type of group therapy for women. She couldn't be more right. From knowing and working with hundreds of left-wing activists and leaders, I can say that a common thread bound us together: damage—the physical and/or emotional trauma we experienced as children and/or young adults.

Feminist activists especially always had a story. Usually heartbreaking, often violent, it could include childhood sexual abuse or sexual assault in their teen years. The multiple-personality disorders of more than one National NOW board member were actually discussed openly at many board meetings, as if the meeting were indeed a sort of group-therapy session. Domestic violence, beatings as children, suicide in the family—you name it.

Dr. Herman considered this "consciousness-raising," or group therapy, to be the manifestation of the modern feminist movement:

It was also no accident that the initial method of the [feminist] movement was called "consciousness-raising" . . . [It] took place in groups that shared many characteristics of . . . psychotherapy . . . a privileged space made it possible for women to overcome the barriers . . . allowing them [to] name their injuries.[36]

Why is this important? Because there is a third stage of recovery that is ignored by feminist and gay special-interest groups—the stage where the group is supposed to concern itself with "reintegrating the survivor into the community of ordinary people."[37] In other words, face your issues, deal with them, get the help you need, and rejoin life. Not as a victim, mind you, but as a survivor and as your ordinary self.

The failure of the Left Elite is that it requires of its leaders and its activists that they not move on to this third stage of recovery. Dr. Herman oddly lauds the fact that the feminist "consciousness-raising groups," full of individuals who clearly needed psychological help because of past traumas, were focused on social change "rather than individual change."[38]

Feminist Blinkers

This is the core of the problem, stated by one of the leading psychologists in the field, but because Dr. Herman is a feminist she was blind to the implications of what she was saying: When your victimhood is your empowerment, recovery is the *enemy*, and working on "individual change" becomes counterproductive, even dangerous to your identity.

When that third stage of recovery is missing—when the group maintains the victimhood of the individual and spurns the last, imperative step—not only is there no reintegration, but something even more sinister begins to happen: the subconscious transference of the injured person's trauma *onto society*. Society and culture end up being subjected to the malignant narcissism of those traumatized during their childhood or youth—which includes the Left's most powerful leaders, activists, and ideologues.

This, I contend, is the monster that haunts the heart and soul of the Left Elite and threatens our future: the fact that the Left is led by a cadre of damaged and powerful individuals who have been condemned by their own politics never to escape their victimhood. Consider an entire wing of politics invested in the victimhood of its constituency, naturally attracting into activism and leadership those who have experienced more than their share of the tragedies that life has to offer and encouraging them to work out their demons on our society.

Is the right wing of American politics devoid of psychological demons? Of course not. Theodore Millon, a professor of psychiatry at Harvard University and a leading authority on personality disorders, describes "puritanical compulsion"[39] as manifesting itself in efforts to dichotomize the world into good and evil, saints and sinners. Of particular concern in politics, puritanical compulsives instinctively seek ever-greater degrees of fundamentalism, "because literalism makes it much easier to find someone who deserves not only to be punished but to be punished absolutely."[40]

All of this sounds pretty familiar, doesn't it? The people of Afghanistan, Iran, and every other Radical Islamic theocracy no doubt could speak about the impact it has when people with this disorder control society. We have our own religious fundamentalists in America, and I would judge that some of them are "puritanical compulsives." However, they do not control our culture. The people who do are the fundamentalists on the other side—the malignant narcissists of the Left.

What I had been unable to articulate about my colleagues on the Left has been expressed by Dr. M. Scott Peck in his discussion of evil in his book *People of the Lie*. Peck, who is unapologetic in his blending of psychiatry and theology, says evil people (as he terms them) have "an unshakable will to be right and will not consider the possibility that they are wrong. . . . Their main weapon, interestingly enough, is the lie with which they distort reality to look good to themselves, and to confuse others."[41] Add to that the phenomenon of groupthink,[42] and you have what the Left offers us today.

It's All Relative

The impact these factors can have on personal decision making is clearly illustrated by a recent *Washington Post Magazine* cover story, which proclaims, "In the eyes of his parents, if Gauvin Hughes McCullough turns out to be deaf, that will be just perfect." The story is astonishingly tragic. A deaf lesbian couple, Sharon Duschesneau and Candy McCullough, both mental-health therapists (of all people!), deliberately sought a deaf sperm donor in hopes that their child would be born deaf like them.[43] As they explained to the *Post* reporter, "It would be nice to have a deaf child who is the same as us. I think that would be a wonderful experience. You know, if we can have that chance, why not take it?"[44]

The reporter, Liza Mundy, spun it this way:

> Sharon and Candy are a little like immigrant parents . . . with a huge and dominant and somewhat alien culture just outside their door. . . .[45]

Immigrant parents? Alien culture? Not quite, but it all sounds so familiar, doesn't it? It's an isolation, an "otherness" that the Left wants its constituencies to feel, and the rest of us to accept. The Left's success in classifying groups into their own little culture, alone and unto their own private, special worlds, obscures personal responsibility. It serves to pound into you the falsehood that you cannot know that way of life, and so you mustn't judge it. In these enforced cultural ghettos, none of us are deemed capable of understanding anyone else—making all decisions and all behaviors morally relative and beyond judgment.

Until fairly recently, no one would have thought of describing deafness as a "culture." It is a disability that condemns the afflicted to a world of silence—without words, without music, without, a great deal of the time, speech. It is undeniably a different world, but is it an alien culture? I think not. No more than being blind or diabetic is a "culture." Is there anything "wrong" with having a disability? Of course not, and most people with disabilities are able to lead fulfilling lives. But what about deliberately inflicting a disability on someone else? The answer to Sharon and Candy's question—"If we can have that chance, why not take it?"—is, Because it's *wrong,* that's why not!

But They're Stylish!

At no point did Mundy ask: If Sharon and Candy wanted a deaf child, why didn't they adopt one? There are 33 children born every day in this country who are hearing-impaired. That's over 12,000 kids a year.[46] There are plenty of deaf children who need to be adopted. If the issue for Sharon and Candy was truly about wanting to share their life with a child like them, adoption would have been the decent answer. Instead, they planned to *create* a disabled child.

And how are you supposed to view this decision? You are supposed to accept it and to respect Sharon and Candy. Mundy presents them as "stylish and independent" college graduates and mental health professionals. That's nice. We've now been told that they know what they're doing, and that they are beyond reproach.

The No-Moral Moral

For Liza Mundy, the moral is that there is *no moral*—it's all relative. In the body of the article, she admonishes us, "In trying to know how to think about Sharon and Candy's endeavor, there are any number of opinions a person might have. Any number of abstract ideas a person might work through in, say, an ethics course. Are the women being selfish? Are they inflicting too much hardship on the child?"[47]

In 1987, for her role in *Children of a Lesser God*, actor Marlee Matlin became the first, and so far the only, deaf person to win an Oscar. The 36-year-old mother of three was asked what she thought about the Duschesneau-McCullough situation. She reportedly shook her head in open-mouthed shock. "My personal opinion," Matlin said, "is that I think it's probably important for God to make that decision as opposed to us."[48] Ms. Matlin did not need to go through an ethics course to come to that conclusion.

I hope these things seem as obvious to you as they do to me. The basics of "right" and "wrong" are easy to grasp and come naturally, but our Cultural Elite have other ideas. They do not want you to feel comfortable about your values. They want you to question whether or not your values are even relevant in today's multicultural society. They want you to believe that the world of two deaf lesbians is so foreign to you that their decision to inflict a disability on a child is beyond the realm of your judgment.

And Gauvin? What has happened to the baby boy whose mother and her lesbian lover hoped he would be disabled? He failed his initial hearing screenings and appears to be quite deaf. Sharon and Candy, from their self-obsessed, Looking-Glass world, consider that to be very good news indeed.

A View from the Front Lines

We Americans have a great capacity to hear the truth. This becomes particularly important when those who are driving our culture do not have our best interests at heart. Freedom of expression and personal liberty are indeed foundational principles of our life, but these principles rely on our *character* to maintain their value.

I have seen firsthand how the agendas of feminism, black power, multiculturalism, and gay advocacy have been consciously used to break down morals and values that the activists saw as obstructions to their achieving, first, cultural acceptance and, ultimately, cultural domination. I observed worlds where "alternative lifestyle" really meant "no limits"; where sexual freedom could not be reconciled with dignity and self-respect; where feminism meant isolating and demonizing men instead of bringing them with us as partners into our independence.

I know these are distortions of what is true and healthy. So do you. And yet, they are at the heart of what drives the Left. Yes, the things that have made this country great are under attack by a Cultural Elite determined to forge a different set of rules for themselves, devoid of decency, responsibility, and honor. The Thought Police effort to keep us from thinking about important social issues is just the first step. The Left's ultimate agenda is to change the very standard by which we view our world.

Don't Look Back!

I was recently asked by a radio talk show host if I thought there was one decade that was the "best" and to which, if we could, we should all wish to be transported. I knew what he meant. Much of the public opposition to the Left Elite comes from people like Bill Bennett, Pat Robertson, and Pat Buchanan. All thoughtful men (albeit sometimes terribly wrong) who at one point or another have identified the 1950s as that time of paradise. Women were in the home (read: bedroom and kitchen), men were in the workplace.

What these men seem to be actually and rightly pining for is a time before political correctness, before multiculturalism, before speech codes, before the death of right and wrong. Part of what they prefer is a time when personal responsibility was not a muddled and dying concept.

I'll tell you what I told that talk show host: We have a duty to be more creative than longing for the past. I believe the best accomplishments of the gay, feminist, and black civil-rights movements in the second half of the 20th century can live alongside the moral clarity that has made America the Shining City on a Hill. These are not mutually exclusive concepts. We do not have to choose one or the other.

> The Left's success in classifying groups into their own little culture, alone and unto their own private, special worlds, obscures personal responsibility.

Our responsibility to ourselves and to future generations is to take the best of what we've become and bring it together. We've had enough of the fundamentalist arguments from both ends of the political spectrum. While religious fundamentalists fantasize about a return to the days of *Ozzie and Harriet,* left-wing fundamentalists are working to create a future reflective of MTV's *Ozzy and Sharon.* Neither option is acceptable. We know we can do better.

Ironically, it was *moral clarity* that brought about the success of the civil-rights movements of the 1960s. And now, according to William Safire, "the ringing phrase *moral clarity* has a clearly conservative political coloration" [49] and is snubbed by many liberals as some freakish concern of the dreaded Right. I submit that moral clarity does not belong to just one side or the other of the political spectrum. The fact that it *seems* to reside on only one side tells us something: It has been *abandoned* by the other. Stigmatized and abandoned by the Left Elite. Abandoned because of moral relativism.

This *can* be remedied—after all, the political Left *owned* moral righteousness during the struggle for civil rights. The fall came when a few of the cynical and self-obsessed decided that morality was too burdensome and that the world would be much more fun without rules. But without rules, there is no perspective, no right and wrong—only relativism, and a culture of self-gratification where everyone loses, especially the generation that must inherit our folly.

The Feminist Ghetto

At this point, I think it's important that I make something clear: I am not a religious woman. I wasn't raised with any religious influence, and, frankly, I have always been rather suspicious of organized religion. I don't identify myself as a Christian, and yet, like the average person, I recognize the extraordinary value of the most basic personal ethics enshrined in the Judeo-Christian tradition. Murder, lying, cheating, betrayal—who can argue with the admonition that these things are bad? Yet we as a society are becoming increasingly uncomfortable with making judgments about issues as obvious as these. Everything, you see, is relative.

Although one may not embrace the institutional structure of organized religion, the Judeo-Christian ethic and the personal standards it encourages do not impinge on the quality of life, but enhance it. They also give one a basic moral template that is not relative, and that's exactly why it so threatens the Left Elite. This basic ethical guide provides standards that people like Bill Clinton, Jesse Jackson, Andrea Yates, and Mumia Abu-Jamal do not meet. But these are the very people who are held up as examples by the Media Elite (serving as foot soldiers for the Left).

I will explain in more detail in the next chapter how I came to appreciate the specificity of virtue, but there is one experience I had that was astonishingly simple and yet played a large part in my own transition. So long as I was part of the Left Elite, I traveled in a pretty narrow circle. The feminist ghetto does not allow for a great deal of mixing, and certainly the "enemy" was never welcomed.

Through my work as a radio talk show host, however, I finally began to meet and talk with people who impressed me, were thoughtful, *and* were religiously devout. My experience contradicted everything I had been taught. The religious (Christians specifically) were supposedly the enemy, but the people I was now meeting were nothing like the rabid, intolerant species I had been told they were. In fact, unlike my leftist colleagues, they displayed respect for others, tolerance, and thoughtfulness, all the while remaining true to their own beliefs and principles. These are values I feel are inherent in true feminism and yet were absent from the world to which I had devoted myself.

I was moved, and changed, by the experience. It made me realize that perhaps there was more for me to consider when it came to the quality and meaning of life. *Something* had to explain why my Left Elite allies were generally miserable, angry, and paranoid (you could put me on that list at that time as well!), while the "enemy" was secure, comfortable, and a group of generally happy (and determined) people. Funnily enough, at that time, values and virtue didn't even occur to me as the missing pieces of the puzzle. Those ideas, along with religion itself, had become so demonized that I had stopped even thinking about them conceptually.

My adventure outside the feminist ghetto was initially born of curiosity, but it became much more than that. I learned the truth about people, something I was never afforded as a member of the Left Elite.

A Community of the Decent

Knowing what's right and how to respond to what's wrong is usually not that difficult. I'm not talking about some of the more complicated issues of our day, where thoughtful people have come to seriously different ethical conclusions. The issues

I'll be presenting to you are morally plain and clear—not just to the devout, but to the *decent*. That's most of us.

The attempt to change that balance can be seen in everything from the lauding of moral terrorists like Eminem, to approving stories about the morally bankrupt in the respected newspaper of our nation's capital, to the praise of assaults on right and wrong presented as "art" or "higher learning." Make no mistake, nothing is *just* entertainment; all these fronts are meant to shape the cultural debate and to change—not for the better—our view of the world.

I'm sure there are a multitude of moments when you have had an immediate values-based reaction to something in the news and were surprised and disappointed when the public debate took a different turn. Perhaps you even wondered

> The Cultural Elite do not want you to feel comfortable about your values. They want you to question whether or not your values are even relevant in today's multicultural society.

if you were "out of touch." Well, when it comes to someone like our "performance artist" Jonathan Yegge and what he has to offer, being out of touch is just fine. It is time to trust your instincts and not be swayed by the Cultural Elite arguments classifying judgment, decency, and morality as irrelevant, passé, or even harmful.

Ultimately, we are engaged in a war to determine the future of virtue. The failure of a culture does not always happen on a battlefield—sometimes a great civilization collapses from within. But we don't have to let that happen. We can be a crew that has decided to survive, and even win. Information is key to this effort, so let's begin.

CHAPTER TWO

The Left's Inquisition

Where there is no God, all is permitted.

—*Fyodor Dostoyevsky,* The Brothers Karamazov

The *Holy Virgin Mary* is what "artist" Chris Ofili titled a collage he presented at the Brooklyn Museum of Art in 1999. In fact, his depiction of Mary was meant to convey something other than holiness. Pieces of elephant dung were stuck all over the image of Mary, and she was surrounded by photos of vaginas from porn magazines. If elephant feces were smeared on the walls of a mosque, it would be a hate crime. Here, smeared on a Christian icon—voilà!—it's Modern Art.

For me, this isn't about dogma. As I explained in the first chapter, although I respect the core values of Christianity, I am not a member of any church. My frustration and concern stem from the fact that Christianity is the target of the Left in this country, while other religions mostly are not. The reason is that Christianity represents to the Left the principal threat to their hollow agenda.

Holy Dung!

Part of the strategy of every activist working to change society is to literally change what things *mean*. Supporters of the aforementioned Ofili work, and the artist himself, have proclaimed that there is nothing negative in his depiction of Mary—elephant dung is a symbol of regeneration in the African world; hence this is actually a positive religious symbol misunderstood by "conservative religious groups"[1] (to say nothing of this feminist lesbian!).

Make no mistake: The degrading of symbols important to Christianity is, among other things, propaganda—propaganda meant to change your view of Christianity as a whole.

You Conservative Religious Hubris-Rotted Clueless Plebe!

A special point, by the way, should not be missed. The pejoratives used to describe those who found the Ofili work worthy of contempt always included the words "religious conservative" in one form or another. Then–New York Mayor Rudolph Giuliani was one of the public figures who had the courage to be outraged by the bigotry in this exhibition. In fact, he threatened to cut the museum's funding if the work was not removed. In a particularly vicious response, Cintra Wilson, a columnist for Salon.com, described Giuliani as "delusional" and as having a "hubris-rotted cop brain."[2] Wilson continued:

> [T]his . . . waste-covered icon is perhaps so moving and terrifyingly effective in its desecration of Roman Catholicism that the shrieking, bat shit-encrusted aboriginal tribe-elder Giuliani feels it is reason enough to fuck up an entire museum.[3]

As long as you haven't been cowed by the moral relativism of the Left, Wilson's screed reveals a great deal about the writer, I think it's fair to say Ms. Wilson has some issues of her own, and she, like Ofili, would do better to deal with them in private. For these leftists, however, that's impossible. Their very identities rely on joining in the cacophony supporting, contributing to, and defending the cannibalization of our culture toward the end of destroying the notion of right and wrong.

Attacks on Christianity in the art world are defended as exercises of freedom of expression (of course) and as complex artistic critical commentaries on religion. One art-world denizen patronizingly argued that there is really no conflict at all, simply "a philistine misunderstanding of the art by its religious opponents."[4]

The you-just-don't-understand strategy is one of the Left's most powerful tools. The Cultural Gatekeepers are in charge, and they *do* understand, so *you* be quiet and *learn* to understand. These classic Thought Police attacks on those who speak up in defense of Christianity certainly send the message that taking such a stand is dangerous and costly, and even perhaps *wrong*. These attacks are part of the effort to condition you not only into silence but even into questioning your own belief system and moral foundation. The religious and/or conservative (God help you if you're a combo!) are truly the newly marginalized, and also, and more menacingly, the new approved-of targets.

Whether you are genuinely religious and conservative, or liberal and simply disgusted by what you see, the put-downs and the name-calling have their effect. When the bashing of Christian symbols is so prevalent, so mainstream, it effectively distorts our views of Christians and Christianity—arguably even Christians' view of themselves.

Not What I Expected

Bear in mind, I am not a religious person; I was not raised with any religious background or encouragement. I remain suspicious of *any* massively organized effort. Whether it be Enron, the federal government, the National Organization for Women, or the Catholic Church, I see the potential for groupthink and bureaucracies-gone-wild.

That being said, the *values* at the heart of an organization or a movement, fortunately, are immune from the follies of its elite. People of faith know this—and so do, dare I say, the Left Elite. You see, it is the cardinal virtues, the immutable *ideas* which are wrapped in the vulnerable bureaucracies representative of Christianity in this world, that are most threatening to the Left. The best way to attack the ideas is to damage the container—the institution and its symbols.

These days, with such things no longer routinely being taught, it's worth noting what I mean when I speak of virtues. I must admit, if you had asked me even five years ago what the cardinal virtues were, I would have looked at you with a blank face. I had no clue. But now, when I speak of transcendent values, or the virtues promoted by Christianity that so intensely threaten the Left, it is the cardinal virtues I speak of: prudence, temperance, justice, and fortitude.

> The *values* at the heart of an organization or a movement, fortunately, are immune from the follies of its elite.

A few years ago, I read for the first time some of C. S. Lewis's essays on Christianity. Lewis was one of the intellectual giants of the 20th century and arguably the most influential Christian writer of his day. What appealed to me about Lewis, and what in my view makes his work so strong, is that he presents a *rational* argument about Christianity that appeals to the intellect.

Although his work overall has made a great impression on me, it has also allowed me the freedom to acknowledge and accept certain aspects of Christianity and Christian values without dismissing my critical assessment of what happens when Man gets his hands on a good idea. Lewis made it possible for me to understand and appreciate the magnificence of the cardinal virtues as an element of Christianity, with it making complete intellectual sense. Lewis does not persuade. He *demonstrates*.

Mere Common Sense

Lewis's *Mere Christianity* is one of the most popular introductions to the Christian faith ever written. In it Lewis offers an explanation of the seven virtues, four of which are the cardinal virtues, with the other three being the theological virtues: faith, hope, and charity. These also, frankly, are nothing to sneeze at. Lewis does a reader like myself a favor, however, by separating the two categories. Recognizing the fact that not all his readers embrace Christian theology, Lewis makes it quite clear how the cardinal virtues apply to everyone and already play a natural role in our lives.

"Cardinal," by the way, does not refer to the men in red robes, but it's essentially the same word. It comes from the Latin *cardo,* meaning a hinge, that on which a thing turns, its principal point. The cardinal virtues are the four principal virtues upon which the rest of the moral virtues turn or are hinged. Classical Greek philosophers identified the foremost virtues as prudence, temperance, courage, and justice. Early Christian theologians adopted these virtues and considered them equally important to all people, whether Christian or not.

Here's how C. S. Lewis explains the cardinal virtues. This is what I'm referring to when I speak of values in this book.

- **Prudence** "means practical common sense, taking the trouble to think out what you are doing and what is likely to come of it."[5] This is a no-brainer, and yet it is a value absent from the attitude and approach of the Left Elite, as of its subset the Art Elite. Obviously, it requires some sense of selflessness and empathy, both of which are quite dead in the narcissist.

- **Temperance** "refers to all pleasures; and it meant not abstaining, but going the right length and no further."[6] When I mention this word to my friends on the Left, they begin to *howl*. "You've *got* to be kidding!" Certainly, this is a word not even spoken on the Left, except perhaps in historical discussions of Prohibition.

Many gay men I know boast of the hundreds of sexual partners they have had. For many, hundreds of anonymous sexual encounters a year is not unusual. These are representative of the people who laugh. They are also the ones who have to remember to take their cocktail of meds in the effort to prevent their HIV+ status from changing into full-blown AIDS.

Let's think about this, though. If there were ever a time when going the right length and no further should be encouraged, it is now. Our culture is one of wretched excess. From SUVs clogging the roads to the epidemic of obesity, we live in a time when there are no restraints. Alcoholism, drug abuse, and sexual compulsion haunt our lives. The Left's rejection of a values-based society compels us to avoid dealing with problems such as these in the context of personal responsibility. Instead, they're labeled disabilities, diseases, or, of course, Alternative Lifestyles.

> Our culture is one of wretched excess. From SUVs clogging the roads to the epidemic of obesity, we live in a time when there are no restraints.

- **Justice** "is the old name for everything we should now call 'fairness'; it includes honesty, give and take, truthfulness, keeping promises, and all that side of life."[7] This seems pretty obvious to most folk. It is a value, however, that I have found missing in the Left's most powerful elite. I think it's safe to say of Bill Clinton, Jesse Jackson, Teddy Kennedy, Gary Condit, Hillary Clinton, and people of their ilk that this virtue doesn't even remotely touch their lives. I know from experience, and you can see from the condition of our culture, that it is certainly not a value embraced by the feminist and gay elites of this country.

- **Fortitude** "includes both kinds of courage—the kind that faces danger as well as the kind that 'sticks it' under pain. 'Guts' is perhaps the nearest modern English. You will notice, of course, that you cannot practice any of the other virtues very long without bringing this one into play."[8]

That's the rub, isn't it? In our culture especially, it takes a certain kind of courage to think of how your actions will affect others, to restrain yourself, and to be fair and honest. It takes a great deal of courage to recognize that perhaps there is a greater good than just your own needs and desires. While the Left exploits our natural concern for others, our struggle has to be to maintain our individuality while remaining constantly aware of our role within the greater good. It's called personal responsibility.

The Church of Malignant Narcissism

Until recently, most Americans would have agreed that the cardinal virtues are obviously good things to apply in our lives. There is nothing Machiavellian about them. They do not ask for money or demand that we do without; they are nonjudgmental; and if applied en masse, they would, without much personal sacrifice, actually solve most of the world's problems. You don't have to be a Christian, as I am not, to see how this is really about common sense and concern for the future.

The religion of the Left, however, the Church of Malignant Narcissism, requires the application of the *antithesis* of these values. The cardinal virtues require an effort made beyond ourselves, with consideration of others. They require personal responsibility, a healthy frame of mind (which takes work and, for some of us, psychotherapy), honesty, and an end to blaming others for everything that goes wrong. By their simple existence, they threaten the very mentality that drives today's left-wing establishment.

The question we all face is what sort of culture we will live in for the rest of our lives and then hand on to the next generation—one that embraces these most basic of values, or one that collapses because of their absence. In the stories that I will be telling, you'll see this is exactly the point of the cultural war being fought right now, as the damaged Left Elite work to transform our culture into a reflection of its disfigured worldview.

That Oppressive Decency

In my years working and sometimes living with activists and leaders in the Left Elite, I always found their hostility toward Christianity somewhat odd. I now recognize it as very revealing of the personal histories influencing our social activism.

Many on the Left describe themselves as "recovering Catholics"; they view the Church as a parent who refuses to offer unconditional love. A disturbing common theme among feminists and gays, meanwhile, was that if the average person continued to view religion positively, it would mean, automatically, that feminists and gays were in trouble. The most threatening aspect of Christianity was its moral certitudes, which were the antithesis of the moral vacuum in which the Left Elite live.

During my feminist activism, I entered into a religion of the Left—a feminist and gay fundamentalism that viewed Christianity, decency, and morality as the enemy, the competitor, if you will, for the soul of America. Every special-interest group needs an enemy—feminists and gays found that enemy in Christianity.

It's key to remember the importance of trauma, nonrecovery, and narcissism when it comes to the mind set of the leftist leadership. With that perspective, it makes perfect sense that the Left Elite feel compelled to demonize and even destroy society's literal and figurative symbols of family and authority.

What Elephant?

As the whole sordid story of sexual abuse by Catholic priests and the hierarchy's efforts to cover it up started to unfold, the *New York Times* appeared simply to be reporting the facts—although it reported them on the front page more often than the new developments in the cases might have warranted. Finally, however, the paper's apparent objectivity fell away in the form of an opinion piece by Bill Keller, a senior writer for the *Times*.

Yes, Keller is just one individual, but he is an influential voice within the newspaper that sets the standard for how

Americans, and indeed the world, are supposed to think about serious social issues. In fact, the coverage of this issue illustrates how a few strategically placed individuals can form and guide the attitudes of the American intelligentsia, and, by extension, of the average American.

In his op-ed column of May 4, 2002, titled "Is the Pope Catholic?" Keller begins by gloating over Pope John Paul's age and infirmity. He then goes on to treat the church today as parallel to Stalin's Soviet Union. Not a nice thing to do, and certainly meant to stir up feelings of immediate revulsion.

> The question we all face is what sort of culture we will live in for the rest of our lives and then hand on to the next generation—one that embraces these most basic of values, or one that collapses because of their absence.

Throughout the piece, Keller's cultural schizophrenia about the church comes through loud and clear. At one point he writes that Vatican II (1962–65) created a more "open and dynamic" church. He then notes that at the time of Vatican II, the sexual revolution was right around the corner. However, he explains, the "aging celibates" in the church hierarchy couldn't reconcile themselves to "equality of women, abortion on demand and gay rights"—which he implies has, somehow, contributed to the scandal of predatory priests.

With this peculiar dance, Keller provides an excellent illustration of how those with the agenda of bashing Christianity and destroying the Catholic Church in particular have an uncanny ability to ignore the elephant in the room.

The more "open and dynamic" church that Keller lauds *did* adapt to the changing mores of our society and *did* run smack dab into the sexual revolution; too many priests *did* find just the wrong way of "reconciling" themselves to it. The *institution* may not have adapted to the feminist and gay civil-rights movements, *but the priesthood sure did*. The result of all that reconciling is what we're dealing with today—predatory gay priests seducing adolescent boys. Ooh, look! An elephant!

Ironic, isn't it? In the 1960s and 1970s the church was condemned for not looking enough like us. So it changed, and now it is being condemned for looking like us. As we face that mirror, we're finding it's not such a pretty sight, and the church is finding out what "damned if you do, damned if you don't" really means.

In a later chapter I'll deal in more detail with the problems the Catholic Church is facing and with the role the Gay Elite have played in the monstrous behavior of gay men with collars. The fact is that the ultimate goal of the Left Elite has never been to *change* the Catholic Church—it has been to *destroy* it.

In one of his more bizarre comments, Keller contends that most Americans don't listen to the pope about some of the more serious social issues. He writes:

> It seems fair to say that a church that was not so estranged from its own members on subjects of sex and gender, a more collegial church, would have handled the issue of child abuse earlier and better.[9]

Do you see the spin here? Keller, through his position, has the *New York Times,* the paper of international record, place the onus on the *church* as being "estranged" from its members, when in fact it's the *members* who are estranged from the church. Last time I checked, people of faith who wanted divorce and remarriage, abortion, sex out of wedlock, and homosexuality weren't "estranged Catholics"—they were called Protestants.

Let me again point out that elephant to Mr. Keller: If Catholics (and many American priests in particular) didn't ignore the pope on these issues, they wouldn't have a child-abuse scandal to deal with. How is it that in one breath you can bash the pope for being dogmatic about issues of homosexuality, as an example, while complaining about the problem of—let's say it—

The fact is that the ultimate goal of the Left Elite has never been to *change* the Catholic Church— it has been to *destroy* it.

homosexuals in the priesthood? *Damn* that elephant—it keeps getting in the way!

In this same op-ed piece, Mr. Keller confesses, "I am what a friend calls a 'collapsed Catholic'—well beyond lapsed. . . ."[10] Surprise. He does not tell us why he hates the pope, or why he's a "collapsed" Catholic. But whatever the reasons, he is in a powerful position to further the agenda of the Left Elite.

The New Dirty Word

On the May 23, 2002, edition of ABC's program *The View,* the network bleeped out the word "Jesus" so that, according to an ABC spokesperson, "viewers wouldn't be offended."[11]

Jesus was mentioned when Meredith Vieira noted that the daily weigh-ins of her dieting cohost, Joy Behar, had ended. "Yes, and thank you, thank you, Jesus, is all I have to say," Behar replied.[12] The broadcast is heard live on the East Coast, so the word "Jesus" was heard in much of the country (shocking!). It was the tape-delayed version of the program for the West Coast from which "Jesus" was edited out.

The spokesperson explained the decision by saying that ABC does not allow Jesus' name to be used in an exclamation. "Under the circumstances, we were concerned it would be offensive to our audience,"[13] the spokesperson continued.

Let's be honest here. ABC's bleeping the word "Jesus" for fear of offending people had nothing to do with fear of offending *Christians;* it was fear of offending their own Elite, and more than anything reflective of the most basic intolerance of any religious expression. The obviousness of this act should send up a flag over how automatic it was for someone at ABC to make that move. Yes, there were complaints after the fact, which is good, but our concern here is with the ruling mentality of those who control our media and design our popular culture. A mentality that feels the need to bleep the name Jesus. Remember, for the Left Elite, "Jesus" *is* a dirty word.

If you think ABC was being sincere about its concern over offending, the guests on *The View* in the weeks after this episode included Chastity Bono, speaking about her new book about lesbianism, and Christian Slater, an actor who has spent time in jail and a drug rehab center after having been arrested for assaulting his girlfriend and a police officer.[14] This also from the network that brings you *NYPD Blue,* replete with bare derrières and plenty of offensive words. I also have some fond memories of ABC's airing a Victoria's Secret "fashion special" in 2001, which, yes, I enjoyed, but it had very, very little to do with fashion.

Does ABC's bleeping the name Jesus make a little more sense now? It's the hypocrisy that gets me, and the fact that the people at ABC think we're going to believe them. Now *that* is offensive.

News vs. Sanctimonious Fatheads

Well, it would be offensive if Christians weren't so "poor, uneducated, and easily led." That characterization, by the way, has a story of its own. It was widely reported in the fall of 1993 that that is the way a *Washington Post* editorial described Christians, or at least evangelical Christians. In fact, the words are those of a Christian being interviewed by the *Post*. He was complaining that that was the message he thought came through in Democratic Party commercials.[15]

It's nice to uncover an urban myth, but it's also unfortunate that it is so easily believed that a comment like that could be a major newspaper's editorial position. The regularity of Christian-bashing in the nation's news media, however, made it all too plausible. Mary McGrory, for example—a longtime *Post* columnist and a Pulitzer Prize winner—had this to say about a very personal way in which some people were responding to the Columbine school massacre: "But when it comes to preventing violence in our schoolyards, some fathead is bound to say that prayer is the solution."[16] Although not guilty of referring to Christians as easily led, the *Washington Post* instead can boast the less subtle insult that Christians and other people of faith are "fatheads."

How does a working journalist cover a pro-Christian rally these days? Here are the comments of Jake Tapper, Salon.com's

Washington correspondent, in his coverage of the Presidential Rally for Family, Faith and Freedom: "And when they were all done, a bunch of us reporters went into town, got drunk and ended up at a local strip joint called Big Earl's Gold Mine. There's only so much sanctimony a guy can take."[17]

There was a great deal at that rally that I also disagreed with, but really, enough is enough. This petty and childish style of attack is based on the kind of bigotry that the Left supposedly finds so appalling. Furthermore, is the liberal thing to do really to get drunk and leer at women who no doubt would prefer not to be taking their clothes off for a brute like Jake Tapper? Oh, but I forgot. This is Bill Clinton's legacy.

Drip, Drip, Drip

Taken on their own, comments such as Cintra Wilson's and Bill Keller's and Mary McGrory's and Jake Tapper's could be dismissed simply as sloppy and juvenile journalism. Like a drop of water, each one, alone, is inconsequential. But taken collectively, story after story, comment after comment, big and small—drip, drip, drip—they can wear away their target, as water can drill through stone.

Ultimately, the solution to the Christian problem is simply to declare that God does not exist. Max Frankel, who was the *New York Times* executive editor from 1986 to 1994, and who currently writes a column for the paper, declared in *Tikkun* magazine in 2000, "I have grown certain that humanity invented God."[18] While believing there is no God is Mr. Frankel's absolute personal right, the fact that someone who for eight years had that much power at the *Times* may explain something about the paper's coverage of religious matters.

Many prefer to consider such disparagements of Christianity as eccentric outbursts that have no real impact on society. It is difficult, after all, to think of Christians as being under attack when part of the Left Elite's drumbeat is that Christianity is the oppressor.

How else do we explain the fact that when Christians protested the play *Corpus Christi*, which features a gay Jesus having sex with his apostles, a *New York Times* editorial condemned the protestors' "bigotry, violence, and contempt for artistic expression"[19] while saying nothing about the anti-Christian bigotry in the play itself?

Drip, drip, drip.

"In painting and sculpture, the bashing of Christian symbols is so mainstream that it's barely noticed," comments John Leo, one of the nation's most prolific and insightful social critics. Leo's examples in his *U.S. News & World Report* column include "the Virgin Mary coming out of a vagina, Mary encased in a condom, Mary in pink panties with breasts partially exposed, an Annunciation scene with the Archangel Gabriel giving Mary a coat hanger for an abortion, Mary pierced with a phallic pipe."[20]

Drip, drip, drip.

The Last Approved Prejudice

Martha Bayles, a professor of humanities at Claremont-McKenna College, has termed this new depravity masquerading as art "perverse modernism." Writing in the *Wilson Quarterly* on the flood of obscenity in popular culture, she made this observation: "To the familiar vices of popular culture—notably, vulgarity and kitsch—perverse modernism has added a new twist: a radically adversarial stance toward society, morality, and art itself. That stance has gone from being the property of a tiny avant-garde a century ago to being part of the cultural mainstream today."[21]

How better for the Cultural Elite to promote their worldview than to use culture itself as a message to Americans that Christianity is not only passé but worthy of denigration? While isolated attacks on an idea through imagery could be considered harmless, what we've been witnessing is a concerted, continual, multifaceted cultural attack on the ideas of decency and values—an attack perpetrated by the few who control the main images in our popular culture.

What we're seeing today is very much the legacy of Andres Serrano. How could we forget Serrano's *Piss Christ*, a photograph of a crucifix submerged in a Plexiglas container of the artist's urine? First presented in 1989, this travesty had a silver lining. It prompted Congress to take a closer look at what the National Endowment for the Arts was funding with our tax dollars. Many Americans felt that this was the big story—the revelation that Serrano had received $15,000 from the NEA, and the subsequent, hotly debated crackdown on the government agency.[22]

After that dust up, however, Serrano did not fade away into obscurity—his work is now considered part of the canon in the art world. It has been shown around the globe and has a place in permanent collections as prestigious as those of New York City's Metropolitan Museum of Art and London's Tate Gallery. *Piss Christ* was actually featured in the second half of the American Century show at the Whitney Museum in Manhattan in 1999.[23]

If you still doubt how legitimate Mr. Serrano is now considered to be (and how desensitized the rest of us have become), in 2001 his work was exhibited in the largest Gothic cathedral in the world, and no one was heard to complain. The Episcopal Cathedral Church of St. John the Divine in Manhattan displayed two series by Serrano through the Lenten season. The program included a series of photos of corpses titled *The Morgue*. This part of the exhibition was housed in one of the cathedral's chapels.

The Reverend Jay Wegman, canon for liturgy and the arts at St. John the Divine, had this to say about the exhibition: "I think you couldn't have a healthy spirit without having art to inform. Art is a window to the divine." Canon Wegman says he focuses on contemporary artists, "especially ones that can be seen through a theological lens," and Serrano's works qualify.[24]

What else has sprung from the twisted mind—er, window to the divine—of the now world-renowned Andres Serrano? His *Red Pope I–III* is a series of photographs of an image of Pope John Paul II immersed in a container of blood. It sold in a 1999 Christie's auction for $70,700.[25] Serrano certainly doesn't need our tax dollars anymore.

And what has become of Mr. Ofili, the man whose "window to the divine" produced the vile image of the Virgin Mary covered with feces and surrounded with pornography? One of his elephant-dung paintings was expected to sell for over $100,000 at a recent Christie's auction.[26]

As my theory would predict, Serrano describes himself as a Catholic. "Lapsed Catholic" would be more accurate, considering that he "hasn't received communion since he was 13 and goes to churches mostly for aesthetic purposes. [He says he goes] 'to churches like they were museums.'"[27] Even with the brief overview I have given of trauma, malignant narcissism, and projection, it is clear that Serrano is projecting his demons onto the popular culture, at our expense.

As moral relativism and narcissism demand, Serrano doesn't contemplate the meaning or the consequences of his actions. "[W]hen I'm working on something . . . I don't ask myself why I'm doing it nor the consequences it will bring about. . . . And all this has nothing to do with morals. I've been accused of being sacrilegious and profane at my work. The morals, the judgment appears once the work is done. What I make has nothing to do with this."[28] A funny thing to say for someone who claims he doesn't think about the consequences, but, somehow, he *knows* it has nothing to do with morality.

Whatever his flaws, Serrano does one thing beautifully: He exposes the dead heart of the Left Elite—one that refuses to look at itself, to face its demons, and to take personal responsibility. Because he is unable or unwilling to integrate back into the society of normal people, he's determined to make society look like him.

Offended, Only at First

Of course, if your agenda is to lead society through the Looking Glass, to a place where everything is the opposite of truth, one must go to the university. And that's exactly what Serrano has done. At Penn State, for example, he spoke to a group of students, to the accompaniment of a slide show of his work, ranging from "shots of blood and milk to 'cum shots' from the artist's very own penis ejaculations . . . used maxi-pads . . . a female prostitute performing fellatio, and a young girl sitting with her legs spread wide to reveal her underpants."[29]

What impact does a presentation of this sort have in an environment where young people are expected to absorb and accept what they are presented? Exactly what you'd think: They absorb and accept. Serving as a microcosm of what happens to all of us at the social level, students reported that they found the presentation offensive "only at first" but then "understood" it.[30] Commented Amy Brennan, then a senior majoring in art education, "Overall, I don't find his work offensive. He takes the vulgar and makes it beautiful."[31]

Jamie Gettle, a junior majoring in advertising, agreed that the presentation was offensive at first, especially the close-ups of bloody menstrual pads. However, "After he talked about them, I understood what he was saying."[32]

For those whose goal it is to twist wrong into right, a good starting point is to convince young people that the vulgar is "beautiful." Once again, all you have to do is ask yourself, What do I want for my children? For the next generation? The young women at Penn State had the instinct to react at first with decency, and then they were taken through the Looking

> For those whose goal it is to twist wrong into right, a good starting point is to convince young people that the vulgar is "beautiful."

Glass. There is a time for understanding, and there is a time for rejection. This is a time for the rejection of what Serrano and his ilk have in store for our future.

Bringing It Home

One of the more vicious ad hominem attacks on a representative of Christianity appeared in the January 4–11, 2001, issue of *Time Out New York*, a local gay rag. John Cardinal O'Connor, the much-loved archbishop of New York, passed away in May 2000. In *Time Out New York*'s feature on the best and worst of 2000, this was cited as one of the "best" things:[33]

> Cardinal O'Connor
> kicks the bucket
> The press eulogized him as a
> saint, when in fact, the pious
> creep was a stuck-in-the-1950s,
> antigay menace. Good riddance!

I've done my share of critiquing the Catholic Church on is-sues of politics and direction. I've had punchy things to say about Los Angeles's Cardinal Mahony, and even about Mother Teresa. I think political discussion and the questioning of au-thority an indispensable part of every system, including organ-ized religion. But really, you don't need to be a Catholic to be appalled by this attack. It's truly embarrassing to be associated with a community that indulges in this kind of tripe. All the big, showy Christian-bashing does filter down eventually to your town, your friends, your family. It's meant to—like a can-cer that spreads despite the fact that the body does not want it.

How do local governments and schools respond to the con-ditioning in popular culture that Christianity is bad? The Catholic League's report for 2001 includes these items:[34]

- In the Seattle area, King County Executive Ron Sims is-sued a memo mandating that county employees use "reli-gion-neutral language" when referring to "the holidays" (i.e., Christmas). He cited as an example, "Holiday Greet-ings." Only after the League protested did Sims withdraw the edict.

- In Arizona, the attorney general defended a decision made by one of her lawyers to ban the display of Santa Claus in her office.

- In New York City, the attorney for the schools chancellor issued a memo saying it was permissible to display Jewish and Islamic religious symbols (the menorah and the cres-cent and star) in the schools but not a nativity scene.

- Minnesota daringly banned red poinsettias from the county courthouse in St. Paul, and kids were forbidden to wear red and green scarves in a middle-school play in Rochester.

The Catholic League cites the following as one of the more bizarre cases it has ever encountered. At the annual Halloween costume party at Sharon High School in Sharon, Massachusetts, two boys dressed as pregnant nuns and a third as the impregnating priest. The faculty awarded the trio *first prize.* In response to complaints from Catholic students in the mostly Jewish school, school officials confessed they were taken aback by the incident. They said they had been particularly on alert to make sure that none of the costumes would be offensive to Muslim students (this being a month and a half after the World Trade Center attack). As an additional corrective measure, the leading Jewish civil-rights group, the Anti-Defamation League, was given permission to sensitize students to bigotry by discussing the Holocaust. [35]

> The underlying message is that Christianity is *offensive* and perhaps even *dangerous.*

All of that is fine and good, but, gee, the case at hand involved an insult to *Christians,* not Muslims and not Jews. Christians, as we're seeing, do not count. Even when bigotry is exposed, we've all been so conditioned to respond to every other special-interest or protected group that it doesn't even occur to us to "sensitize" students to anti-Christian bigotry.

I am convinced that these examples, which do not make the evening news, are the mutant children of the Left Elite's popular-culture campaign to marginalize not religion per se, but Christianity specifically. Banning red and green colors, forbidding a nativity scene but allowing other religious expression, controlling religious speech—all are symptoms of the malignancy moving through the body. The underlying message is that Christianity is *offensive* and perhaps even *dangerous.*

"Christians are regularly targeted for ridicule and vilification by a significant portion of America's cultural elite, a situation all the more striking in view of the prevailing hypersensitivity toward other religious, ethnic and lifestyle groups,"[36] write Vincent Carroll and David Shiflett in their book, *Christianity on Trial.* They couldn't be more right. While the Left Elite push through hate-crime legislation to benefit their favored groups, when it comes to bashing Christianity, anything goes—especially if you call it "art." Why this double standard?

Simply because, in the context of American history and society, it is Christianity—not Judaism and not Islam (and not Buddhism, or Hinduism, or Zoroastrianism)—that is the last bastion of morality, values, and decency. And Lord knows, we can't have that!

No, values, decency, and morality must be snuffed out because the Left Elite have so much work to do. Their moral vacuum, like the Energizer Bunny, wants to keep going, and going, and going until our culture and society looks just like them—vague, empty, and lost.

CHAPTER THREE

Then and NOW:

Feminists and Killers and Men. Oh My!

Only crime and the criminal, it is true,
confront us with the perplexity of radical evil;
but only the hypocrite is really rotten to the core.

—Hannah Arendt

In November 2000, Monica Berger filed for divorce from Gregory Berger, her husband of 14 years. Two years earlier, Monica and Greg had adopted a newborn baby they named Joseph. At the time his adoptive mother started divorce proceedings, Joey, as he was called, was a lively, happy little boy.

Greg was known to be loving and caring toward Joey, so Monica couldn't accuse him of being a violent or inadequate father when seeking custody. Instead she argued in court that Joey had life-threatening food allergies and that Greg would not provide the kind of care he needed.[1] Monica's argument worked. She received temporary custody of Joey and moved to Louisville, Kentucky. She left behind her estranged husband in

Jasper, Indiana, where both of them had grown up and where they had planned on raising their adopted son.

No one could have imagined the kind of "care" Monica would be giving Joey. On July 6, 2001, as divorce proceedings were under way, Monica Berger killed her son, stabbing the little two-year-old 30 times with a butcher knife. Leaving the mangled body in her condominium, she went out for a walk. When police who were routinely patrolling the area came upon the bloodied woman, they went with her to the condo finding the carnage she had left behind.[2]

The situation is pretty clear. If it were a man who in the midst of divorce proceedings murdered his child, even in our current judicial climate he would be heading to the electric chair or, at the least, to a very long prison term. But not Monica. In February 2002, Circuit Court Judge Ken Conliffe *dismissed* murder charges against this killer. Why? She was found to have been mentally ill at the time of the murder because she had stopped taking her medication for Addison's disease.

Addison's disease is what afflicted President John F. Kennedy. A disorder affecting the adrenal glands, it causes fatigue and muscle weakness, loss of appetite, and weight loss. Sufferers crave salty foods.[3] It also can cause irritability and depression—but insanity sufficient to excuse the brutal murder of a trusting child? It's hard to swallow, but in today's morally bankrupt culture so-called feminists, like the leaders of black and gay special-interest groups, have made it their number-one priority to remove their constituents from your judgment. Women are not to be judged even if they kill their children. Because, gosh, they must have had a good reason. And you have no right to assume otherwise.

> In today's morally bankrupt culture so-called feminists have made it their number-one priority to remove their constituents from your judgment. Women are not to be judged even if they kill their children.

This is the legacy of years of establishment feminist rhetoric positioning women as victims of society, victims of motherhood, victims of family, victims of religion, victims of men, with the ultimate betrayal being the portrayal of women as victims of their own femaleness.

Feminists and Twinkies

What persuaded Judge Conliffe that a depressed woman probably craving some beef jerky should not be prosecuted for stabbing a little boy beyond recognition? How is it that—only for women, mind you—being depressed gives you a license to kill?

Prior to dismissing the case against Monica Berger, Judge Conliffe, like all of us, had been assailed by the media frenzy surrounding Andrea Yates, the Houston woman who drowned her five children in the bathtub. In the months leading up to Judge Conliffe's bizarre decision, representatives of NOW could be heard on virtually every major news show in the country jabbering about how women suffering from depression need to be let off the hook for whatever they may do. Including murdering their children.

In all its horrifying reality, the Yates case exposed for us NOW's commitment to using whatever tools may be available to promote their own morally vacuous agenda. Yates became a tool of a Left Elite determined to convince us that convicting a woman who kills her children is wrong. The dismissal in the Berger case shows us exactly how serious the consequences can be.

In one of NOW's press releases about Yates, the organization's president, Kim Gandy, complains, "The overheated dialogue and the repeated characterization of Andrea Yates as 'a monster' and 'evil' interfere with the kind of clearheaded dialogue we must have."[4]

What had led to the "overheated dialogue" and characterization as a "monster" to which Gandy took such exception?

On June 20, 2001, Andrea Yates systematically drowned her five children in the bathtub. When her eldest son, Noah, age seven, came into the bathroom and saw his six-month-old sister, Mary, lying deadly still in the water, he asked, "What's wrong with Mary?" Yates, facing her last surviving child, replied by telling Noah to get into the tub. In a desperate effort to save his own young life, he ran. Tragically, he could not escape his mother and became her fifth victim.[5] In the course of her interrogation by the police, Yates revealed that as she began to drown her son, he asked, "Mommy, have I done something wrong?"

If there was *ever* anything to get overheated about, if there was *ever* anything representative of evil, it is the acts of Andrea Yates. Kim Gandy's confusion about right and wrong in this case should indicate at the very least how rotten to the core a once truly great organization has become.

Despite (or perhaps because of) its depravity, the Yates case became a perfect gimmick for the Feminist and Left Elite to use in marketing their special brand of moral relativism to the public, including people like Monica Berger's judge. What a coup it would be if the Feminist Elite could persuade the American public to accept the murder of children as something that must be "understood." Motherhood is more difficult than you can imagine, they argue, so you must not judge women who are driven over the brink.

Yates became NOW's poster child for postpartum depression. NOW insisted that Yates murdered her children not of her own volition but because of the effects of postpartum psychosis. This is a new version of the "Twinkie defense," a term coined in 1979 when a lawyer successfully defended a man accused of a double homicide by saying his client's diet of junk food, primarily Twinkies, was what had caused him to commit murder.

When Good Organizations Go Bad

It wasn't always this way with NOW. When I joined the organization in 1986 I was attracted by its history of correcting actual wrongs against women. Changes spearheaded by NOW in the 1960s and 1970s benefit women across the board, regardless of political affiliation.

Some of you may not remember that it was not until 1973—after a five-year campaign by NOW, including three and a half years of litigation of a NOW complaint—that the U.S. Supreme Court finally issued a ruling prohibiting sex-segregated employment advertisements. I kid you not. It took a lawsuit, the Equal Employment Opportunity Commission, and the U.S. Supreme Court, but because of NOW's work, when your daughter or wife or sister is looking for a job, she now can apply for whatever job she wants, not just for things determined to be "woman's work."

It was only in 1970 that United Airlines halted its "men-only" executive flights between New York and Chicago, which NOW had protested as a form of sex discrimination in public accommodations. That same year, NOW chapters in California lobbied for a bill introduced in the California legislature to permit girls to work as newspaper deliverers at the same age as boys. Until then, state law allowed boys to begin delivering newspapers at age 10 but girls only at age 18. Girls were not allowed as pages in Congress until NOW intervened.

These may seem like simple things, but I chose them, among so many other successes, to give you a sense of the absurd situation that existed at the time of NOW's founding in 1966. To those of you who are too young to remember that situation, it probably seems incomprehensible to you. Things changed for the better because of NOW, because of feminists.

Over the last two decades things have changed again, and not for the better.

While in 1970 NOW rushed in to halt those United Airlines' "men-only" flights, in 2001 the Houston area chapter of NOW rushed in to establish the Andrea Pia Yates Support Coalition.[6] Part of its mission was to collect money for a legal defense fund set up by Yates's lawyers. The group also provided courtroom supporters for Yates and held candlelight vigils on her behalf.

I was president of Los Angeles NOW from 1990 to 1996. During my presidency we, too, organized coalitions, offered courtroom support, and held candlelight vigils. But our efforts were on behalf of women who were *victims* of violence. Never would I have thought, even in the age of the death of right and wrong, that a NOW chapter would be defiling those legitimate activists' tools to help a murderer.

This rallying around postpartum depression, of all things, strongly suggests an antichildbirth and even antichild attitude in the modern feminist movement. Certainly not an authentic feminist approach, this is, however, reflective of a movement that desires the complete extirpation of any role for men in women's lives.

You see, with men come marriage and children (hopefully in that order). And with children many women choose to lead lives not sanctioned by professional feminists. Putting family first—children and husband—is the ultimate blasphemy and must be fought against. That fight includes painting childbirth and the pressures of motherhood as something that drives women mad. Literally.

The Left's Needy, Depressive, Stressed-Out, Sympathetic Child-Killer

Newsweek columnist Anna Quindlen carried that banner for the morally bankrupt Feminist Elite. In one of her "Last Words" columns, she declared it was the "insidious cult of motherhood" that caused Yates's actions.[7] It is, she wrote, "the hideous sugarcoating of what we are and what we do that leads to false cheer, easy lies and maybe sometimes something much, much worse, almost unimaginable."

The Internet magazine Salon.com characterized Yates—a woman who was confronted by her seven-year-old son about the horror of what she was doing, and who drowned him while he struggled—as "guilty of little more than extraordinary need and dangerous fragility."[8] That says it all, doesn't it? This column was titled "The Andrea Yates Verdict Is Insane." Another Salon.com report was called "She Killed Her Kids, But We Must Forgive Her."[9]

NOW's exploitation of postpartum depression in the Yates case is a bitter pill from behind the Looking Glass. The betrayal of women in all of this is mind-boggling. NOW's message was essentially this: Women get postpartum depression, and, without proper help, we are so fragile, so unhinged, that we'll succumb to the temptation to drown our children like kittens.

Would you trust a creature who was that fragile and easily undone in the Senate, in the White House, or in the boardroom of a Fortune 500 company? *That* is the new message about women, courtesy of NOW.

And why this new message? Because it's part of the agenda of the new style of "feminists" to tear down the "stereotypical" role of women as childbearers and nurturers, in an effort to "free" them. The Feminist Elite ignore the fact that many women choose, and love, that life and deserve to be supported by feminists. But the Elite's commitment to "choice" ends up being just a slogan.

Of course, exploiting women, even to the point of damaging the image of the entire gender, is worth it to the new "feminists" if it allows them to move the culture a little closer to accepting their agenda. Kim Gandy admitted using the Yates case to draw attention to NOW. Gandy told Eleanor Clift of *Newsweek* that NOW was using Yates to publicize the seriousness of postpartum depression "in the same way the death of Nicole Brown Simpson focused public attention on domestic violence."[10]

> NOW's message was essentially this: Women get postpartum depression, and, without proper help, we are so fragile, so unhinged, that we'll succumb to the temptation to drown our children like kittens.

Well, that's a surprising comparison. Nicole Brown Simpson was the victim of violence; Andrea Yates was the perpetrator. Ironically, I resigned my position as president of Los Angeles NOW in 1996 partly because of the way I was attacked by so-called feminists (specifically National NOW's president and vice president at the time, Patricia Ireland and Kim Gandy, respectively) for my efforts to raise awareness about domestic violence during the Simpson trial.[11] It's fascinating to see Gandy now refer to that well-regarded effort in order to justify her organization's support of a mass murderer.

If Yates's lawyers were bent on using postpartum depression (when you can't claim you didn't do it, claim insanity!), the authentic feminist response—the progressive and supportive feminist response—would have been to remind the nation of a few facts. A large number of women who give birth (some reports indicate the figure may be as high as 80 percent) suffer to some degree from the condition (commonly called the Baby Blues)—*but nearly all of them manage to not kill their children.* Postpartum psychosis, the more severe form, strikes about one in 1,000 new mothers[12] *and they don't kill their children either.* First used as a defense in the United States in 1930, postpartum depression has shown up in the courts only five or six times in the last 20 years.[13]

In 2001, the year that Yates murdered her children, there were approximately 4 million births in the United States.[14] That one in 1,000 figure translates into *4,000 women* experiencing postpartum psychosis—and only one killed her children. These numbers refute the claim that Yates killed her children because of the condition. It just doesn't happen.

Could NOW have realized that this would have been the more feminist, more appropriate, and more truthful way to approach the issue? Of course not. Their world is wrapped in victimization, irresponsibility, bad news, and oppression. In their subconscious (and sometimes conscious) efforts to bend society to their warped view of the world, it becomes impossible to do the right thing.

As Gandy and her colleagues indicated, their work was intended to reach beyond the Andrea Yates judge and jury. The campaign was meant to influence other judges and other juries, and the public at large. And to a shocking degree it has succeeded. Little two-year-old Joey Berger will never get justice because malignant narcissists have hijacked our culture.

Sally Satel, in an article for the *Wall Street Journal* titled "The Newest Feminist Icon—A Killer Mom," said it best when she wrote:

> Andrea Yates is not a symbol of motherhood under duress nor of the embattled state of the American woman. To portray her as such is a cynical move that trivializes a serious mental illness and misinforms women about their risk of committing one of humanity's most unspeakable acts.[15]

NOW They See It. NOW They Don't.

After NOW's intense campaign about the dangers of postpartum depression, I began to wonder, How much work had NOW been doing on the issue prior to their support of Andrea Yates?

From their battle cry that postpartum depression was America's ignored epidemic, I thought they must have had some project that had gone unnoticed; they must have been toiling for years without recognition in their efforts to save women from the madness that would consume them once they had children. Even knowing what I do about the hypocrisy of the Left Elite, I was surprised by the result of my search. If one can rely on the organization's own Web site, prior to the Yates murders, NOW had done *nothing* on the issue.

NOW puts everything it possibly can on its Web site. Posted are press releases, conference resolutions, "actions," news commentary, and the organization's newspaper. Everything NOW has ever produced is supposed to be there. Although I was pretty sure that during my time with NOW the organization never uttered a word about postpartum depression (I certainly never received any action notices, nor was it ever a conference issue), the Web site, started in 1995, would have material on whatever they had been doing since my departure. Here's what I found on the NOW.org Web site regarding the subject they claimed was a life-and-death issue for women and their children: Of 4,762 posted documents, the keyword "postpartum" brought up only nine documents, all written after the Yates murders and relating in one way or another to Andrea Yates.

What's of interest here is less what we see than what we *don't* see. Not only is there nothing about the issue *prior* to the murders, there is nothing about it *after* Yates's sentencing either. It's as though postpartum depression magically popped up and then went away. The last out-of-touch whimper from NOW about the issue was released after the Yates verdict, when Kim Gandy announced:

The National Organization for Women is troubled by the March 12 guilty verdict in the Andrea Yates trial and its implications for the one in 1,000 new mothers who will suffer from postpartum psychosis.[16]

The Feminist Elite are "troubled" by a verdict that tells society that if a woman kills her children she will go to jail. NOW may not have succeeded in freeing Andrea Yates, but the fallout from their brainwashing has only just begun.

And what of Houston NOW—the chapter that organized the support coalition for Yates? Following the verdict, their e-group posted a message from their president lovingly describing "A Note from Andrea." The message reads, in part, "I received a note from Andrea. I have been sending her cards and she expressed appreciation for them and for the support she has been given."[17] Members are then given Yates's prison address so they, too, can enjoy being her pen pals.

It won't surprise you to learn that another message from Houston NOW's coordinator, posted at around the same time, reads, "Pledge [of Allegiance] declared unconstitutional—it's about time." There was also a posting referring members to a Catholic-bashing Internet site. Giving emotional support to a mass murderer while cheering attacks on Christianity and on public mentions of God is not my kind of feminism, but it does make perfect sense for the malignant narcissists who infest the feminist establishment today.

Breaking Their Own Promise

Some think NOW's disintegration into a cabal of so-called feminists against men, religion, and progress is a return to the past. On the contrary. The past is when NOW's leadership was actually feminist. The organization I described for you, as it was in the late 1960s and through the 1970s, was driven by a Statement of Purpose that has actually been *disowned* by the current gang. Here are the first few lines of the brilliant original document, along with the disclaimer added by today's NOW:

THE NATIONAL ORGANIZATION FOR WOMEN'S
1966 STATEMENT OF PURPOSE

NOTICE: This is a historic document, which was adopted at NOW's first National Conference in Washington, D.C. on October 29, 1966. The words are those of the 1960's, and do not reflect current language or NOW's current priorities.

We, men and women who hereby constitute ourselves as the National Organization for Women, believe that the time has come for a new movement toward true equality for all women in America, *and toward a fully equal partnership of the sexes* [emphasis mine], as part of the worldwide revolution of human rights now taking place within and beyond our national borders.

The purpose of NOW is to take action to bring women into full participation in the mainstream of American society now, exercising all the privileges and responsibilities thereof *in truly equal partnership with men* [emphasis mine].[18]

This was the promise of NOW when it began. It clearly no longer is. The hostility to the idea of an actual partnership of the sexes is exhibited all too clearly in that truly sad disclaimer.

In the proposal for a *new* Statement of Purpose, all positive references to men have been eliminated. This version is openly sexist. The new reference to men is as follows: "We envision a world where patriarchal culture and male dominance no longer oppress us or our earth."[19]

It would be worthwhile for the women toying with such sentiments to realize that it is the actions and choices of *men* during the past 40 years that have helped women succeed in our fight for equity. Remember, social progress only happens when those in society's privileged classes *choose* to give up their status. Certainly, activism on the part of the unenfranchised can influence those in power, as it has done throughout our country's history and as it does now. But without those in power choosing to make a difference, nothing would ever happen. *White men* voted and died to free black men. *Men* voted to give women the vote. *Men* acted to change the world, so women could act with them. How dare the so-called feminists still claim that ours is a "patriarchal, oppressive society" when it is due in great part to actions of men that we have the freedom and equity we enjoy today.

Trying to Break Men's Promises

You can imagine, given NOW's current attitude toward men, how excited the Feminist Elite were at the emergence of the men's spiritual group Promise Keepers.

The Promise Keepers is essentially a Christian ministry for men on a mass scale. The organization holds conferences in stadiums across the country, attracting tens of thousands of participants. The conferences are for men only, and they promote traditional Christian values, but with a special hook: the need for men to become more responsible, not only in their relationship with God, but also in their relationships with women.

> How dare the so-called feminists still claim that ours is a "patriarchal, oppressive society" when it is due in great part to actions of men that we have the freedom and equity we enjoy today.

The only thing feminists needed to know in order to condemn the effort was the fact that it was a men's movement based in Christian theology. Think of it! Promoting marriage and God and decency! Empowering men! The sky was indeed falling. But the jackpot came with the discovery that the Promise Keepers promoted men being head of the household, essentially "in charge" when it comes to their relationships with women.

This is clearly based on the New Testament, although many practicing Christians today believe the injunction for men to be in charge and women to obey them was tied to a particular culture and needn't be taken literally—any more than most Christian women today feel obliged to cover their heads when they go to church.

For women and men who do not subscribe to the more fundamentalist strains of Christianity, no harm, no foul. For myself, as you know, I'm not a Christian, and I don't subscribe to certain ideas, like one person or the other in a relationship getting the job of boss. But I'm all for men making a commitment to be better husbands, boyfriends, fathers, sons, and brothers to the women in their lives. For Christian women who have chosen that life, having this support must be wonderful.

Of all the material I've read about the Promise Keepers, the most important is an assessment by feminist John Stoltenberg. A male feminist, you ask? That's exactly my point. Under NOW's current leadership, he would be considered just another patriarchal oppressor.

John wrote about his experience covering a Promise Keepers rally in an essay titled "Christianity, Feminism, and the Manhood Crisis," published in Dane Claussen's book *Standing on the Promises: The Promise Keepers and the Revival of Manhood.*[20]

John, a seminary graduate, has written several books on ethics and masculinity. He was the editor of *On the Issues,* a magazine whose readers were mostly women. He is also a friend of mine and someone I greatly admire. John reports on positions promoted by the Promise Keepers that are progressive and should be embraced by all feminists. Consider this exchange between John and Dr. E. Glenn Wagner, the Promise Keepers' vice president for national ministries:

> **John:** Have sexual harassment and date rape ever come up?
> **Dr. Wagner:** Oh, absolutely. With sexual harassment the main thing we've been teaching men is that they're to honor and esteem women—whether it is their wife within the home or women within the workplace—that they are not objects, they're not toys, they are individuals to be esteemed and respected as God's creation, and so you have no right to demean anyone.[21]

This is just one exchange, but from my research it is very indicative of the Promise Keepers' general attitude toward women. Would I prefer they let go of the "man is boss" angle? Sure. But overall, for many women, this approach is—dare I say—a godsend. Really, who can argue with a movement that exhorts men to keep their promises, to be good fathers, loyal husbands, and decent people? Apparently the Feminist Elite can.

In one of the more paranoid screeds I have ever read, Patricia Ireland cautioned the nation that the Promise Keepers' efforts were nothing less than a real-life version of Margaret Atwood's *The Handmaid's Tale,* a story where the "religious right" take over and condemn women to a life of imprisonment, slavery, and servitude to men. (Hmm. Sounds a bit like the Taliban.) Ireland wrote:

> We hear of Promise Keepers vowing to spend more time with their families. So what is the problem? . . . The Promise Keepers seem to think women will be so thrilled that men are promising to take "responsibility" in their families that we will take a back seat in this and every other area of our lives. . . . Feminists will not be fooled by the many recent public disclaimers about this feel-good form of male supremacy with its dangerous political potential.[22]

Wow! But NOW didn't stop there. The organization provided opinion pieces in newspapers, ran articles in its own publications, and staged protests. Ireland herself became a regular talking head on television, warning America about the danger posed by the dreaded Promise Keepers. It was a campaign that reflected the Feminist Elite's panic at a genuine Christian message being embraced by Americans. This panic actually is well grounded. After all, what room is there for the current NOW's malignant narcissism in a world where responsibility and decency reign?

Do some of the leaders of the Promise Keepers hold some of the more extreme views associated with fundamentalist Christianity? Probably. Like all of us, they are imperfect, and in my opinion they could benefit by a less literal view of the Bible.

Still, considering what I've outlined here in just one chapter of one book, it's clear to this feminist that NOW has become more dangerous to the lives of women than the Promise Keepers could ever be. Remember Andrea Yates's children.

Consider also a striking hypocrisy in NOW's denunciation of the Promise Keepers, pointed out by John Stoltenberg:

> There was a serious fallacy in NOW's depiction of Promise Keepers as having a right-wing "misogynist" agenda. . . . [I]n order to keep faith with NOW's pro-choice allies on the sexual-liberal left (the American Civil Liberties Union, various Democratic party bigwigs, the pro-porn and pro-S&M gay-rights movement), NOW engaged in hollow anti-right mudslinging, all the while keeping conspicuously mum about the misogynist agenda being propagandized by the sex industry.[23]

In all of my time at the local and national levels of NOW there was a refusal to engage in direct action against pornography and prostitution. Pornography was determined to be a "free speech" issue, and there were even discussions about how pornography and prostitution were simply other "career choices" available to women. Porn stars and prostitutes, preferring to call themselves "sex workers," were an organized element in NOW, always agitating for the "No position" position regarding porn. It was the epitome of moral relativism, and it carried the day.

I'm saddened by the fact that even Los Angeles NOW, which under my leadership assailed pornography and the harm it does to women, recently held a fund-raiser at the Playboy Mansion here in Los Angeles. Thus is the state of today's establishment feminism.[24]

By the way, as of this writing, if you search the NOW Web site under "Promise Keepers," you will find 75 documents, none of which, shall I say, are complimentary. If you look up "pornography," you will find 15 articles, none of which deal with porn in any comprehensive manner. In fact, one article *lauds* a bookstore owner who went to court and successfully "sued the Colorado State Legislature when a 1981 law banned a display of books containing sexual content in stores open to children. The so-called 'harmful to minors' provision was subsequently dropped from the legislation."[25]

Last time I checked, making sure children had access to sexually explicit material was the antithesis of the feminist agenda. How things have changed.

Supporting a murderer of children and ignoring the bane of pornography, while demonizing a Christian organization that is devoted to getting men by the hundreds of thousands to become better husbands—that is NOW today. And our stroll through the Looking Glass with the new feminists has just begun.

NOW Finds Religion

You might be as surprised as I was to find that in April 2001, just before they were distracted by postpartum girl Andrea Yates, Patricia Ireland and NOW issued a statement—in fact, a flurry of press releases—in support of religion. Well, not just any religion. In fact, what they were demanding was "an end to oppression of Falun Gong practitioners."[26]

In case it hasn't crossed your radar screen, Falun Gong is a quasi-religious movement based in China that engages in occult practices.[27] It was founded in 1992 by a man named Li Hongzhi. Adherents say that Falun Gong has 20 to 80 million followers worldwide (this in just 10 years), that Falun Gong practice groups can now be found in more than 40 countries (including the United States), and that Li Hongzhi's writings have been translated into 10 languages. Li himself claims his group is simply a spiritual movement that combines Buddhist meditation and Taoist Qigong exercises for the sake of promoting physical and mental health.

Sounds dandy. But that's not the whole story. Li, who lives in New York, has told Western reporters that humanity will soon be wiped out, that space aliens are already on Earth trying to replace human beings with clones, and that he personally is invested with supernatural powers allowing him to move through dimensions.[28]

Yes, indeed, this is a "religion" NOW can like.

NOW says it supports Falun Gong in part because most of its followers are women. Here again true feminism is dangerously abandoned by NOW. Many of the Falun Gong supporters are indeed women, but it is also women (and children!) who have been directed to kill themselves by public self-immolation to protest the Chinese crackdown on the cult. Mass suicides of followers have also taken place.[29] There are reports of women and children being murdered by other cult members because they had expressed a desire to leave, as well as followers murdering their families in order to send them to "paradise."[30] It makes you think Jim Jones would have had a friend in NOW, if only he had come along a few years later.

Li writes that he can heal disease and that his followers can stop speeding cars using the power of his teachings. He writes that the Falun Gong emblem exists in the bellies of its practitioners, who can see through the celestial eye in their forehead. Li believes "humankind is degenerating and demons are everywhere." (No, those aren't demons—just the Feminist Elite, the Clintons, and Jesse Jackson.) Extraterrestrials are everywhere, too, and Africa boasts a 2-billion-year-old nuclear reactor. (Whoa!) Li also says he can fly (without an airplane, of course).[31]

Let Them Eat Christians

So, why is NOW compelled to get downright protective toward Falun Gong? Consider this line from Ireland in a NOW press release: "The U.S. government should be taking strong action against the religious persecution of Falun Gong practitioners by the Chinese government. The White House should be taking the lead. Since they will not, we must." Ah, the grandeur!

NOW's statement perfectly reveals its hypocrisy when it comes to concern about religious freedom. It's one thing to say we oppose any government restraint on adherence to any belief, and quite another to single out a fringe sect like the Falun Gong while completely ignoring the long-standing and hardcore oppression of Christians in China.[32] The transparency of the double standard is truly stunning.

To really get the flavor of this cult, let's listen to the Falun Gong leader himself. Here's what Li had to say in an interview with *Time Asia* (an interview that was not released in print here in the United States, as far as I could determine, where the numbers of Falun Gong followers are increasing):

> *Time:* Have you seen human beings levitate off the ground?
> Li: I have known too many.
> *Time:* Can you describe any that you have known?
> Li: David Copperfield. He can levitate and he did it during performances.[33]

Hmm. Maybe Li is just a nutty David Copperfield fan. There's no crime in that. Well, try this on for size:

> *Time:* Why does chaos reign now?
> Li: . . . [S]ince the beginning of this century, aliens have begun to invade the human mind and its ideology and culture.
> *Time:* Where do they come from?
> Li: The aliens come from other planets. . . . Some are from dimensions that human beings have not yet discovered. . .[34]

Li eventually explains that the ultimate alien takeover of Earth will occur through cloning. Now, many Americans have religious objections to cloning, but Li's are, well, unique. He believes that clones will have no soul, allowing aliens to take over the body. That is why the aliens took control of scientists—so they could develop cloning, so the aliens would have more bodies to inhabit. Got it?

So, maybe the Left Elite really *are* from another planet.

Li's friends include not only the loopy current version of NOW, but also some apparently normal people, like former Houston mayor Robert C. Lanier. On October 11, 1996, Mayor Lanier proclaimed the date to be Li Hongzhi Day. Can you imagine the outcry if he had proclaimed the date to be Jesus Day?

NOW's antifeminist agenda and commitment to the death of right and wrong could not be more apparent than in their support for Falun Gong. If they were truly concerned about the women followers of this cult, they would be supporting the Chinese government's action and warning Congress about the growth of Falun Gong here in the United States. The majority of the victims at Jonestown were women and children.[35] The majority of the Falun Gong victims are women and children, and more will be hurt by the spread of a new cult hell-bent on getting rid of the aliens in our midst before the apocalyptic end of the world.

By the way, Qigong, the discipline of which Falun Gong is a mutant offshoot, is practiced to clear the mind of all thoughts. Perhaps that explains NOW's behavior.

Amazing Themselves

The schizophrenia of the Feminist Elite can be pretty astounding. Consider this statement made by Kim Gandy on May 15, 2002:

> I never cease to be amazed that anyone would actively oppose the marriage of any two people who want to make a legal commitment to love, honor and support each other.[36]

Well, that seems right on. So Gandy and NOW must have supported the Statement of Principles from the Smart Marriages Conference in June 2000. In part, the Statement pledges:

> [I]n this decade we will turn the tide on marriage and reduce divorce and unmarried childbearing, so that each year more children will grow up protected by their own two happily married parents and more adults' marriage dreams will come true.[37]

Children protected by two happily married adults; marriage dreams coming true—who could disagree with that? Certainly not Gandy. After all, she's already said she would be amazed at anyone actively opposing the marriage of two people who want to make a commitment to each other.

Well, apparently she's in the business of amazing herself. Here's her response to the Smart Marriages pledge: "Single moms are being demonized. . . . NOW is committed to exposing and organizing against this deliberate return to the days of unchallenged male control."[38]

What can explain these two diametrically opposed positions on marriage?

Well, it turns out Gandy's first quote is about *same-sex* marriage! It's women who want to engage in *heterosexual* marriage that are so dangerous and threaten to throw us all back into the Dark Ages. It would be laughable if it didn't so accurately reveal the soulless heart of today's Feminist Elite.

Those Stupid Poor Women

But it doesn't stop there. Marriage, as a natural reminder of the importance of men in women's lives, must be attacked whenever it rears its ugly head. And attack is exactly what NOW did in 2002 when faced with George W. Bush's fantastic Marriage Initiative.

Of course, with NOW's Looking-Glass mentality, President Dubya's Marriage Initiative is the ultimate attack on the sacrosanct right of women to be alone, free from men and their all-consuming desire to turn us into Stepford Wives.

So what's so evil about the Marriage Initiative? It promotes healthy, two-parent households, as opposed to the situation fostered by our welfare state over the last three decades. The welfare system, up until now, has encouraged illegitimacy by punishing recipients with reduction or elimination of aid if they marry. The Initiative attempts to give poor women in this country the same chance of marrying the men they love that their middle-class and wealthy counterparts enjoy.

The Marriage Initiative includes premarriage counseling, fatherhood training groups, and education for young women to prevent teen pregnancy. It even enhances the enforcement of child-support payments.

Of course, upon hearing of a plan from a Republican administration that does the unspeakable—embraces the fact that men are important in women's lives—the Feminist Elite became crazed Chicken Littles. A media blitz warned of everything from women being forced to marry men who beat them up to the administration engaging in wide-scale "social engineering." The sky would fall, and cats would start sleeping with dogs, too.

You know you're in trouble when you have to engage in double-talk about the facts to further your agenda. Gone are the days when reality fed the feminist movement. Now, the bogeyman has to be constructed out of whole cloth. Kim Gandy demonstrated this when she appeared on *The O'Reilly Factor* to discuss the issue.

Bill O'Reilly, a really fair guy, kept trying to get Gandy to explain why exactly NOW is against the initiative, but to no avail:

> **O'Reilly:** But you would admit that if you're a single mom and . . . your—you know, whoever . . . fathered your child leaves, that you're likely—more likely be poor, because the statistics are unbelievable. You know that.
>
> **Gandy:** Right, there's no question. And to say to these women, who the father of their children has abandoned them or abused them, to say, You've got to track him down and marry him or your child's not going to get into Head Start, or your check is going to be reduced, that's a terrible . . . package. [39]

But that isn't what the Initiative says. It is about counseling for women and men who love each other and want to marry, in order to help them have successful, healthy unions. But the fact that the Initiative doesn't *force* a woman to marry a certain man, even if he's the father of her child, doesn't suit NOW's agenda, so they will say whatever they need to in order to manipulate the public—accuracy be damned.

Besides "forcing" women to marry men who beat them up, NOW's other doomsday complaint about the initiative is that a poor woman, if offered money, will marry the wrong man, instead of waiting for a man she loves. In other words, poor women are stupid and will do stupid things for money.

Fortunately, I had the opportunity to appear on *The Factor* with Bill O'Reilly and counter Gandy's pathetic message about poor women. I'll tell you what I told Bill: I know poor women have more agency, more control over their lives than that, and I will not insult them by suggesting that because they're having a rough stretch, they've become mindless, controllable welfare-mom automatons, ready to roll over for some cash. That, it seems, is NOW's impression of them.

> By casting men as unnecessary if not downright evil, the Feminist Elite have made it very hard for the average man to accept feminist concerns as legitimate.

As for NOW's impression of men, feminists used to be stereotyped as hating men. The old NOW fought against that stereotype; today's NOW is bringing it right back.

What's important about all this nonsense is that it has real social repercussions. There are many fronts in this war to change our world. One of them is to tarnish our view of organizations like the Promise Keepers, which remind people of the important relationship women and men share. On another front, Christian ideas are attacked, along with society's view of traditional relationships, while anti-Christian, anti-Western organizations and gurus are praised and supported. If actions such as these don't have a serious impact on young people, and especially on young women, it isn't because NOW isn't trying.

"A Woman Needs a Man like a Fish Needs a Bicycle"

That's Gloria Steinem's line, and it truly reflects the agenda I've been describing. One of the goals of the Feminist Elite is to reinforce to women the idea that men are obsolete. The mantra, spoken or unspoken, is: Your true life can only be achieved by yourself. But we still must ask why the response to the suggestion that marriage is a good option for women is so vitriolic.

- First, it is a manifestation of the modern feminist movement's twisting the authentic feminist agenda from equality *with men* to independence *from men*. We saw that in NOW's repudiation of their original 1966 Statement of Purpose.

One of the biggest problems with the modern feminist movement is its failure to bring men along with us. By casting men as unnecessary if not downright evil, the Feminist Elite have made it very hard for the average man to accept feminist concerns as legitimate.

- Secondly, marriage is certainly a moral issue, but it is also one of personal choice. It ties in directly with the notions of individual liberty and limited government, which are the kiss of death to the Left's special-interest groups.

Consider this: When a woman becomes pregnant without being married, or if a woman's husband dies or her marriage fails, she may have no rational choice other than to turn to the welfare state, which tells her, We'll take care of you and your baby. For women who turn to welfare, Big Brother becomes Husband. These women, and their families, are then likely to turn to the party that supports the welfare state and reliance on big government. They potentially become more responsive to messages about "victimhood" and more open to the left-wing special-interest groups, like NOW, that assure them that their victimhood is their power.

Indeed, poor women seem to be the last "victim" group that NOW's leaders feel they can exploit. With a membership base that is disappearing faster than you can say David Copperfield, they are desperate to hang on to that base of the poor and disfranchised by keeping them poor and disfranchised. The last thing NOW wants is to see the cycle of dependency broken.

President Bush is right. When the government stops rewarding illegitimacy and single parenthood, while making it possible for women to marry the men they love, the door to freedom, true equity, and a bright future opens up.

Imagine being on welfare, already having a sense that you do not have as much control over your life as you'd like, and then hearing a message of concern from women who are supposed to have your best interests at heart. And what is the feminist establishment's message? The government is coming to force you to marry some brute. But if you join or support NOW, you will be protected from the Big Bad Wolf. That's what NOW's leaders want these women to think. Fortunately, I do believe, as I told O'Reilly, that poor women have more agency than that and recognize that wolf despite the disguise.

NOW's message does seem to be losing some of its power. The organization's membership is in free fall; current and past national board members have shared with me the desperation at board meetings as they try to figure out how to stave off bankruptcy.

As women's lives expand, the deceit of the posers currently in charge of establishment feminism becomes clear and undeniable. At this point, its leadership must feel that everyone is out of step but them. They must see the writing on the wall, however, when even a committed lesbian feminist like me has had enough.

So if NOW is in such dire straits, why do I think it is still dangerous? Because its representatives can still get on national programs like *The Factor* and attempt to draw us into NOW's moral vacuum. You don't need reality on your side to have a great deal of influence. You just need access.

Hey! Fish Do Like Bikes!

I was shocked, just *shocked,* the other day when, as I was feeding my goldfish, I noticed they had a brand-new Schwinn! Tenspeed, the whole deal. As goldfish are apt to do, they were sharing the new speed racer, taking turns making laps around the bowl.

Of course, I shouldn't have been so surprised. Gloria Steinem got married not too long ago. Patricia Ireland is married, and so is Kim Gandy. Ditto the leadership of the feminist think tank Feminist Majority—Eleanor Smeal, its president, has been married for ages, and Katherine Spillar, its vice president, has also wed. None of these are the same-sex marriages that these women tout. No, they are regular heterosexual marriages (with the silly exception of Ireland also having had a girlfriend), the kind that will ruin the lives of poor women and unleash male domination. Funny how the Feminist Elite like to indulge!

When Steinem married, I became curious about what the default leader of the Feminist Elite was up to these days. Maybe her tune had changed. Perhaps, since fish were riding bikes, she had decided men would be okay for regular women to enjoy as well. All right, I admit it, I'm an eternal optimist.

Of course, Steinem is a socialist,[40] so her primary concern is not with the quality of women's lives at all. She apparently is still awash in how awful this country and the "patriarchy" really are. In her contribution to the death of right and wrong, she projected some of this rot onto the landscape in Florida early last year.

Speaking at a charity luncheon for the YWCA of West Palm Beach County, Steinem blamed pretty much everything awful that had ever happened—ranging from the September 11th massacre, to the sex-abuse scandal in the Catholic Church, to Adolf Hitler—on male domination. She started her speech with a coy "I hardly know where to begin. . . ."[41] Oh yes she did.

Steinem first parroted the Left Elite's myth that the Catholic Church's rule about celibacy is the cause of the predatory practices of some priests. Steinem declared:

> To create a hierarchy of authority and sanctity and then suppress sexuality as a natural form of expression and subject these men to total control . . . well, it's almost natural that some of them will then seek control over people lower down in the power structure.[42]

Priests molesting adolescent boys is almost natural? This has been the usual strategy—to blame sexual abuse by priests on their celibacy, a.k.a. Church dogma. You see, according to Steinem, you've got to get it out of your system, you've got to act on it, otherwise it will become a monster, turning you into a homosexual and forcing you to prey on young boys.

Here's the truth: As I'm sure Steinem knows—considering all her years as a feminist activist—but as you may not know, rapists and molesters, serial and otherwise, usually have sex readily available to them. Most rapists and molesters—whether their victims are male or female—are in fact married or have girlfriends.[43] This is a basic fact known throughout the feminist community, in academia and within the rape crisis networks. For Steinem to ignore this fact is truly reprehensible. It places women and children at risk by misrepresenting where danger truly lurks.

The Cult of Fish with Bikes That Are Too Masculine

In her post-9/11 speech to the YWCA, Steinem condemned "the cult of masculinity" and offered examples that are supposed to prove how masculinity causes death and destruction.[44] Do you see what's happening here? This kind of rhetoric is meant to drive another guilt nail into the coffin of the American character, condemning both men and women to mistrust of each other, less self-esteem, less confidence, and general confusion. It is meant to manipulate you into acquiescing to the destructive politics of identity and victimhood. Keeping you off-balance is an indispensable tool of the Left Elite in pursuing the death of right and wrong.

Steinem and her colleagues in the Feminist Elite are attempting to push the people of this country further into an abyss where distrust, paranoia, lack of confidence, and self-hate rule the day.

Let's use Steinem's own illustrations, but view them from *outside* the Looking Glass.

■ She brings up Hitler as an example of what a "strong, patriarchal, authoritative structure" produces. The question must be asked then: Why was there only one Hitler? Why weren't all the national leaders brought up in that same "strong, patriarchal, authoritative structure" just like him?

- Regarding the crisis in the Catholic Church, if celibacy "naturally" makes you into a predator, why is it that only a small percentage of priests are involved in the tragedy? Why aren't nuns going batty and molesting girls?

- Serial killers, Steinem declares, tend to be male, white, middle-class or above, and heterosexual. This means, she emphasizes, that what they share is membership in the class of Americans who are most likely to have been brought up believing they have a right to control others. So, according to the 2000 census report, 211,460,626 Americans are white. Around 49 percent (some 104,000,000) of those are male. Being less than generous, let's say 90 percent are heterosexual, and let's say 50 percent are middle-class. That leaves 47,000,000 Americans who should be inclined to be serial killers. With a pool of that size, why aren't we all dead?

- Steinem points to the fact that the killers in our high schools have also been male, white, middle-class or above, and heterosexual. In a country where millions of high-school-age boys fit that description, why have there been less than a dozen perpetrators?

I certainly don't mean to belittle the importance of even one murderer being free. Even one serial killer is too many. But let's get real here and look at these accusations with some common sense. If Steinem were right, we should have hundreds of thousands of Hitlers, high-school maniacs, abusive priests, and serial killers, *but we don't*.

By pointing out that these predators tend overwhelmingly to be white, middle-class, heterosexual males, but *not* pointing out what a tiny percentage of white, middle-class, heterosexual males they are, Steinem is attempting to move the false message that men (at least, white men) are out of control and cannot be trusted by women. She and her colleagues in the Feminist Elite are attempting to push the people of this country further into an abyss where distrust, paranoia, lack of confidence, and self-hate rule the day. They are attempting to make you feel just like them!

Steinem did offer a solution to her cartoonish problem of the Awful Man. "The cult of masculinity is the basis of every violent, fascist regime," she said. "We need to raise our sons more like our daughters, with empathy, flexibility, patience and compassion."[45] I see. Steinem's version of womanhood is of the Donna Reed variety, and even more frightening is that she thinks we should turn men into Donna Reed as well. If she goes to any gay pride parade, she can see her fair share of men dressed and acting like their favorite female movie star, but I certainly don't think she'd want some guy dressed as Dolly Parton running the Department of Defense.

Here's a news flash for Ms. Steinem: Women come in all shapes, sizes, and mentalities, just like men. The women I admire are like the men I admire. Margaret Thatcher, Dianne Feinstein, Lynne Cheney, Condoleezza Rice—they have the same qualities I see in Franklin Delano Roosevelt, Ronald Reagan, and Winston Churchill. They can wage peace, wage war, send men and women to their deaths if necessary for the country's survival, while improving the quality of life for everyone.

Today's so-called feminist leaders, as they sing their dirge of doom, truly hate the honesty, bravery, and courage of the average person. With the light of who you are, with all your hope and trust and pride, you are to the Feminist Elite what sunlight is to Dracula. They need to damage you, to defame the sense of who we are as Americans, so they can feel better about themselves and protect themselves from the truth.

The real story about Americans is that we saved the world twice over in the 20th century. Americans of previous generations gave their lives so that we in the 21st century could wage this debate. The Feminist Elite, as they do their march down the road of moral relativism, pollute the memory of those who went before us. They should be ashamed of themselves.

CHAPTER FOUR

First the Culture, Then the Children:

The Agenda of the Radical Gay Elite

Every major horror of history was committed in the name of an altruistic motive. Has any act of selfishness ever equaled the carnage perpetrated by disciples of altruism?

—*Ayn Rand*

For the gay establishment, the death of right and wrong began when gaining civil rights ceased to be enough. As the Gay Elite found Americans willing to tolerate and even accept their divergent lifestyle and point of view, they started exploiting that compassion. Thus began the furtherance of a campaign that, although promoted in the name of tolerance, understanding, and compassion, has nothing to do with acceptance of homosexuals and everything to do with eliminating the lines of decency and morality across the board. Instead of being about tolerance and equal treatment under the law, today's gay movement, in the hands of extremists, now uses the language of rights to demand acceptance of the depraved, the damaged, and the malignantly narcissistic.

Today's gay activists have carried the campaign a step further, invading children's lives by wrapping themselves in the banner of tolerance. It is literally the equivalent of the wolf coming to your door dressed as your grandmother.

The radicals in control of the gay establishment want children in their world of moral decay, lack of self-restraint, and moral relativism. Why? How better to truly belong to the majority (when you're really on the fringe) than by taking possession of the next generation? By targeting children, you can start indoctrinating the next generation with the false construct that gay people deserve special treatment and special laws. How else can the gay establishment actually get society to believe, borrowing from George Orwell, that gay people are indeed more equal than others? Of course, the only way to get that idea accepted is to condition people into a nihilism that forbids morality and judgment.

> The radicals in control of the gay establishment want children in their world of moral decay, lack of self-restraint, and moral relativism.

It is, in fact, about power and control. It's that simple.

Although the radical gay agenda seems to be everywhere in our culture, there is actually a quite small number of individuals constituting what I term the Gay Elite. They, like other left-wing leaders, are the fundamentalists of their movement—usually the most damaged and the most determined. They work to the detriment of all the decent, responsible gay women and men in this country, for whom they claim to speak.

Who are "they"? They're the leaders of groups like the Gay and Lesbian Alliance Against Defamation (GLAAD), the Gay, Lesbian and Straight Education Network (GLSEN), the Human Rights Campaign (HRC), and the National Gay and Lesbian Task Force (NGLTF). All have tremendous cultural and political influence.

The leadership of gay and lesbian activist groups in major cities—such as the organizers of Gay Pride marches and festivals in New York, Los Angeles, and San Francisco—enjoy considerable authority in their communities. Finally, there is a growing number of openly gay and lesbian politicians, many of whom have moved from leftist special-interest groups and pursue extreme agendas using their elected office. They, too, are part of the influence loop.

I'm not contending here that these people are all meeting secretly and concocting plans together. However, with common problems and goals, they can act through tacit agreement on their strategy for subverting—or what they term "changing"—the culture.

The Depraved Alternative

During my activism in the feminist and gay communities, the conditioning was nonstop. The effort, using the mass media primarily, was and is to brainwash the public into believing that certain sexual practices are merely "alternative lifestyles." I had my first shock during a meeting for an AIDS action group in 1990. We were planning a protest geared to gaining more media awareness of the need for AIDS research funding when the discussion suddenly shifted to the need to show more support for our "sisters" involved in sadomasochism. One participant, a young lesbian dressed in leather and with virtually every visible part of her body pierced, demanded that the AIDS action include "S&M Visibility."

You see, according to her warped view, the fetish for pain and violence that she and her girlfriend shared was simply another alternative lifestyle within the gay alternative lifestyle. I was dumbfounded, but keeping my mouth shut has never been one of my strengths. I sat there for a while and listened to a stream of politically correct nonsense about how the use of violence and the infliction of pain on one's lover was simply— voilà!—another lifestyle choice. Finally I spoke up.

I said that the desire to inflict pain on someone was sick; that S&M had absolutely nothing to do with homosexuality; and that the fact that no one else (there were about 18 people at this meeting) had spoken up to challenge what was being said was in itself very disturbing.

Well, you can imagine how that room erupted. It actually became a shouting match. I was predictably condemned as intolerant and self-loathing and as a danger to the community. I was told that my describing S&M as a sickness put gay people at risk. Why? Because if any "alternative" sexual practice was condemned, there would be the "slippery slope," and no gays would be safe from all those maniacal Christian fundamentalists. By default, it was argued, we had a responsibility to embrace and support *anyone* who challenged the sexual and social status quo.

That idea took hold, and now all manner of sexual perversion enjoys the protection and support of what was once a legitimate civil-rights effort for decent people. The real slippery slope has been the one leading into the Left's moral vacuum. It is a singular attitude that prohibits any judgment about obvious moral decay because of the paranoid belief that judgment of any sort would destroy the gay lifestyle, whatever that is. You see one very public display of this "big tent" approach when you watch news coverage of any of the major Gay Pride marches. Have you ever noticed how big the parade banner is?

In the old days, the banners declared the parades were for "Gay and Lesbian Rights." That's rather straightforward. Today, reflective of the any-perversion-is-our-perversion mentality, the banners read "Gay, Lesbian, Bisexual, and Transgendered Rights." I think the only reason the words "and Women Who Love Their Cocker Spaniels Too Much" haven't appeared yet is that the organizers simply ran out of room.

Men Trapped in Men's Bodies

The idea of "transgendered rights" dismays me the most. I spoke up in many a meeting challenging the idea that those with so-called Gender Identity Disorders (GID) somehow belonged within a gay-rights movement. My cautions about this issue were always met with the same dismissal as my warnings about the S&M crowd.

Men with "gender problems" consider themselves to be women trapped in men's bodies. Once they have had their "reassignment surgery," many—surprise!—identify themselves as lesbians. So, in other words, they were men who wanted to become women who sleep with women. In my opinion any man who thinks simply having his penis removed, having breast implants, and taking hormones turns him into a woman needs to be in a psychiatrist's office, not in a parade.

I will always remember a radio interview I did for a program geared to a gay audience. The engineer and interviewer, who was called Tina, was a man dressed as a woman. He wore a wig in the *That Girl* Marlo Thomas style and dressed in the burlesque-ish way only drag queens have mas-

> There is a quite small number of individuals constituting what I term the Gay Elite. They work to the detriment of all the decent, responsible gay women and men in this country, for whom they claim to speak.

tered. Of course, the female names they choose for themselves are either the most delicate or borrowed from the sex goddess movie stars of the past. Imagine a man who looks like Arnold Schwarzenegger taking a name like Tina or Marie. There are also more Marilyns, Glorias, Lolas, and Lanas in the transgendered community than you can shake a stick at. It is indeed a distorted male idea of what a woman is and exposes the misogyny in that particular "gay" subgroup.

Nothing could disguise the fact, however, that Tina was 6 foot 4 and had wrists the size of mangoes. He was a man trapped in a man's body. Nothing a doctor could do to him would ever change that.

He switched on the machine for the recorded interview. I was there to promote *The New Thought Police,* but the first question out of Tina's mouth was "Would you date a transsexual?" In other words, would I, as a gay woman, date a man who had had his body surgically mutilated so he could pretend he was a woman? I was indeed Alice in Wonderland that day—the Mad Hatter, I was sure, was just around the corner.

My answer was an emphatic No! I explained that if I wanted someone masculine, I would date a man who had elected to remain a man. I also said bluntly that having your penis removed and taking hormones did not make you a woman. A woman's identity comes from her complete history. All of our experience living lives treated as girls and then as women works toward forming our female identity. Ironically, the idea of becoming a woman through surgery and hormones could only appeal to men who are truly clueless about what it means to *be* a woman.

Tina, in all his glory, was shocked. Not surprisingly, that interview never made it on the air.

Destroying Themselves Is Not Enough

If Tina had thought this up all by himself, I wouldn't bother to write about it here. But the tragedy of transsexuals rests with the psychiatric and medical communities who participate in the charade by legitimizing "gender identity" disorders. It also sits squarely with the Gay Elite for creating a cultural environment that makes serious discussion and analysis of psychological problems politically incorrect.

As we've seen, these problems don't remain personal and private. The drive, especially since this issue is associated with the world of "gay rights," is to make sure your worldview reflects theirs. To counter this effort, we must demand that the medical and psychiatric community take off their PC blinders and treat these people responsibly. If we don't, the next thing you know, your child will be taking a "tolerance" class explaining how "transsexuality" is just another "lifestyle choice."

Already, the agenda of indoctrinating children is being implemented. If you think this issue is too far-fetched, too freakish, to touch your life or your children's, consider the plans offered by a medical doctor, Anne Lawrence, associated with a group called Transsexual Women's Resources.

Lawrence, who, by the way, is also a transsexual, suggests lowering the age at which "treatment" of GID can begin to 16 years.[1] The first red flag here is that this presses the idea that GID actually exists *in children*. And, sure enough, one of Lawrence's other nifty suggestions makes this explicit: She advocates providing "puberty-delaying hormones," which can only mean treating children *as young as 9 to 12 years old*[2]—that is, prior to the onset of the process that begins the development of our adult sexual identities. Prepubescent children don't *have* a sexual identity in the adult sense and consequently do not need hormones, unless, of course, your goal is to legitimize your own illness by forcing it onto everyone else, including children.

By the way, in the passage where Dr. Lawrence says that adolescents should be considered eligible for hormonal therapy, she adds, "preferably with parental consent."[3] *Preferably?!* How considerate of her.

While you may view Dr. Lawrence as being on the fringe, she is not. She writes prolifically on GID and works feverishly with the gay establishment to influence society and the medical establishment.[4] It is important to remember that it is a very few individuals in our country who work for direct social change. Those who do, have an impact. Sometimes all it takes is one person to profoundly reshape social attitudes and even medical standards.

Not My Kind of Big Sister

If you still think any effort to reach children with this perversion is an anomaly, consider the following. One of the events Dr. Lawrence participates in is an actual transgender "conference." For the past 12 years, the Esprit Gala,[5] as it's called, has provided a wide variety of activities for attendees, including a fashion show, a dance, and a number of workshops. In between taking Corsage Making and Choosing the Right Wig Style, attendees can enroll in courses such as Sex and the Cross Dresser—Bedroom Issues, Crossdressing 101, Man! I Feel like a Woman!, and Sexual Reassignment Surgery.

If adults want to delude themselves in this manner, that's up to them. The outrage is the fact that the conference agenda includes—get this!—a Big Sister/Little Sister Program. Here's how the Task Force chair, Miss Dixie Darlington (I'm not kidding), describes the program. (Remember, with this group, references to "girls" and "sisters" actually mean males.)

Esprit also has a wonderful program designed to help those who want to come out but might need a little help getting started. We call it the Big Sisters/Little Sisters. We take little sisters, girls who are just getting started and match them up with big sisters. Big sisters are girls who have been out for a while and can give you a helping hand.[6]

I think it's safe to say this is the kind of helping hand that no parents want for their child. While there's no reference to age groups or the involvement of adolescents in this event, co-opting the name of the well-known and respected children's mentoring organization leaves little doubt about the agenda.

In fact, the organizers of the Esprit Gala specifically make accommodation for children. The Web site admonishes attendees that those in charge of Esprit "pride ourselves to be a family friendly event so please keep your hard-core, fetish wear at home or at least in the privacy of your room."[7] Gee, how nice of them.

The participation of people like Lawrence, who have actively promoted the inclusion of children as potentially transgenderable, also makes it clear that children are a target, as they are for any group that wants to remake society in its own image.

> I believe this grab for children by the sexually confused adults of the Gay Elite represents the most serious problem facing our culture today.

I believe this grab for children by sexually confused adults represents the most serious problem facing our culture today. We see this focus on projecting their issues onto children throughout the efforts of the radical gay movement. Recall the deaf parents I wrote about in chapter 1. Now imagine a pair of transsexual parents putting their child into GID treatment instead of Little League—and imagine that child is one of *your* child's classmates.

Of course, there are those rare individuals who are born with a chromosome abnormality that produces legitimate gender issues. What I'm talking about here is something very dif-

ferent: men, and sometimes women, who have been so traumatized that they are unable to accept themselves. Psychologically
they feel the compulsion to disappear themselves by changing
their very existence. How all this works has not been studied
with a serious and objective psychological eye. In fact, researchers supportive of "reassignment surgery" readily admit
that there is really no research addressing the possibility that
"gender identity disorder" is in fact a mental illness, to be
treated as such rather than taken as a cue for surgical transformation. One report explains it this way:

> [M]embers of the DSM-IV Subcommittee on Gender Iden-
> tity Disorders [a subcommittee of the Child Psychiatry
> Work Group] have noted that the question of whether dis-
> tress is inherent to transvestism or imposed by social pres-
> sures is not resolved. . . . It is again not clearly defined
> who is ill and who is not, the judgment resting upon the
> personal values of the evaluator.[8]

That's a worry. Consider that many of the people relied on
to make those judgments are willing participants in events like
the Esprit conference—the same people who had to be asked to
leave their fetish wear at home. Theories that rest on the sub-
jective "personal values" of a researcher instead of on concrete
scientific definitions are a cornerstone of moral relativism. They
have condemned many who simply need psychiatric help to believing that mutilating their bodies will solve their problems.

The Red Badge of AIDS

One would think that with the scourge of AIDS loose in the
world, the gay community itself would have taken a stand
and demanded a change in the gay male lifestyle, which is
largely one of promiscuity and unprotected intercourse. The
epidemic presented a terrific opportunity for the community's
leaders to realize that integrity not only could be a part of gay
men's lives but could enhance them. Instead, the exact opposite has occurred.

The fact that promiscuous sex has been the essence of gay male liberation is an important point. This promiscuity is truly a gay *male* phenomenon and not characteristic of homosexuality per se—or you would find lesbians in bathhouses looking for easy sex with scores of partners. That's not happening because women behave differently from men, in the gay world as in the straight world.

My early activism included work with the group AIDS Coalition to Unleash Power (ACT UP). Known for outrageous actions designed to focus media attention on the issue of AIDS, the members of ACT UP were mostly HIV-positive men (joined by a few women) who were determined to increase funding for research.

By now, scores of young men I grew to love and admire are dead from AIDS. They contracted the disease in the 1980s, before anyone even knew it existed. They led lives of "sexual liberation," not taking seriously the dangers of promiscuous anal sex that were known, including epidemics of rectal gonorrhea, syphilis, and hepatitis B. In the decades preceding AIDS, these contagions, while treatable in themselves, depleted immune systems and opened the door for the pandemic.

These men had been lulled by treatable diseases into a blissful ignorance. For most of my friends, their biggest health worry pre-AIDS was not a worry at all. They saw no reason to address their promiscuity or face their demons.

AIDS changed all that—for a time. Public-health authorities in most cities moved to close the bathhouses (over the protests of the very activists who were demanding AIDS research), and many gay men heard the wake-up call for "safe sex." Some settled down with a single partner; others at least started using condoms.

What a difference treatment makes! As researchers succeeded in developing ever more effective drugs, AIDS became—like gonorrhea, syphilis, and hepatitis B before it—what many consider to be a simple "chronic disease." And many of the gay men who had heeded the initial warning went right back to having promiscuous unprotected sex. There is now even a movement—the "bareback" movement—that *encourages* sex without condoms. The infamous bathhouses are opening up again; drug use, sex parties, and hundreds of sex partners a year are all once again a feature of the "gay lifestyle." In fact, "sexual liberation" has simply become a code phrase for the abandonment of personal responsibility, respect, and integrity.

In his column for Salon.com, David Horowitz discussed gay radicals like the writer Edmund White. During the 1960s and beyond, White addressed audiences in the New York gay community on the subject of sexual liberation. He told one such audience that "gay men should wear their sexually transmitted diseases like red badges of courage in a war against a sex-negative society."[9] And did they ever. Then, getting gonorrhea was the so-called courageous act. Today, the stakes are much higher. That red badge is now one of AIDS suffering and death, and not just for gay men themselves. In their effort to transform society, the perpetrators are taking women and children and straight men with them.

Even Camille Paglia, a woman whom I do not often praise, astutely commented some years ago, "Everyone who preached free love in the Sixties is responsible for AIDS. This idea that it was somehow an accident, a microbe that sort of fell from heaven—absurd. We must face what we did."[10]

The moral vacuum did rear its ugly head during the 1960s with the blurring of the lines of right and wrong (remember "situational ethics"?), the sexual revolution, and the consequent emergence of the feminist and gay civil-rights movements. It's not the original ideas of these movements, mind you, that caused and have perpetuated the problems we're discussing. It was and remains the few in power who project their destructive sense of themselves onto the innocent landscape, all the while influencing and conditioning others. Today, not only is the blight not being faced, but in our Looking-Glass world, AIDS is romanticized and sought after.

HIV Is Fun and Erotic!

Today, the leading gay activists are no longer with ACT UP, agitating for more research and for AIDS education and awareness. No, today's leaders are the "bareback" activists, who advocate anal sex without condoms. The message is: It is hip and glamorous to have unprotected sex. And that message is particularly appealing to the age group that is most inclined to take risks anyway. "If someone has AIDS or HIV, that kind of lionizes them. It's heroic, like fighting the battle," says an HIV-negative sophomore at the University of Florida. "When you get with someone who has HIV, it's like being with someone greater than you are."[11]

The ghastly bareback movement is being oddly lauded in the gay community. *Poz*, a magazine for HIV-positive people, featured a bareback activist on its cover not long ago, glamorously presenting him naked and smiling atop a saddleless horse. The phenomenon has become so widespread that the *New York Times* and *Newsweek* have covered it. *Newsweek* tried to explain the trend by saying, "Danger can be erotic, even the threat of contracting a deadly disease."[12] In other words, gay men are essentially resorting to suicide in order to have an "erotic" experience. Are you still looking for the definition of sick and depraved or the death of right and wrong? There you have it.

Gay men are using the term "bareback" on Web sites and at singles clubs to find other men willing to engage in the practice. Internet chat rooms and personal ads in magazines also keep the bareback community's wheels greased. It must be considered that barebackers, even subconsciously, are seeking out the virus. Barebacking got its biggest boost with what is termed the "morning after" pill. It is a combination of powerful AIDS drugs that must be taken for 28 days. Some studies have shown this course of treatment may actually prevent the AIDS virus from taking root.[13] Meant initially for health-care workers who were exposed accidentally or via an attack by an infected patient, it is now being marketed to gay men.

The strangest and most disturbing development of all is the small but growing minority of gay men not only risking infection but *seeking* it.[14] In the community these men are known as "bug chasers." On the right side of the Looking Glass, this idea sounds incomprehensible. Unfortunately, in the context of trauma, malignant narcissism, and projection, it makes all the (deadly) sense in the world.

- Victimhood is your empowerment—hence the desire to become infected and infect others.

- You work to have AIDS become normal and inevitable by leading a life that spreads the contagion, thus forcing society to assimilate with you.

- You then demand that all the world accept your behavior and suppress judgment, perpetuating moral relativism.

Here comes that elephant again: Almost without exception, the gay men I know (and that's too many to count) have a story of some kind of sexual trauma or abuse in their childhood— molestation by a parent or an authority figure, or seduction as an adolescent at the hands of an adult. The gay community must face the truth and see sexual molestation of an adolescent for the abuse it is, instead of the "coming-of-age" experience many regard it as being. Until then, the Gay Elite will continue to promote a culture of alcohol and drug abuse, sexual promiscuity, and suicide by AIDS.

I mentioned what I've just told you at David Horowitz's birthday party last year. A number of the Worth Knowing were present, including Congressman David Dreier. It was to him that I made this observation. Fred Dickey, who was writing a story about me for the *Los Angeles Times Magazine,* later wrote, "I am holding a tape recorder in front of Bruce, and I'm thinking, 'Do you have any idea how this will look in print?'"[15]

Yes, I sure do. For so many gays and lesbians, it looks like the difficult truth, which we've avoided for far too long and must begin to seriously address. The only way that's going to happen is if we begin to actually say it, out loud.

The Preventable Plague

Barebacking is the equivalent of setting off a bomb in an office building. The latter is illegal, and so should be knowingly spreading the AIDS virus. Let's be honest. There is a way to stop the spread of AIDS—it's called abstaining from sex. Unlike with Alzheimer's disease, Parkinson's disease, or diabetes, you can make a decision to not get AIDS (with a few unfortunate exceptions, like the child of an infected mother or the victim of a contaminated blood transfusion). Considering its preventability, there is no excuse for AIDS being the biggest health crisis we as a people face.[16]

> Considering its preventability, there is no excuse for AIDS being the biggest health crisis we as a people face.

In a rare event, one gay male was honest enough to address the lack of personal responsibility as a factor in the spread of AIDS. Charles Bouley, whose partner had been HIV-positive for 12 years and had died of a heart attack, noted in a column for *The Advocate,* the premier gay and lesbian news magazine in the country, the fact that AIDS cases are rising. Remarking about the Centers for Disease Control's announcement that gay men, ages 16-25, are the number one group getting those new infections, Bouley states:

> . . .They are ignorant to a disease that has been around over 20 years. And if they are gay and male, they doubly deserve it. We've seen firsthand what it can do but choose to ignore that in favor of our own carnal desires.[17]

But Bouley's prescription is based much too much on common sense and morality to gain much of a hearing.

Of course, AIDS also became a huge crisis because our society has been gagged by political correctness and the Thought Police. Because tolerance of homosexuals has become generally accepted, and because the sexual compulsives I am talking about are a subset of homosexuals, one dare not suggest that they change their behavior pattern. And yet the gay radicals may be pushing it too far. With such slick expressions as "Membership has its privileges," bandied about by HIV-positive men concerning their status, it is not unreasonable for the average person to become resentful of the billions of dollars spent every year by the government (in other words, by us taxpayers) for

AIDS research, medical care, and disability payments. There is a point where all of us become nothing more than enablers.

Men purposely infecting one another while expecting lesbians and straight Americans to fund the death party is truly bizarre and unacceptable. Of course, the silence about this continues because society has been brainwashed into believing that suggesting people behave with some decency is an affront, and suggesting to a gay man that he stop having anal sex is homophobic.

The Gay Elite supposedly want to confront homophobia. At this rate all they need do is look in the mirror. Their abandonment of their own out of political correctness, cowardice, and narcissism has condemned tens of thousands to death.

Lying: The Good Deed

"I lied because I felt very strongly about the fact that I should not allow the homophobic policies of this organization to keep me from helping my fellow men/women."[18] What is the awful homophobia that this noble gay man is seeking to circumvent by lying? It's the Red Cross's rules to keep the national blood supply free from HIV, the virus that causes AIDS. His remarkable statement was presented by *The Advocate* in a poll of its readers about donating blood in the aftermath of 9/11.

In 1985, when scientists finally reached a consensus on how HIV is spread, the Red Cross established a rule banning men from donating blood if they had had sex with another man since 1977. This rule was established because gay men who are sexually active are more likely than the general populace to be infected with diseases such as AIDS and hepatitis. It's that simple, that reasonable, and that important.

For malignant narcissists, however, other people's lives mean nothing. Everything is about them. They're offended. They're insulted. Me me me me meeeeee!

The rationalization of the man quoted by *The Advocate*, who lied about being in the highest-risk group for HIV, was that he did it in order to "help" other people. This is a perfect illustration of how far some gay men will go to break the rules.

In their self-obsessive grandeur, they refuse to consider the danger in which they are placing other people.

It was only after September 11th that a number of gay men who had never donated blood finally learned of the restriction, and their true nature came wailing out. One of the more shocking episodes was when a Harvard student leader encouraged gays to violate the Red Cross policy.

Clifford Davidson, then-leader of Harvard's BOND (Beyond Our Normal Differences), a student group self-described as "geared toward those who may not be 'straight,'" sent an e-mail to his membership on the day our nation was attacked. According to *The Harvard Crimson,* his e-mail read, "On the Red Cross's form, you will be asked: 'Are you a man who has had sexual contact with another man since 1973?' This applies to many of you. You should lie."[19]

The public protests complained that the Red Cross was "prejudiced" and that "bigotry" was at the heart of its policy. These protests ignored everything about AIDS transmission known to the medical community and to gay people. The fact is, there is a window of at least six months between the time a person is infected with HIV and the time it can be detected. Which means you could be HIV-positive and test HIV-negative.

Some have complained that the Red Cross's rule was developed at a time when we knew much less about HIV/AIDS than we know now, and when anxiety about the disease was high. Other gay critics say that the policy, a mandate from the U.S. Food and Drug Administration, is "outdated" because current testing methods can detect HIV and other contagions in donated blood.

Given this mentality, it would be futile to remind these men that AIDS was quietly spreading for years (if not more than a decade) before anyone even knew of its existence. Do we really think AIDS is the last unknown killer lurking out there? Given the ability of viruses to mutate, who knows what new resistant HIV strains or bacteria mutations may be developing in response to the newly developed drugs?

The medical community understands this. "The risk is not so much with the diseases we can test for. It's for the diseases we don't know about,"[20] is how Professor Dr. F. Blaine Hollinger explained why health specialists oppose allowing sexually active gay men to donate blood. This concern, however, means nothing to the men who are willing to pour their blood into the nation's supply in a vain effort to deny the reality of their lives.

In the normal world, anxiety about this plague is still high. In 2000 Sandra Thurman, AIDS policy advisor to then-President Clinton, described the HIV pandemic as comparable to and potentially worse than the bubonic plague. "This is clearly the worst public health crisis we've seen . . . and if the epidemic continues to escalate at its current pace it will absolutely make that epidemic pale in comparison."[21]

That seems not to matter to another gay man who participated in the *Advocate* poll. "Being a volunteer EMT (Emergency Medical Technician) for 8 years plus and an American Heart Association CPR Instructor I know from medical facts that the Red Cross's policy on Donating Blood is outdated and morally wrong. Therefore, I always lie when asked about my sexual history in order to continue my good deeds."[22] On his side of the Looking Glass, potentially exposing innocent strangers to the plague is a "good deed." If you were thinking the malignant narcissism of some members of the gay community could never affect your life, it's time to think again.

GLSEN Wants Your Children

For people whose entire identity and reason to live is based in their sexuality, what do they need to do in order to fit comfortably into our society? They must work to sexualize every part of society—and, as every good marketer knows, that effort must begin with children.

The Gay, Lesbian and Straight Education Network describes itself as "the leading national organization fighting to end anti-gay bias in K–12 schools." This organization, which cloaks itself in a mantra about "tolerance" and "understanding," is implementing programs in public schools that are aimed at nothing less than sexualizing your children.

The efforts of gay establishment organizations, if the future is really their concern, should be focused on persuading the horde of bacchanalian boys to change their lifestyle. Instead, they are demanding that we accept their degeneracy, and the destruction of our future in the process. We dare not judge them. We dare not question their actions. And we are to hand the nation's children over to them.

Keep in mind, GLSEN claims as its mission the protection of so-called gay, lesbian, and transgendered children from harassment and discrimination. Think about this. Gay and lesbian children? Transgendered children? GLSEN states it is working to make sure all primary- and secondary-school students "accept all of their classmates—regardless of sexual orientation and gender identity/expression." Gender identity/expression in kindergarten?

I for one, and no doubt you as well, believe we should let children be children without having to "learn" about homophobia, especially when it's used as a pretext to gain access to a child.

Every Parent's Nightmare

On March 25, 2000, the Massachusetts Department of Education, the Governor's Commission, and GLSEN cosponsored a statewide conference at Tufts University called "Teach-Out." One workshop was titled What They Didn't Tell You About Queer Sex & Sexuality in Health Class: A Workshop for Youth Only, Ages 14–21. Education professionals would receive credit for attending, and teenagers and children as young as 12 attended as well.[23]

In this "workshop," the discussion revolved around what homosexual sex actually is. The answer, for these people, amounted to filling a bodily orifice with genitalia. (I guess they haven't gone to the Bill Clinton School of how to get away with denying ever having had "sexual relations.")

Given this definition of sex, it shouldn't be surprising that the workshop presenters found it necessary to describe how lesbians have sex. Dildos were discussed, with tips on how you (a 14-year-old) would know if the dildo was too large or too small. At that point, gay "resources" about similar subjects were offered to the kids.[24]

Of course, there was role-playing, too. One female student acted the part of a lesbian attracted to another girl. In addressing the topic "Cum and calories: Spit versus swallow and the health concerns," the presenters said, among other things, that male ejaculate is "sweeter" if the man eats celery.[25] Remember, this conference was supposed to be about "tolerance" and accepting those who are different from you. In fact, it appears to have been nothing more than indoctrinating students into sex—homosexual sex.

Surely, in the age of AIDS, if the presenters were encouraging children to be sexually active, they were also educating them on some basic precautions? By now, you know the answer is No. One 16-year-old boy shared his idea about how to avoid HIV/AIDS transmission while giving oral sex. His suggestion? You should not brush your teeth or eat coarse food for four hours before you "go down on a guy."[26]

To make the parents' nightmare complete, the presenters answered some questions that supposedly had been submitted by children in the audience before the program began. One of the presenters read the first question for the panel: "What's fisting?," a sex act which involves the insertion of a fist and forearm into the vagina or rectum of the partner.

If this was a question submitted by a child, then I'm Elizabeth Taylor. And even if it had been, the adults involved should have rejected it. But they did not, because it specifically suited their agenda. The *Weekly Standard* reported that a "helpful and enthusiastic" presenter responded by offering the proper hand position for the act, while another described fisting as "an experience of letting somebody into your body that you want to be that close and intimate with."[27]

Thousands of Foot Soldiers

This is what GLSEN has in mind for your children. This is what decades of conditioning have allowed a state's public school system and department of health to condone. The death of right and wrong has so permeated our culture that the institutions we rely on to protect children now willingly participate in attempts to destroy them.

Make no mistake, this isn't some isolated quirk of funky Massachusetts. GLSEN is a national organization with one thing in mind: getting to your child through the open door at school. Take it from GLSEN. Their Web site states, "Thousands of volunteers participate in our national chapter network. These chapters work with local school boards, principals, educators and school librarians to create positive change in hometown schools," while "GLSEN's student organizing project provides support and resources to youth in *even the most isolated of places* [emphasis mine]. We support students as they form and lead gay-straight alliances—*helping them to change their own school environments from the inside out* [emphasis mine]."[28]

How does a group like GLSEN survive? With corporate sponsorship, of course! GLSEN, a nonprofit organization, proudly announces the list of corporations that fund it, many of which are among this nation's most powerful corporate entities (all publicly held, by the way).[29] Major supporters include AOL Time Warner, General Motors, IBM, and Pacific Bell. I wonder how many of the executives, let alone stockholders, of these corporations are aware that their money is helping to teach "fisting" techniques to children, while encouraging gay male sex during the plague?

It's time we demand that radical gays leave children alone, no matter how politically incorrect the argument becomes.

Conferences like the one in Massachusetts are just part of GLSEN's program. The organization is also responsible for the proliferation of over 700 Gay-Straight Alliance clubs on high-school campuses across the nation. It has also blasted the recent U.S. Supreme Court decision upholding the Cleveland school district's private-school voucher program. The GLSEN Web site complains that the voucher decision "undermines efforts to ensure the safety of lesbian, gay, bisexual and transgender (LGBT) students."[30]

Please. The only thing it undermines is GLSEN's ability to infiltrate schools with their propaganda. That's what drives them crazy. They will not have the same kind of access to children at private and religious schools as they have gained in the public-school system. That's another fantastic reason to support school vouchers—to get these parasites out of schools and away from children.

For decades now, a major front in the culture war has been over who makes decisions concerning your children. The belief that your children are not yours but the government's was given a new twist by Hillary Clinton, but it began, with whatever good intentions, as far back as the Supreme Court decisions on school busing in the 1970s. It is an ideology that permits the government to use children in the attempt to remake society, with or without their parents' consent. It's time we demand that radical gays leave children alone, no matter how politically incorrect the argument becomes.

It's Elementary

GLSEN isn't alone when it comes to using children and the school system to promote the radical gay agenda. A documentary film called *It's Elementary: Talking About Gay Issues in School* offers a look at that agenda in action. The film, which actually uses children to move its message, is supposed to show teachers and other educators how to advocate homosexuality to children in grades one through eight. In perhaps a more subtle way than GLSEN's conference, *It's Elementary* endorses the idea of homosexuality, bashes religion, and mocks people who believe homosexual activity is wrong.

At one point, it offers a montage of supposed homophobia as depicted by Hollywood. One clip features Jim Carrey responding with disgust after his character in a film mistakenly kisses a man.[31] What's the underlying message here? That Jim Carrey's reaction was wrong, so consequently a man kissing a man must be just fine. Obviously, for many men it is, but this message, in fact any message about sex, does not belong in a child's life.

According to *It's Elementary*, those who take traditional views of homosexuality are ignorant (a teacher remarks that to be homophobic means to think homosexuality is contagious), racist, and violent (a fifth-grader announces that "some Christians" want to "torture" gays).[32]

Just like GLAAD and GLSEN, the film's producers coyly describe their work as an effort to help end bigotry and intolerance. They argue that teaching children about homosexuality will keep them from turning into homophobes later.[33] This promotes, as the Left is wont to do, the idea that inside each of us is a little homophobe waiting to strike out. The distrust of the average American is fed by a victim mentality that has become absolutely astonishing.

This film, by the way, isn't languishing in some basement without a hope of being distributed. It has already been aired on 100 stations of the Public Broadcasting System (PBS), and the film's producers delight in informing us that it has been acquired by nearly 2,000 educational institutions.[34]

Interestingly, it's the choice of music at the very end of the documentary that gives away the underlying attitude of the whole Left Elite regarding children. Brent Bozell of the Media Research Center, writing for NewsMax.com, points out that the song heard over the closing credits says, in part, "Your children are not your children. . . . They come through you, but they are not from you, and though they are with you, they belong not to you."[35]

As you can imagine, I have a deeply personal interest in people learning to at least be tolerant of homosexuals. My life depends on it. And as I wish to be left alone, I realize it is not in my interest to interfere with how other people choose to lead *their* lives, or raise their children. All totalitarian arguments that restrict people's freedom have been based in the it's-best-for-everyone framework.

In all honesty, the real issue here isn't whether you willingly accept homosexuality, think homosexual activity is a sin, or are even homosexual yourself. While that question is certainly an important one, the striking development here is the fact that it's being presented to children at the elementary-school level.

These issues about sex, values, and even tolerance belong in the hands of parents, not of school administrators and faculty. Educators have been charged with teaching your child how to read and to compute two plus two—not what to think on important moral and social issues. And these issues certainly don't belong in the hands of agenda-driven documentary producers.

It's worth reiterating that a discussion of homosexuality has simply no place in elementary school. There is no overriding claim worth usurping the moral right of parents to determine how their children will be raised and with what values. Americans have been raising their children the best way they know how for over 200 years, and gay people are doing quite well and are pretty darn safe in this country. The promotion of so-called tolerance of homosexuals in this way is nothing more than an excuse to move the idea itself into your child's world without your interference.

Bashing the Boy Scouts

Where do you think your 14-year-old boy would be safer for the weekend—at a camp run by a bunch of Catholic priests or at a Boy Scout retreat? It's a shame, but the answer is obvious for all of us. I address the Catholic Church's homosexual sex scandal in chapter 7, but a discussion of the gay agenda would not be complete without addressing the assault on the Boy Scouts of America (BSA).

Unlike the Catholic Church, the Boy Scout organization made a deliberate decision to not knowingly allow homosexual men to hold official positions of trust and authority over young males. The BSA has taken a lot of flak for that principled decision, but it has been proved right by the tragic counterpoint of the Catholic scandal.

David Kupelian, vice president and managing editor of WorldNetDaily.com and of *Whistleblower* magazine, has written some of the most important and informative articles on this problem. He reports that "the Scouting folks know what everyone with half a brain understands: that adults interested in sexual contact with young people gravitate toward careers and volunteer positions allowing proximity to their prey, positions such as coaches, teachers, scoutmasters—and priests."[36]

How do you reconcile this with what you've heard coming from the slick gay-activist PR machine? Their mantra is: Gay men are not pedophiles. Technically, they're right, but it really is just a cynical spin of semantics. Pedophilia indicates attraction to those 12 years old and younger. In fact, the problem the Boy Scouts have avoided by excluding gay men as Scout leaders is ephebophilia, or an attraction to adolescents.

What the gay establishment does not want you to think about is the fact that adult men being attracted to female adolescents is called "heterosexuality," while adult men being attracted to male adolescents is called—surprise!—"homosexuality." Now, based on the many gay men I've known, I feel safe in saying that most gay men are not ephebophiles either. Still, reasonable gay men should recognize that they have a responsibility to respect the Boy Scouts' concern over what some of their gay brethren are wreaking.

Unfortunately, many Americans have responded to the anti–Boy Scout drumbeat. In part this has happened because we care. We are a nation committed to equity, and once again narcissistic activists have manipulated that compassion in order to destroy something that dares to put children first, even ahead of the leftist agenda and political correctness. Kupelian reports that many individual Americans, along with businesses and other organizations, have withdrawn their financial and moral support from the Boy Scouts of America, condemning the organization as bigoted and hateful. Many United Way chapters have ceased to fund the BSA, and some local governments have declared it to be discriminatory.[37]

Those reactions are dramatic, and when juxtaposed with the American revulsion at the Catholic Church scandal, they indicate how controlled we are by what the media, and left-wing special-interest groups, choose to tell us. We are struggling in a swamp of groupthink, fearful of offending and refusing to face the devastation wrought by the sexually compulsive.

The real story about the Boy Scouts is that their policy of banning gay men has allowed them to manage the problem of molestation and avoid allowing the massive destruction of lives we see in an organization that has been unwilling to face reality. They have saved children's lives, and for this they remain under attack.

The Gay Trojan Horse

The hypocrisy among gay men and the larger community about the Boy Scout issue is spectacular. Come on. The gay culture does not grow men who are desperate to be Scout leaders! The Gay Elite know this, and so does every self-respecting gay person. Any gay man who truly embraces the Boy Scouts' tenets would understand the concern and would consequently be compelled to respectfully walk away. By contrast, those who threaten and demand and huff and puff about their exclusion expose their real agenda as inherently anti-Scouting. If the Catholic Church had been as eager to defend its principles as the Scouts have been, so many lives would not have been damaged or destroyed.

Frankly, even before the depth of the Catholic Church's problem became known, it was common knowledge that many gay men pursue sexual relationships with adolescent boys. Why? Based on my experience in the gay community, I believe it's due in part to the fact that so many gay men had their first sexual experience as an adolescent with an adult male. That is a traumatic experience, and as long as the wound remains untreated, the victim feels compelled to continually reenact the experience so as to master it or project it onto others.

> If the Catholic Church had been as eager to defend its principles as the Scouts have been, so many lives would not have been damaged or destroyed.

The other reason actually discussed in the community is that, because of the AIDS crisis and the emergence of drug-resistant strains of contagions like herpes and gonorrhea, gay men are compelled to seek new, untouched young men. Think about it. If you want to have condomless "safe" sex, whom can you choose that will almost certainly be absolutely, perfectly safe? Only a virgin suits your needs, and in today's world the best bet is a boy under the age of 16. Of course, the same consideration drives heterosexuals who lack a moral compass, leading both to the same pursuit of adolescents here at home (as I discuss at greater length in chapter 7) and to the horrible traffic in young girls for "sex tourism" in the Far East.

That knowledge did not stop the radical gay-rights movement from goose-stepping into action against the Boy Scouts:[38]

- Lobbying and threatening corporate sponsors to get them to discontinue their support

- Urging then-President Clinton to step down as honorary president of BSA

- Persuading a few members of Congress to try to revoke the organization's honorary charter (this effort failed)

- Urging Clinton to sign an executive order to evict the Boy Scouts from federal lands and facilities (this effort succeeded)

All this, in spite of the U.S. Supreme Court's decision that the BSA had every right to make and implement their ban on gay Scout leaders. Frankly, the reason for keeping gay men out of the Boy Scouts is the same reason men are not allowed to participate in the Girl Scouts. Yes, there is an important element of bonding in those environments, but really, wouldn't your red flag go up if a man was *desperate* to be a Girl Scout leader? Mine would. Self-respecting and Scout-respecting heterosexual men understand that the Girl Scouts are beyond their purview. They accept this and move on.

One reason the Left Elite hate the Boy Scouts is that the Boy Scouts have standards—standards that in the past have produced some of our best and brightest.

I know countless gay men and lesbians who recognize the benefits of the Boy Scouts.

- 63 percent of U.S. Air Force Academy graduates were Scouts.

- 68 percent of West Point graduates were Scouts.

- 70 percent of Annapolis graduates were Scouts.

- 85 percent of FBI agents were Scouts.

- 26 of the first 29 astronauts were Scouts.[39]

My life as an American has been made richer because of the contributions of an organization with standards that has produced extraordinary men.

Ironically, the gay establishment's argument is that the BSA's current policies teach Scouts to hate gay people. This libel needs to stop. It is not gays who are being defamed and tarnished in this effort—it's Scouts. Freedom demands a constant reassertion of values. The absence of righteous anger can be devastating to a culture. You and I need to go out of our way to support the Scouts and not let another battle in this culture war be lost.

To Hell with Those Vows

I don't wonder why the Boy Scouts are concerned. I don't wonder why the average American does not want gay people to adopt children. All I have to do is look around.

Consider this revealing look at the death of right and wrong, provided by *The Advocate*. This gay news magazine is considered quite mainstream and is highly respected. Heck, they've even published Yours Truly. Knowing that, consider the following story.

Stephen E. Goldstone, a medical doctor, responds to readers' questions in the magazine's "Health" column. His byline describes him as an openly gay physician in New York City. Gosh, that sounds pretty respectable—a professional, successful gay man reaching out with advice to the gay community. Advice from a source such as this should be highly reliable.

In June 2002 an elderly man signing himself as "James" wrote to Dr. Goldstone explaining that he is married (to a woman) and yet has been in a relationship with another man for eight years. He was writing to actually ask the doctor what medicines he could take to lower his sex drive. He wanted to change his libido to make it easier to break off his adulterous affair. In James's words, "[A]t 84, it is time I stop this double life."[40]

Certainly a little late, but a sentiment worth respecting and encouraging. So how did Dr. Goldstone reply to James?

> The fact that you still have a desire to have sex and have a fulfilling sexual relationship with a 45-year-old man is wonderful and should not be wished away. . . . Ending the relationship could cause illness and depression, and you could end up blaming your wife for the decision you made.[41]

The doctor then urges James to find ways to "come to terms" with his sexuality that will help him feel less guilty, so that he can "continue to find fulfillment with [his] male partner as well as with [his] wife."[42]

This is depravity, stripped bare and with no shame. While the betrayal of a vow does not bother the doctor, it has evidently started to bother James. And what about the health risks faced by James's wife? If James has such an active libido, it's a good bet he and his wife still share their own intimacy. How do women get AIDS? Is there any concern over how an elderly woman would deal with getting a strain of virulent herpes or gonorrhea?

What makes this particularly shocking is that it is not coming from some fringe "sex-positive" freak who thinks getting AIDS is a cool thing to do. No, this advice comes from a medical doctor in a suit and tie (he has his picture online with his column), giving apparent legitimacy to this kind of moral degeneracy.

Keep in mind, this advice is not just for James. It is in a column meant to be read by thousands of men and women, many of whom may also be leading double lives. They, too, are being encouraged to continue to lie and cheat, and to do so in a world full of awful ailments, none of which you want to have visited upon your home.

What else does this "resident physician columnist" for *The Advocate* offer? "[M]edical advice about alcoholism and libido, the safety of sex toys, sex for couples with mixed HIV status, and overcoming childhood abuse."[43] Ah, that's nice—let's make sure we deal with sex toys and how to enjoy cheating on your wife before we get to that pesky childhood abuse issue.

Here Little Boy, Have a Syphilis Sore

Okay, so now we have a medical doctor encouraging elderly men to maintain a life of lies; radical gay propaganda in schools; billions of taxpayer dollars continuing to fund research for a plague spread wantonly, and sometimes even deliberately, by gay men; and organizations that challenge the Gay Elite, like the Boy Scouts, being libeled and punished.

What's left? Oh, let's add the distribution of squeeze toys representative of a sexually transmitted disease. If you think that's impossible, it's already begun.

In the face of a rise in sexually transmitted diseases (STDs), and syphilis in particular, among gay men, the San Francisco Department of Health unveiled a new public-service ad campaign to try to stem the increase. Titled "Healthy Penis 2002," this campaign used the motto "Making Every Penis a Healthy Penis."[44] The ads used a cartoon image of a smiling, friendly erect penis. Bumpy red syphilis sores, all determined to harm the Happy Penis, were also drawn as cartoon characters with personalities, faces, and attitudes. One sore, named Phil (get it? as in syPHILis?), wore silver shoes and an earring.

What's the problem with this campaign? First of all, the San Francisco health authorities apparently believe that gay men are so immature they need cartoon characters to admonish them to deal with the red sores they may have on their penises. (It's important to remember that although syphilis is treatable with antibiotics, syphilis sores serve to transmit AIDS.)

That alone is pathetic enough, but here's the more dangerous situation: Treating gay men like children means reaching out with messages that are noticed *by* children.

You remember all the outrage about the use of Joe Camel by Camel cigarettes? The legitimate complaint there was that the use of a cartoon figure was meant to appeal to children. So what kind of message do you think a smiling, friendly erect penis sends to children? It makes the adult penis a fun, friendly kinda guy. Suddenly a man's penis isn't something children shouldn't see—it actually becomes their *friend*. A plaything, if you will. As today's children grow up, the world of gay promiscuity, disease and all, will have been normalized and legitimized by campaigns such as this.

Has anyone objected to the campaign for that reason? No. The impact on children isn't even broached because we've been brainwashed into thinking that protecting children from messages about gay sex is nothing more than homophobia. Los Angeles County health authorities did decline to use that particular campaign—not because of the effect on children but because they felt it objectified *gay men!*[45]

> As today's children grow up, the world of gay promiscuity, disease and all, will have been normalized and legitimized by campaigns such as this.

Instead, Los Angeles chose to run a "Stop the Sores" campaign without the Happy Penis. Phil is the star of this campaign, being featured in all manner of public places, including full-page newspaper ads. In fact, Los Angeles County seems to be doing even *more* than San Francisco to make its campaign kid-friendly. It has commissioned 40,000 three-inch Phil squeeze toys and two people wearing Phil suits as mascots of the character that will make appearances throughout Los Angeles.

Whoever these toys and mascots are meant to influence, we're all in a lot of trouble. Either the gay male community has indeed become a mindless walking penis, reachable only through cartoon images, or the Gay Elite now have carte blanche to attempt to draw children into their world. And why not kill two birds with one stone? Legitimize and treat as normal gay men who choose to ignore contagious diseases—and heck, let's make the disease fun for kids, too!

In fact, Dr. Jeffrey Klausner, director of Sexually Transmitted Disease Control in San Francisco, said his office favored the "Healthy Penis" campaign, which would cost about $50,000, specifically because its messages are "fun."[46]

Yes, indeed, these messages are fun. Certainly more fun than making promiscuous gay men face the fact that they are sick and need help. No, we need fun, and ignorance and pride, and squeezable plush toys commemorating our debauchery.

AIDS on Sesame Street

At the 14th International AIDS conference in Barcelona in July 2002, Joel Schneider, vice president and senior adviser to the Sesame Street Workshop, announced a new *Sesame Street* character—the world's first HIV-positive Muppet. This Muppet, named Kami, debuted as a regular on South Africa's *Takalani Sesame* in September 2002. Schneider explained the need for an HIV-positive Muppet for South Africa because one in nine people there has the virus.

Kami, which means "acceptance," is a female mustard-colored furry "monster" Muppet like Grover or Elmo, the least human-like of the *Sesame Street* cast. While Schneider said that there would be no explicit mention of sex,[47] *Time* magazine reports:

> When Kami bounces onto the screen, she will come across as a perky, fun-loving and healthy HIV-positive character with a wealth of information about HIV/AIDS to share with her inquisitive friends.[48]

I have one question. If Schneider is serious and there will be no discussion of sex associated with an HIV-positive Muppet, what "wealth of information" about HIV/AIDS can be shared? Presumably Kami will not be telling her friends that AIDS is a disease you can choose to not spread. She will not be telling them the reason why so many women and children in Africa have the disease—because of irresponsible men spreading it to the women in their lives, or intravenous drug abuse.

Consequently, the only message Kami can send to the two-to-four-year-old crowd (the prime target audience of *Sesame Street* and all of its international franchises) is that HIV is just a thing that, somehow, some way, fell out of the sky, infecting vulnerable, unsuspecting women and men. Gone will be the moral imperative of personal responsibility, and entering the picture will be a generation of children who think AIDS is like cerebral palsy. It's not anyone's fault, it just happens. This it-can-happen-to-you lie about AIDS—the Gay Elite's favorite motto—is now being passed on to the youngest children courtesy of *Sesame Street.*

If they can't bring up the reality of AIDS and how people get it, at least they *can* make children not afraid of the virus itself—they can make it . . . fun! And okay, and *normal.* Sesame Street Workshop confirmed that Kami will be used to "de-stigmatize" people with HIV/AIDS.[49] Who are they kidding? A two-year-old doesn't even have a concept of stigma. Are they concerned about all the three-year-old skinheads out there looking for gay men to beat up?

No, four-year-olds aren't contemplating the philosophical and social impact of the AIDS virus, nor are they making judgments about people with AIDS. This is simply another Trojan Horse to get to the minds of children as early as possible with the message that a plague wrought by promiscuous gay men and intravenous drug-users is okay. Even if you do things that spread the plague, that's okay, too. Everything is good. Nihilism rules the day.

At what point can we allow children to simply be children? If they're ready for HIV, why not weekly messages about adultery and anal sex? Hey! Let's throw in a Phil toy for every precocious youngster who can spell s-y-p-h-i-l-i-s.

Exploiting and Using the Innocent

Of course, children with HIV are indeed innocent. But how the virus got to them is not an innocent process. It's there because Daddy brought it home and infected Mommy, or because Mommy uses needles to inject her drugs.

Initially, even the Sesame Street Workshop was reluctant to create the new Muppet because they admitted they hadn't done appropriate research on the issue.[50] But that didn't worry the Workshop's "production partners," who insisted on Kami's development.

Those production partners include the South African Education Department; Sanlam, one of the country's major insurance companies; and—get this—the U.S. Agency for International Development. USAID describes itself as "an independent government agency that conducts foreign assistance and humanitarian aid to advance the political and economic interests of the United States."[51]

USAID work is funded with our tax dollars. Which means *we* paid for Kami to be created. The *Sesame Street* people had originally stated that the HIV-positive character might appear on the U.S. program. After some outrage, they backtracked, saying the producer of the program "misspoke." [52] So, instead, they've used American tax money to develop this travesty, which they can tweak after assessing the response of children in South Africa, and then move through other countries' programs as a guest Muppet.

The use of South African children as guinea pigs is unforgivable in itself. After Schneider made the initial announcement, the president of the nonprofit Kaiser Family Foundation, which studies health issues in South Africa and the United States, said the new Muppet could be helpful for young people or could be "a really bad thing."[53] We don't know yet, of course, because the study is being done on the children themselves.

Time for Action

Between GLSEN, the Happy Penis, Phil, and now Kami, I'd say the Gay Elite have your children as a captive audience. Whether you like it or not, they have appointed themselves as your children's moral tutor.

Oh, you don't like that? Then take some action. Here are some suggestions:

- *Recognize* that the radical Gay Elite do not represent the average gay man, and certainly not the average gay woman, in this country.

- *Think:* Is what is being presented to your children *really* about tolerance, or is it intended to introduce a sexual message? Think carefully, and then trust your conclusion and respond accordingly.

- *Remove* your child from any school that allows a sexual message to be presented. It will most likely be presented under the guise of tolerance or preventing the spread of disease. Don't be fooled.

- *Ask* your congressperson and senators to tie AIDS prevention funding in the gay community to a decline in the spread of the disease among *gay men* specifically. Tell them you're tired of subsidizing promiscuity and irresponsibility.

- *Contact* your city's department of health and go on record as opposing ad campaigns that use cartoon images in dealing with STDs. The men who are supposedly the targets of the campaign are grown-ups—how they deal with their diseases should be discussed in private with their doctor, not in public in front of your child.

- *Support* the Boy Scouts.

- *Realize* that wanting to be your child's moral tutor does not make you a homophobe—and don't be silenced by bullies who try to exploit your compassionate nature.

The agenda of today's radical Gay Elite not only harms you, it also does an extraordinary disservice to all the gay women and men in this country who are decent people, leading remarkable lives. It's time these decent people who happen to be homosexual take a stand against the hypocritical and destructive agenda of the radical Gay Elite. I consider this exposé of the corrupt in our community to be my first shot in the rejection of the depravity of the few in the name of the many.

Enslaving Their Own:
Betrayal by the Black Elite

There is a class of colored people who make a business of keeping the troubles, the wrongs and the hardships of the Negro race before the public. Having learned that they are able to make a living out of their troubles, they have grown into the settled habit of advertising their wrongs—partly because they want sympathy and partly because it pays.

—*Booker T. Washington, 1911*[1]

Why are people like Louis Farrakhan and Jesse Jackson, who claim to be working to improve the quality of life for blacks in this country, actually doing the opposite? How is it that Al Sharpton, Johnnie Cochran, and Maxine Waters became leaders of their community by working to condemn its people to hopelessness and despair? The answer is the Cult of Victimhood, and its operations in the black community provide some of the more graphic and distressing examples of how much damage can be inflicted on the concepts of right and wrong when malignant narcissists are in charge.

121

122 • ENSLAVING THEIR OWN

The brutal Mike Tyson and the bizarre Michael Jackson are lionized by the Black Elite as showing what the young black man can achieve. Cold-blooded murderers Mumia Abu-Jamal and H. Rap Brown are held up as examples of how Whitey tries to keep good men down.

Blacks in this country have a remarkable array of genuine role models to emulate, from Michael Jordan to Colin Powell, Condoleezza Rice to Halle Berry. The Black Elite have no excuse for protecting, supporting, and celebrating the sickest and most dangerous of their community instead of these positive figures.

Booker T. Washington was only partly right. Yes, there is money to be made off oppression and victimhood. In *The New Thought Police* I detailed why I call today's Black Elite the Misery Merchants. But I contend that the Black Elite are also motivated, whether consciously or subconsciously, by a deep-rooted hatred for their country and themselves, which leads them to attempt to destroy the future of their own people and, indeed, everyone else.

The Dilemma

The Black Elite have a serious dilemma: How do you subjugate a people while convincing them that you are working tirelessly to protect their rights? You must keep up the drumbeat that there is no hope; that white people are the enemy who would as soon tie a black man to the back of a truck as look at him; that the government is conspiring to distribute crack cocaine to young blacks; that black men are targeted for genocide by the white justice system.

Those who claim to lead the black community perpetuate these falsehoods about our culture in part because it helps create a climate of moral relativism After all, how else can you keep a straight face while demanding the release of a cop killer? How else can you condition Americans to accept the idea that murderers and rapists are the victims?

Why do the role models held up to the black community include killers, rapists, and other violent, abusive men? Is it because black people as a group fall disproportionately into these categories? Hardly. Yet that is exactly the image projected by the morally bankrupt Black Elite. Just as the image of the average gay person has been stained by the agenda of the Gay Elite, black Americans are facing nothing less than libel at the hands of their so-called leaders. The compulsion of those leaders to support murderers in their midst would be inexplicable if we didn't understand that it's the death of right and wrong that drives them.

Black youths are besieged with the message that personal responsibility, self-control, and respect for others are outdated concepts. They are also constantly drilled with a message that can only bring hopelessness and anger: Whitey is out to get you and won't stop till he does.

Professor Walter Williams has collected some outrageous expressions of this message. From David Bell, Harvard law professor: "Black people will never gain full equality in this country." From the late columnist Carl Rowan: "Racism remains a terrible curse on this society, and . . . nothing in sight suggests that that curse will end soon." From New York Representative Charles Rangel: "Black men are not the problem. Black men are the victims." From Jesse Jackson: "We [blacks] are under attack by the courts, legislatures and mass media. We're despised. Racists attack us for sport to win votes." From New York Supreme Court judge Ivan Warner: "The entire United States is a racist society."[2]

> The compulsion of the Black Elite to support murderers in their midst would be inexplicable if we didn't understand that it's the death of right and wrong that drives them.

Williams analyzes these demoralizing statements by the Black Elite: "These comments, observations and counsel are just a tiny sample of three decades' worth of defeatist poison bestowed on the black community by leftist politicians, civil rights leaders, professors and teachers. . . . The victimization counsel of black and white liberals is debilitating. . . ."[3] However, for the Black Elite, as for the Feminist and Gay Elites, keeping your constituents hopeless and angry makes them infinitely more controllable and exploitable. After all, if everyone else is the devil, they won't dare question you or your motives.

When I speak of the Black Elite, I mean black men and women in politics, entertainment, and sport who deliberately use their position to draw their black sisters and brothers into their abyss of hatred and blame. Among the guilty are Louis Farrakhan, Jesse Jackson, Julian Bond, Kweisi Mfume, Maxine Waters, Mike Tyson, Al Sharpton, Jim Brown, Johnnie Cochran, academics Cornell West and bell hooks, and every "gangsta rap" performer, promoter, and producer.

These people dare to say that they do the bidding of the average black American, that they care and are working to improve the quality of life for blacks. I believe the opposite is true. From what I have seen and will detail for you here, it appears they do their own bidding, furthering the subjugation of the average American who happens to be black. Because it pays. Because it forces society to integrate with their hopeless worldview.

Why Aren't Things Getting Better?

I remember a particularly honest young man at a speech I gave at the University of Southern California, my alma mater. After my speech, he rose and identified himself as a proud leftist and explained his politics were based in wanting to make life better for those in this country he felt got the short end of the stick, blacks especially.

He then looked down, and for the life of me I never would have predicted what his question was going to be. He said he believed the Left truly wanted to make things better for people in the inner city. Then he continued: "I've been frustrated, though, that things don't seem to be getting better. We're all working so hard [his fellow student volunteers and idealists] but nothing's getting better. Why is that?" Both the professor and a reporter there to cover the event were astonished not only that he noticed the lives of those on the fringe weren't improving but that he felt comfortable asking *why*.

I expanded on what I've just told you here—those who proclaim themselves advocates for the poor and minorities (the two unfortunately are in the same sentence more than any of us would like) have a vested interest in things not changing. Blacks in this country in particular have been relying on Democrats and leftists for decades now, while the quality of life for those most in need has declined. At what point will others who have been hoodwinked by the Left be as brave as that student and ask themselves that same question? The truthful answer will lead them away from malignant narcissists and finally into the future.

Leftists, now in control of the Democratic Party, have simply co-opted issues of importance to all Americans, including black civil rights. But the proof of a real commitment isn't seated in rhetoric—it's in action. Which is probably why it took a fairly conservative president, George W. Bush, to finally appoint black people to real positions of power. Jimmy Carter didn't. Bill Clinton didn't. It didn't take a village, Hillary—it took a Republican.

Muddy Waters

You may have noticed that this is the first chapter in which I've mentioned power-players in music and sport as a key part of the Left Elite. Although all the Left's special-interest groups use their superstars in various fields to soldier their message along, black youth emulate music and sports stars more than, for example, young gays or feminists do. But before we turn to these black "heroes," let's look at an elected leader of the black community.

Consider Congresswoman Maxine Waters. Normally I would not ask such a thing of you because of the unpleasantness of the request, but in this case it is necessary. Waters is a perfect example of how those trusted to keep alive the flame of the civil-rights movement handed it over to individuals with a very different agenda.

Waters's own congressional Web site declares that she is considered "one of the most powerful women in politics today."[4] Unfortunately, I'm afraid that's true. She has served on the Democratic National Committee since 1980. She has led the Congressional Black Caucus. She was a key player in five presidential campaigns, and she seconded the nominations of Senator Edward Kennedy (1980), the Reverend Jesse Jackson (1984 and 1988), and Governor Bill Clinton (1992).[5]

She also has an uncanny ability to simultaneously create and exploit victimhood. Her determination to malign her fellow black Americans revealed itself most dramatically when she declared the 1992 Los Angeles riot to be a "rebellion"[6] of oppressed black people and an outbreak of black "civil unrest."[7] Neither statement is accurate, and both rely on the presumption that black people in the city are violent, out of control, and so desperate to end their oppression that they've turned into anarchic beasts.

The fact is, as a RAND Corporation analysis stated a few months after the riot, and as I noted in *The New Thought Police,* "This was clearly not a black riot."[8] Some blacks took part, but it was mostly opportunistic Hispanics who looted and burned the city, for no other reason than that they wanted free stuff. I'm a native of Los Angeles, and I believe the black people of this city still deserve an apology from Waters for her demagogic portrayal of them.

What's ironic is that Waters represents the 35th Congressional District, which includes Inglewood and South Central Los Angeles, both areas significantly affected by the riot. She of all people knows the community and must have known that the vast majority of her constituency were not remotely poised to launch into a race riot, even after the fateful Rodney King verdict.

Many people in this city were appalled by that verdict. But for Maxine Waters, it was conveniently marketed as an issue of black versus white.

To further her own agenda, Waters was willing to portray black people as vandals eager to loot and burn their own community. She also reinforced that falsehood to the black community itself. You see, although most of her constituents knew that *they* had not participated in the orgy of destruction, perhaps *their neighbor* had. It wasn't a difficult misrepresentation to maintain. The black community, like all of us, relies on news coverage for information, and local, national, and even international news media—thanks in great part to Waters's rantings—repeated and amplified the falsehood that this was a "black rebellion."

As a feminist and a civil-rights advocate, I still find it hard to grasp, despite everything I now know about the real agenda of the Left, that anyone who claims to want to improve the quality of life would deliberately do things to destroy it. And yet, by portraying rioters as an oppressed underclass of blacks who can't help striking out, Waters achieves the malignant narcissist's dream combo—she reinforces the victim mentality among her public and pits black people against everyone else. The coup de grâce of this strategy is to indict the American government, and indeed the whole American system of freedom and democracy, as ultimately responsible for the riot.

But even that wasn't enough. While some modicum of decency would at least have compelled her to come to the aid of the Korean store owners in her district who suffered so greatly at the hands of opportunistic looters, she did the opposite. Instead of embracing the truly victimized among her constituency, she gave her sympathy to those who ransacked and robbed the innocent:

> There were mothers who took this as an opportunity to take some milk, to take some bread, to take some shoes. Maybe they shouldn't have done it, but the atmosphere was such that they did it. They are not crooks.[9]

How dare she cast those who ruined hardworking people's lives as desperate mothers looking for milk? If it weren't so revolting it would be hilarious. It also exposes how deep her disdain is for the concepts of right and wrong.

Mad Maxine

One of the most extraordinary urban myths in the black community is that AIDS was created by the U.S. government to kill black men. I say *one* of the most extraordinary, because Waters has had a grand old time promulgating another myth along much the same lines. This is the myth that the Central Intelligence Agency deliberately sent crack cocaine into South-Central Los Angeles to destroy the black community. Here it is from the, er, horse's mouth during a congressional hearing on the matter:

> "The origin of the crack cocaine trade in this country was led and designed by the CIA and their paid Nicaraguan agents—who introduced crack cocaine to South-Central Los Angeles. . . . The consequences of this wholesale dumping of cocaine into inner cities by CIA-organized agents has been widespread homelessness, violence, the destruction of families, and death."[10]

So there you have it. Homelessness, drug addiction, and the destruction of the black family have nothing, absolutely nothing, to do with the epidemic of personal irresponsibility among black men. No, they're victims, and of the CIA to boot!

Think about the extraordinary narcissism and destructiveness of this statement. First, Waters seems to think the government (and I suppose the rest of us) are so obsessed with black men as to spend a large chunk of resources on a plot to destroy them.

Then, by spreading this story, Waters infects her own public with a paranoia and distrust that only draws them further into the pit of hopelessness. For crying out loud, if your own government wants you dead, why make an effort to succeed? And so victimhood and blame take up the space where integrity and character should be. But of course in a world where you can trust no one else, you'll always need Maxine Waters.

After she made this absurd charge, she pledged: "I vow to leave no stone unturned in an effort to punish those responsible for creating the devastating drug addiction, sales, gun-running, violence, and death associated with crack cocaine throughout this nation."[11] Really? Then she had better be prepared to hold responsible black and Hispanic gang members across the country. Those young men are the ones who control the drug trade and gun-running in the inner cities and are responsible for the deaths associated with crack cocaine.[12]

This situation directly or indirectly affects all of us, not only those who believe what Maxine Waters tells them. Drug use is at the root of much urban crime, such as burglary, mugging, and carjacking. These impose a direct cost, financial and emotional, on their victims. In addition, welfare, law enforcement, prisons—everything society uses to combat crime—are paid for with our tax dollars.

The contributions young black men might make are erased when the Black Elite give them a free pass to prey on society, including their own people. And Maxine Waters is in the vanguard of those who encourage the predators at the expense of the one culture that could save them—a culture of decency and responsibility. But then she'd be out of a job.

Another Looking-Glass Hero

A familiar adage offered up with the death of right and wrong is that when a black man kills a police officer, it's not murder— it's self-defense. It is argued that after all these awful years of the infamous, ubiquitous, and unending oppression of the Black Man, the need to fight back to the death is inevitable.

In chapter 1 I described the obscene lionization of Mumia Abu-Jamal and the subsequent radioactive fallout on our society. To make Abu-Jamal, O.J. Simpson, and other killers actual role models for young people is a coup that guarantees a generational moral relativism that will ultimately send us back into the Dark Ages (and guarantee jobs for life for the malignant narcissists who rely on social chaos). The latest in the Black Elite's parade of killers as role models is H. Rap Brown.

> A familiar adage offered up with the death of right and wrong is that when a black man kills a police officer, it's not murder—it's self-defense.

Many of you will remember Brown from the 1960s, when he served as a leader of the militant Student Nonviolent Coordinating Committee and as Justice Minister of the Black Panthers. It was 1967 when he uttered his most famous line: "I say violence is necessary. It is as American as cherry pie."

In the 1970s Brown converted to the Dar-ul Islam movement and changed his name to Jamil Abdullah Al-Amin while serving a five-year sentence for his role in a robbery that ended in a shootout with New York police. After that stint in prison he emerged as a Muslim cleric.[13]

We saw in chapter 2 how the Left Elite bash traditional religion and try to undercut it as a force in society. This is key in the rush to moral relativism. Another strategy is to co-opt religion for their own purposes. By donning a clerical mantle, they gain access to the ultimate environment where true evil can thrive. How is this possible? If there is any entity that demands complete trust, it is organized religion. Put that power in the hands of the wrong people, and, well, you get Jamil Abdullah Al-Amins and Jesse Jacksons in your midst. Al-Amin, in fact, leads one of the nation's largest black Muslim groups, the National Ummah, which has formed 36 mosques around the nation. When he got out of prison in the late 1970s, he started his own mosque, along with a grocery store, in the west side of Atlanta.

In March 2000, Fulton County Sheriff's Deputies Ricky Kinchen and Aldranon English arrived at Al-Amin's store in order to serve him with an arrest warrant on charges of receiving stolen goods and impersonating a police officer. When Kinchen and English approached the car in which Al-Amin was sitting, he pulled an assault rifle and opened fire, wounding both deputies.[14] As if that weren't enough, Al-Amin then produced a 9 mm handgun and shot Kinchen three times in the groin as he lay bleeding in the street.[15] English survived, Kinchen died.

Both deputies, by the way, were black. The chief of the Atlanta Police Department, which led the hunt for the killer, is black and female. The Black Elite's war on decency clearly does not discriminate—it first dooms their own.

The industry that exists, ready to stand and support the most heinous, was there for Al-Amin. Of course, a support committee was immediately established. It includes two other famous leftist convicts, Bobby Seale (Seale's former lawyer represented Al-Amin)[16] and the ubiquitous Mumia Abu-Jamal. In one of his dispatches from jail, Abu-Jamal wrote:

Imam Jamil has lived a good and rich life in service to his spiritual and ethnic community. He richly deserves the fullest support in all efforts leading to his freedom, so that he may return to the community.[17]

For Abu-Jamal, the dead and wounded black law officers aren't even worthy of mention.

Andrew Young, former congressman, former U.S. ambassador to the United Nations, and past mayor of Atlanta, is not in jail and was able to testify at Al-Amin's sentencing hearing. And so he did, but not on behalf of English and Kinchen. No, he came forward to help Al-Amin. What exactly did Young tell the jurors? At this trial for a man who, in front of a mosque, murdered one sheriff's deputy in cold blood and seriously wounded another, Young ludicrously told the jury that Al-Amin should be shown mercy because he *had helped to reduce crime and clean up his impoverished neighborhood.* I kid you not.

Al-Amin was eligible for the death penalty, which was meant for crimes like this. Instead, the jury gave him life in prison without parole. Although a conviction of any sort is more than we've seen with some other high-profile killers, the trial served, and now the incarceration, like Abu-Jamal's, will serve as a rallying point for the moral relativists in their crusade to condemn the next generation.

Personally, I think monsters like Al-Amin should get what they give. Mercy is obviously not part of his repertoire. Now that we are squarely facing the Looking Glass, we can't be shocked anymore, but we have a duty to be outraged.

We should also be very concerned. Al-Amin's supporters threw fund-raisers for him during his trial, set up Web sites claiming, "The case of this civil rights and Muslim leader of Atlanta has generated a growing grassroots movement amongst Muslims," produced fund-raising "scripts," and organized an "International Day of Solidarity."

Let's be honest. Most American converts to Islam learned about it, as Al-Amin did, in prison. The foundational rhetoric of the American Muslim movement is typified by the Nation of Islam's Louis Farrakhan and includes comments like the following.

About white people:

- "White people are potential humans . . . they haven't evolved yet."[18]

- According to an account in a Jackson, Mississippi, newspaper, "Farrakhan called 'the white man' the 'anti-Christ' to rousing applause."[19]

About Jews:

- "[T]hey exercise extraordinary control, and Black people will never be free in this country until they are free of that kind of control."[20]

- "You are wicked deceivers of the American people. You have sucked their blood. You are not real Jews, those of you that are not real Jews. You are the synagogue of Satan."[21]

Yes, it's good Al-Amin was convicted. But the importance of this story is that he is not an anomaly. He commanded a level of support that should serve as an indicator of how many other potential Al-Amins are out there, being fed and nurtured by the death of right and wrong.

Al-Amin came from a leftist milieu that continues to draw young people into an abyss of hatred, division, and moral corruption. No one is safe from this threat—not black lawmen in Atlanta and certainly not Jews or white people generally in New York or elsewhere. Farrakhan has made his point of view on that subject well known, and on September 11, 2001, so did Radical Islamists.

Thinking Out of the Box

I am lucky enough to be invited on occasion to give speeches to groups that have an interest in culture and public affairs. Business groups have asked me to speak about how to deal with thought police in their ranks and in policy-making positions, and student groups have invited me to speak about individual liberty and civil rights.

On one such occasion, I was speaking at a law school in California as a guest of the Federalist Society, a nonprofit membership organization dedicated to bringing conservative and libertarian ideas into law schools and the organized bar. When I speak at law schools, I tend to focus, among other things, on how racism—understood as discrimination by whites against other races—is fast becoming an ancient relic in this country. I also discuss how blacks who have not succumbed to the victim culture have been, are, and will be doing quite well—all on their own, without handouts, affirmative action, and other patronizing measures.

At the end of my speech, one of the first hands that shot up belonged to a professor who, although very diplomatic, seemed sure that he was going to expose the inconsistency of my argument about racism. "How can you say that?" he began. "All the statistics show that blacks still get lower test scores in elementary schools, they're underrepresented in college admissions, the unemployment rate for blacks is sky high, and the poverty level for blacks still outpaces that for whites? What else can explain this other than white racism?"

> Blacks who have not succumbed to the victim culture have been, are, and will be doing quite well—all on their own, without handouts, affirmative action, and other patronizing measures.

What else can explain it? Consider the moral void that propels young black men into hopelessness. Consider black racism and the depraved Black Elite serving as role models. Consider the vested interest certain black leaders have in maintaining the victimhood of their constituency. I also reminded the professor that we've all been brainwashed into believing two fundamentally wrong things about the lives of blacks in this country. First, blacks are in trouble and victimized at every turn. Second, it's all Whitey's fault.

This message isn't intended only to make white people feel guilty; it's also meant to reinforce paranoia and despair in the black community—all to the benefit of those who have found power and money in the bleakness of lives that are lost before they begin.

Are there tensions between the races? Of course there are, for a variety of reasons, including the stoking of those tensions by Black Power Grand Pooh-Bahs who profit from them. You really do have to look far and wide to find white people who actually believe that their race is superior. Those kinds of sentiments are mostly expressed by people who are still wearing white robes and hoods and have been appropriately stigmatized.

The Complicity of Rap

If it's not white racism that keeps black kids from getting good grades, what else could it be? How about a culture that denigrates doing well in school while romanticizing and rewarding violence and crime?

A Harvard study, in fact, ties rap "music," now euphemistically termed "hip-hop," to a drop in reading and math test scores among black youth a decade ago, just as they were narrowing the gap with white students.[22] Citing a radical change in after-school habits, Professor Ronald Ferguson of Harvard's John F. Kennedy School of Government noted, "There was tremendous progress in the 1980s in reading and math scores for black youth. Sometime between 1988 and 1990 the progress stops."[23] Ferguson said he was struck by the way the halt in progress coincided with the rise of hip-hop's popularity. He noted that in 1988, 40 percent of black students questioned said they regularly read for pleasure, but by 1992 that figure had dropped to just 14 percent.[24]

Hip-hop, rap, Gangsta Rap, or whatever you term it is nothing more than acid on the fabric of our culture. It helps draw young black men especially into a nihilistic moral void. One would think that black leaders would be leading the fight against music that glorifies criminality and violence. We know they can do it. There have been innumerable actions by black leaders to get cigarette and alcohol companies to stop targeting blacks. The NAACP threatened to boycott the three major television networks if they didn't include more blacks in programming, noting the impact entertainment images (or the lack thereof) have on self-esteem and confidence.

Yet it isn't whether or not there's another black family comedy on the WB network that holds the key to a bright future for a young black man or woman. No, it's the so-called music that pervades the black community, glorifying everything from murdering police officers to killing your neighbor, that has a deadly affect on black youth. When it comes to the most horrific, the most damning material, the Black Elite, specifically including Al Sharpton, Jesse Jackson, Maxine Waters, and Louis Farrakhan, systematically support, defend, and legitimize this cultural rot, and all the while they deliver their daily dose of the we're-all-in-trouble-because-of-white-racism shtick.

The Death of Music

While the Feminist and Gay Elites use television and film to move their messages of subjugation, the Black Elite have a special niche all their own. Popular culture provides a myriad of options with which to further the death of right and wrong. Music in particular is marketed to black youth, with rap performers elevated as heroes.

This racist, violent, and misogynistic music makes a mockery of the optimistic transformative promise of the arts, while its millionaire promoters and performers lure today's inner-city youth into a bottomless pit of nihilism. Rap and hip-hop have made fortunes for so-called artists who foment hate, violence, and criminality.

As we've seen, it is not unusual for the damaged to be attracted to the obscene and destructive. But what impact does this have on the rest of us? Decent, normal people have nodded our acceptance primarily because the Left Elite have drilled into us that rap and hip-hop are simply cutting-edge urban performance "art." And as the violence promoted by the Black Elite comes out of the recording studio and explodes in people's lives, the first victims are likely to be good, hardworking people in the black community.

Rap and Murder and Profit

On March 14, 1992, Patricia Harris, aged 42, was beginning another day as the proud matriarch of a well-liked and highly regarded family in Sacramento, California. She got up early that morning and started preparing for a party to celebrate the birth of her new granddaughter. Children were Patricia's first love. During the day, she worked at the local high school, and she was active in the PTA. She was the kind of woman kids in the neighborhood would come to visit and adult neighbors knew they could count on.[25]

Her husband, William, was a hard worker. He came home at 8 A.M. every day like clockwork after his graveyard shift as a dispatcher for a private patrol company. When William got home the morning of the 14th, he enjoyed watching his wife flutter about the house getting ready for the party. They had been married for 25 years.

The celebration began at 5 P.M., with 40 children crammed into the tiny home. There were balloons everywhere, and Patricia sang and danced with the children through the evening.

At 2:15 A.M., with William off at work, Patricia was awakened by an unusual noise. She dashed from her bedroom into the hall and was immediately shot in the chest. She struggled back to her bedroom and, surrounded by pictures of her family, she died.[26]

Eventually, four 17-year-olds were arrested and convicted. It was determined that the punks who had invaded the Harrises' home had vowed to kill anything that moved while they looked for rival gang members (there were none).

Rich, Famous, and Trigger Happy!

Among those convicted for Patricia Harris's murder was one Anerae Brown. To the California Department of Corrections, he is No. K17737. In the world of hip-hop, he is known as X-Raided.[27]

Throughout his trial Brown insisted he was innocent, but his so-called music presented the truth of the situation. In early

1992, just prior to the murder, he had recorded a number called "Tha Murder," which may be found on the album *Psycho Active*. Brown—er, X-Raided—who describes himself in this "song" as a "trigger-happy nigger," raps these lines:

> I'm kicking down doors
> I'm killing mamas, daddies and nephews
> I'm killing sons, daughters and sparing you.[28]

Another rap on the same album, titled "Shoot Cha in a Minute," has this to say:

> Letting fools know X-Raided ain't playing
> Tha Murder, yeah, I got something to do with it
> Cause I shoot cha punk ass in a minute.[29]

During the trial of Brown and his three fellow gang members, some members of Congress expressed concern over the negative impact of rap music on the culture and on real people's lives. Maxine Waters chimed in, but her remarks truly came from the other side of the Looking Glass.

"It would be a foolhardy mistake to single out poets as the cause of America's problems,"[30] she scolded her fellow lawmakers. Described by the *Los Angeles Times* as "an outspoken supporter of rap music,"[31] Waters cozily added, like a big Mother Hen, "These [rappers] are our children and they've invented a new art form to describe their pains, fears and frustrations with us as adults."[32]

This pathetic statement of aid and comfort was made just two years after Patricia's brutal slaughter by one of these Frustrated Poet Children. Decency demands a repudiation of this. The least Patricia Harris deserved in her death was the sympathy of Professional Angry Black Woman Maxine Waters. Instead, the pit from which Patricia's murderer sprang became a well of "art." This is moral relativism and the abandonment of a community staring you in the face. Waters is romanticizing and giving the cachet of her important position to a "poetry" that costs people, black people primarily, their lives, while she and her ilk point the finger of racism at others. And who was it that called the congressional hearings in the mid-1990s to deal with this scourge? White Man, Republican, and then-Senate Majority Leader Bob Dole. Only the mind-numbing effects of the death of right and wrong keep so many black people thinking Maxine Waters is on their side.

A few months before the killing of Patricia Harris, Sacramento-based Cedric Singleton had produced a local antigang benefit record, *Silence the Violence.* Singleton also owns the 12 tracks that make up X-Raided's *Psycho Active* album. This man who supposedly was concerned about gang violence also marketed an act called "Homicide." When asked by a reporter from the *Sacramento Bee* if he felt comfortable releasing the X-Raided tracks on his record label, Black Market Records, Singleton wasn't sure. He had concerns. Ah, finally, you think, some common sense! Some decency! Unfortunately, not so. Singleton told the paper, "One dilemma I have is whether they're gonna use the record as evidence against him."[33] The album also included tracks titled "Still Shootin'" and "Everybody Killa." "If they want to force me, they'd have to subpoena it,"[34] he offered. So much for silencing the violence!

The Real Issue

My concern here is how the spread of moral relativism keeps good people from being comfortable with their judgments or even sure about what kinds of judgments to come to. How do we respond to the corruption that comes out the door of moral relativism and kicks in Patricia Harris's door in the middle of the night? Consider the result of Anerae Brown's trial.

Eventually, he was convicted of first-degree murder and sentenced to 31 years in prison *with the possibility of parole.* This is what I'm speaking of. This is the goal of the Black Elite. Even if someone is convicted of a premeditated, completely un-provoked murder, somehow that doesn't merit even life in prison, let alone the death penalty. I deal with our increasingly immoral justice system more fully in chapter 9, but it's sentences like this that make you realize how deeply infected that system is. Because of the moral relativism of the judge and jury, "Trigger Happy Nigger" Brown, the man who took Patricia Harris away from her family and community forever, will be eligible for parole, probably by 2010.

A light sentence, though, isn't the end of it. Brown's first album wasn't a fluke, and being in prison hasn't kept him from pursuing his career. In 1996 X-Raided released his second album, *Xorcist*. It was recorded over the telephone from the Sacramento county jail.[35] In 1998 he released his third album, *Unforgiven Vol. 1*, recorded on a DAT (digital audiotape, a cheap, high-quality cassette). He also cowrote rap songs and recorded them with other inmates. In 2000 his *Speak of Da Devil* was released, under the name Nefarious. *Vengeance Is Mine* was released in 2000, and two more recordings were released in 2002. By 2000 Brown had made approximately $100,000 on the albums he had cut since he went to prison.

Death to Law & Order

Since rap mostly isn't what stores and airports and other public places choose to pipe in, many of us never hear it. It's easy to forget how big a role this arm of the entertainment industry plays in conditioning young people of every race and ethnicity into its immorality. Remember, if you want to change the world, you must begin with the children.

As I discussed in *The New Thought Police*, political correctness and speech codes are quickly applied to anyone who dares to judge, to dissent, to challenge those who would throw acid onto the fabric of our culture. The longer we wait to criticize, the harder it becomes, and the lower the odds that we will ever express our judgment. As time goes on, what once appalled starts looking normal. Consider society's relative silence in the face of the violence offered up by thugs posing as artists.

It was in the late 1980s that gangsta rap took hold, notably with the work of Ice-T and Niggas With Attitude (who could forget that lovely group of young men?). The continued success of the rap industry, more than a decade and a half after it declared war against decent society, confirms our growing inability to say no to cultural and human degradation.

In addition to putting pearls on these swine and making them filthy rich, the Left Elite open other doors for them. Ice-T is a perfect example of the new rule that Wrong is Right. Famous for some of the more brutal so-called lyrics in rap, here are a few lines from his "Cop Killer," released in 1992:

> COP KILLER, I know your family's grievin' . . . FUCK 'EM! . . .
> . . . I got my stereo bumpin' . . .
> I'm 'bout to kill me somethin'

These words are followed by this particularly special refrain:

> DIE, DIE, DIE, PIG, DIE!
> FUCK THE POLICE!

How has the Left Elite rewarded this vile man? Since the release of "Cop Killer," Ice-T has had roles in 59 films, has produced 3 films and a TV series, has made guest appearances on 18 television shows, and is currently directing a film based on one of his "songs."[36] For a last dose of irony, this man who wrote a song encouraging the murder of police officers now stars as a police detective in the NBC television series *Law & Order: Special Victims Unit*.

In this instance, it seems as if our culture is the special victim.

Depravity Masquerading as Poetry

"We'd rather talk about the militia. We'd rather talk about the Oklahoma City bombing. They start talking about gangster rap. Gangsters don't rap and rappers are not gangsters. That's nothing but diversion."[37] This is what Misery Merchant Jesse Jackson had to say at, ironically, a rally supporting affirmative action. In this instance, Jackson's feeble attempt to distort reality doesn't fly. The depravity and concomitant success of the rap industry demonstrate the extent to which it is both pusher and manifestation of the death of right and wrong.

There is national news coverage whenever a famous rap thug is murdered, as when Tupac Shakur was shot down in Las Vegas in September 1996. High-profile killings of rap stars and violence associated with rap's producers and "artists" happen at a rather frequent clip, providing an indication that the violent words of this "new art form" are more than just lyrics—they represent reality.

- In February 1996, a few months before the murder of Shakur, rapper Snoop Doggy Dogg was acquitted on a charge of murdering a rival gang member.[38] Both Dogg and Shakur recorded for the rap label Death Row Records (now known as Tha Row), whose CEO, Suge Knight, was arrested for assaulting gang member Orlando Anderson on the night of Shakur's murder.[39] Knight was convicted and was in prison in March 1997 when the Notorious BIG (a.k.a. Biggie Smalls), who recorded on a rival label, Bad Boy Records, was murdered in Los Angeles. A car belonging to Death Row Records was linked to the murder scene.[40]

Come on now, how obvious do these people need to be! But of course, in order to effectively desensitize all of us into moral oblivion, they *have* to be obvious, and as destructive as possible. Here are a few other examples Jesse Jackson would prefer us not to discuss:

- In June 2002 Carlo "South Park Mexican" Coy, a rapper and the CEO of Dope House Records, was sentenced to 45 years in prison for sexually assaulting a 9-year-old girl who had spent a night at his home.[41] During the trial, eight women testified that they had had intercourse with Coy when they were 12, 13, or 14 years old. Coy's response? He said "most" of them lied.[42]

BET.com reports that at the 2000 Houston Press Music Awards, Coy was named Musician of the Year and Best Rap/Hip Hop Artist, and one of his recordings won the Album of the Year award. He went on to sign a major distribution deal with Universal Records.[43]

- C-Murder (born Corey Miller) was indicted in March 2002 on charges that he killed a 16-year-old boy, Steve Thomas, with a single shotgun blast to the chest.[44] According to a civil suit filed by Steve's parents, Steve and Miller were both taking part in a rap contest when Miller became enraged because Steve was getting more favorable attention than he was.[45] Although there were plenty of eyewitnesses, police had difficulty obtaining a definite identification of Miller as the gunman. As one news report put it, "[P]olice have suggested that many witnesses were reluctant to come forward given Miller's influence and reputation for violence."[46]

How is this killing portrayed to teens by a heavily read music Web site?

[*Trapped in Crime*] also signaled the launch of Tru Records, C-Murder's new label, which promises to be accompanied by a clothing line and successive releases. His 2002 release, *Tru Dawgs,* was a test for the label but was preceded by tragedy when C-Murder was arrested for shooting someone in a nightclub.[47]

Tragedy? Shooting "someone"? How about "preceded by the shotgun murder of a 16-year-old named Steve?" It seems the rap industry has become proficient in the use of euphemisms when it comes to describing murder and mayhem. Then again, I suppose it is easier to not know the names of the victims as the body count rises.

Miller was eventually picked up at the House of Blues in New Orleans' French Quarter because of a disturbance there.

Once in custody he was charged with Steve's murder, and police learned that there were also outstanding domestic violence charges.[48] At the time of Steve's murder, this remarkably out-of-control man was *free on a $100,000 bond* for allegedly attempting to kill a nightclub owner.

- In March 2002 Snoop Doggy Dogg received the Stoner of the Year award from a magazine that focuses on legalizing marijuana. When asked at a press conference whether he thought pot would be legalized in his lifetime, he said, "I already legalized it! . . . We doing s*** they said we couldn't do, and they sitting up here taking pictures of it, loving it. Put this on the front of *USA Today*!"[49] The report noted that the Stoner of the Year seemed "clueless" throughout the evening. Gee, I wonder why?

- Antron Singleton, (a.k.a. Big Lurch) is described by Black Entertainment Television's Web site as an "an up-and-coming rapper."[50] But Singleton is not just any up-and-comer. He allegedly did something not yet attributed to any of his peers—eating his victim.

  In May 2002 Singleton was ordered to stand trial for the murder of 21-year-old Tynisha Ysais. Los Angeles Police Detective Raymond Jankowski testified that when he found Ysais's body in her apartment, her chest was ripped open.[51] Pieces of her right lung appeared chewed and torn, he said.[52] According to the *Los Angeles Times*, Jankowski also testified that a medical examination shortly after Singleton was arrested found blood and flesh not belonging to him in his stomach. Ysais's friend Alisa Allen testified that about noon she saw Singleton naked in the street. His chest, abdomen, and mouth were covered with blood.[53]

As If He Really Cared

It is difficult, even with all we know, to understand why anyone would voice support for an industry that promotes this kind of behavior. Music, which once stood for beauty and truth, summoning us to our better selves, now serves to encourage the heinous in their debauchery.

Of course, the answer is in plain view. Those who support the misery usually profit from it in one way or another. They get reelected to Congress because, after all, Whitey is out to get you, so you'd better have Maxine Waters in Washington. Organizations that feed off victimization and racism, like the NAACP, ACLU, and Urban League, among others, continue to get members and funding only if the supposed race war continues. You have only to read Kenneth Timmerman's *Shakedown* if you want to learn to what extent Jesse Jackson has his own self-interest at heart.

But there's another motivation as well. Some activists are driven by a positive—their concern for other people. Leftist activists, however, operate on a negative basis—their hate for others. It seems Jackson, like so many of his colleagues, is motivated less by caring about black people than by hating white people.

All one needs to do is go a bit into the past to know what really drives Jesse Jackson. With what we know today it seems he is an opportunist without peer, a malignant narcissist angling for the most money and the best way to inflame racial tensions. Of course, he denies these things, but a brief and disgusting admission made in 1969 is quite illustrative of the man's character.

In a November 1969 *Life* magazine article[54] he admitted that when he worked as a waiter at a hotel in Greenville, South Carolina, he spat into the soups and salads of white customers. "[Spitting into the food] gave me a psychological gratification," Jackson said.

He obviously hasn't changed much. These days, instead of serving people food, he works at serving us our culture, spitting in it all the while.

Spitting Up on CNN

Why would anyone in his right mind (and we must presume Jackson is) publicly support a cultural genre that condemns his own constituency? Well, it seems for Jesse it's all about the fame.

Here's a little corporate background. Bear with me—it's these kinds of connections that help make sense of things. Consider the fact that in 1987 Time merges with TCI, the country's largest cable operator, to in effect bail out Ted Turner's overextended Turner Broadcasting System and Cable News Network (CNN). In 1989 Time merges with Warner Communications, becoming Time Warner.[55] In 1990 Time Warner enters into a partnership with Interscope Records, then and now one of the biggest distributors of "rap" and "rage" music.[56] Yes, rap producers, writers, and performers would now be funded and supported by one of America's largest corporations as they went about their marketing of death and destruction. But that's the way it works, you see. A malignancy doesn't stay put. It metastasizes and infects every part of the body. The entertainment industry, which I discuss in more detail in chapter 8, can't help salivating at the profit to be made, even at the cost of people's lives and hope for the future.

In 1992 the heat was turned up on Interscope/Time Warner by, among others, myself, as president of Los Angeles NOW,[57] and C. Delores Tucker,[58] chair of the National Political Congress of Black Women and a woman not afraid to confront the black establishment. Tucker and I, in separate actions, denounced Time Warner's gangsta rap artists for promoting violence and denigrating women. What else happened in 1992? CNN, another part of the Time Warner media conglomerate, hired Jesse Jackson to host his own program, *Both Sides with Jesse Jackson,* which aired from 1992 to 2000.[59]

So, Jesse gets hired by a media conglomerate that has a financial interest in the success of rap, while he continues to tell us that the reality of rap's crime and violence and racism and misogyny is a "diversion," and that there are other more important, more relevant targets for activism. Do I have any direct evidence of a payoff here? No, I don't, but the appearance of impropriety is stunning.

Jackson's Rainbow/PU$H Coalition's Web site tells us, "Reverend Jackson has been called the 'Conscience of the Nation.'"[60] It's time we begin to refuse to let that be the case.

In 1995 Time Warner finally severed its ties with Interscope, which is now part of the Universal Music Group. How did Interscope, under the tutelage of Universal, eventually deal with the fact that rap and rage were aimed at a black audience? They introduced Eminem, a young *white* man, to carry the rap banner of hate and violence. No more could it be said that black youth was being targeted. No, we could relax—this cancer is now being pushed to everyone, making it truly equal opportunity.

Just like Julie Andrews

That's what X-Raided is, at least to major book and record retailer Barnes & Noble. A normal person who hadn't studied the record charts would think it didn't matter that X-Raided was allowed to make records in prison because the material can't go anywhere. And C-Murder and Big Lurch, the rapper who allegedly murdered and ate part of his victim—what decent retailer would sell anything made by these men?

Frankly, when I started researching this segment, that's what I thought, too. I wondered, How the heck am I gonna get my hands on this junk? After just a few minutes of doing general research on X-Raided, it became painfully obvious. My first step was to do a basic Internet search. Of course, I found various Web sites about X-Raided, but then an *advertisement* from Barnes & Noble appeared right on the search page promoting that murderer's CD! That's right. On shelves next to Julie Andrews, Diana Krall, Billie Holiday, and Stevie Wonder sits the murderer of Patricia Harris.

> Individuals make those decisions, and they have a responsibility to the public at large to act with some deference to common decency. Freedom of expression does not equal cultural anarchy.

A friend of mine told me it was difficult for him to blame a retail store for making decisions about what to sell. After all, it's all about making a profit, right? I reminded him about the core of this book. Yes, we have the freedom to do as we please, but it only works because we don't do *everything* we might please—we should exercise some degree of personal, and corporate, responsibility. Corporations are not inhuman robots making impersonal decisions about what to carry. Individuals make those decisions, and they have a responsibility to the public at large to act with some deference to common decency. Freedom of expression does not equal cultural anarchy.

Barnes & Noble doesn't sell everything ever recorded. Its executives and buyers make decisions every day not only about what to carry, but conversely about what *not* to carry. It's time we demand they make responsible decisions. We can, and should, judge the intentions of a corporate entity just as we would those of an individual. Unfortunately, the Enrons and Global Crossings of the world have brought this point home to too many people.

In addition to X-Raided, you will find C-Murder and Big Lurch at Barnes & Noble. Amazon.com offers X-Raided and C-Murder, but, to its slight credit, does not offer Big Lurch's recordings. It's a small consolation considering that the point here is now undeniable—what should be stigmatized and condemned has instead become celebrated and acclaimed. With the complicity of mainstream society.

What does this say to your children? When this unspeakable material is available at respected mainstream retail outlets, the message is reinforced to all of us that it must be okay. This lends an extraordinary credibility to these thugs. It represents success and, yes, *normality*. That is, after all, the point of the death of right and wrong.

Black When Convenient

Standards still do, on occasion, rear their head. That's exactly what's happening to Michael Jackson. His career, once at a remarkable zenith, sputtered and came to a halt when accusations of child molestation were made. He was never brought to trial or convicted, of course, but the charges seemed all too plausible, considering what a circus sideshow that man has made of himself.

As his albums started to fail, instead of accepting the fact that he had gone beyond even the growing moral relativism in our society, he decided it was "racism" that was ruining his career. Not charges of child molestation, not his multiple plastic surgeries in what seemed to be an attempt to look as much as possible like a mutant cross between Diana Ross and Peter Pan. No, it was Whitey who was out to get him. Just like O. J. Simpson, Michael Jackson suddenly morphed into a Black Man when it became beneficial. After all, you can't blame Racist America for discriminating against you if you're not, well, black, sort of.

Enter Al Sharpton, a man who has been found guilty of defamation for falsely accusing a white man of the imaginary rape of a black girl.[61] This is a man who has proved he will do everything he can to propagate a race war because it benefits him personally. How? Someone like Sharpton would be selling shoes if it weren't for the Big Lie of a racist, oppressive America where all black people are at risk.

No wonder Michael chose Sharpton's National Action Network office in Harlem as his venue for pointing the Racism finger at his record label, Sony.[62] Michael offered this explanation of why his career has, well, petered out: "The recording companies really, really do conspire against the artists—they steal, they cheat, they do everything they can." An interesting complaint about how morality affects the decisions people make considering he's a man who dangled a baby over a fifth floor hotel balcony and settled a lawsuit accusing him of child molestation. Of the chairman of Sony Music, Michael complained that he is "mean, he's racist, and he's very, very, very devilish." Well, those are certainly characteristics that Michael Jackson and Al Sharpton should recognize.

A Window into the Soul

I wish one of you guys had children so I could kick them in the f——g ass and stomp on their testicles so you could feel my pain. 'Cause that's the pain that I have waking up every day.[63]

This wish to do unspeakable violence to children comes from adulated maniac Mike Tyson. I share it with you because sometimes it takes someone as uncouth as Tyson to be honest. The Farrakhans and Jesse Jacksons of the world are too smooth to say something like this in public, but Tyson isn't. He exposes more directly than anyone else my point about the damaged rising to the top with the desire and ambition to do you, and your children, torturous harm. Tyson, in fact, provides a window into the soul of the Black Elite.

Former world heavyweight champion, rich beyond our wildest imaginations, held up as a role model for millions of young black men in this country, Tyson is also a convicted rapist and a man violently out of control. But once he had served his sentence, he was again rewarded with boxing matches, and with fame and admiration worldwide.

The elevation of Tyson is reflective of our own collective conditioned amorality on issues of culture, drilled into us by the Left's multicultural and victim-based worldview. Generations of brainwashing have kept us from feeling comfortable judging anything a black person does. The cry of racism isn't even really necessary any more. We've all been lobotomized and shell-shocked into silence. Mike Tyson is part of the mosaic that represents how far down the hole we've collectively fallen.

Tyson's torture wish for children was made after a reporter challenged him over earlier comments that he doesn't like to talk to female reporters unless they'll have sex with him. Tyson had this to say about the episode:[64]

> I asked this lady a lewd question because I'm in a lot of pain, too. You know, I'm in some pain that I'm gonna have for the rest of my life. And by some way, a little bit, I'm trying to give some of that pain to you all.[65]

Except for Tyson's astonishing candor, how is this different from others of the Black Elite, who condemn their own people to the enslavement of hopelessness, drug abuse, and violence because they want everyone else to wake up into their world of pain?

The Great Black Hypocrite

Well, at least Tyson's honest about his corruption. He wanted sex from women if he was going to do something for them—like give them an interview. There's no respect for them, no thought for anyone but himself. How is he different from others in the Black Elite? Not much. Going just on what we learn from the news, the least we know is that the "Reverend" Jesse Jackson fathered an illegitimate child with a woman to whom he gave a job. He was also carrying on that adulterous affair at the very time he was counseling President Clinton over the Monica Lewinsky affair. Former Congressman Kweisi Mfume, now the head of the NAACP, has fathered five illegitimate children.[66]

Since 1970, out-of-wedlock birth rates have soared. In 1965, 24 percent of black infants and 3.1 percent of white infants were born to single mothers. By 1990 the rates had risen to 64 percent for black infants, 18 percent for whites.[67] In fact, for black women, the proportion of first babies either born or conceived before the woman's first marriage doubled from 43 percent in the 1930s to 86 percent in the 1990s.[68] These are numbers that men like Jesse Jackson and Kweisi Mfume have recklessly contributed to. How can these men claim to be addressing problems in the black community, a major one of which is men impregnating women they're not married to and then taking a hike? It's called hypocrisy—another wonderful lesson brought to black America by its shakedown artists.

Even more revealing is the truth about one of the most highly regarded black men in this country, a man who is applauded precisely as representing family values, and who was even awarded the Presidential Medal of Freedom, the highest honor an American civilian can receive—Bill Cosby.

The *New York Post*'s "Page Six" drew attention to Janice Dickinson's new book, *No Lifeguard on Duty: The Accidental Life of the World's First Supermodel.* As "Page Six" puts it, "Bill Cosby—who promoted Dickinson's failed singing career—became nasty to her in 1984 when she turned him down for sex, claiming she was tired."[69] Here's her account of her exchange with America's Family Man:

After dinner he asked me back to his room, and I went. But I stopped myself at the door. "I'm exhausted," I said, begging off. His eyebrows went a little funny. "Exhausted?" he asked, and it was clear he was trying hard to keep his temper in check. "After all I've done for you, that's what I get? *I'm exhausted.*"

"Well, gee, Bill," I stammered. "If I had known it was going to be like this—" He waved both hands in front of my face, silencing me. Then he gave me the dirtiest, meanest look in the world, stepped into his suite, and slammed the door in my face.[70]

He might have gotten the Medal of Freedom, but he didn't get Janice. Good for her.

Yes, a Baptist minister, a former congressman turned special-interest-group president, and an American icon can't hold a candle to Mike Tyson when it comes to honesty. And the message they send, either implicitly or explicitly, is abuse, infidelity, and personal irresponsibility are no worry. You don't need a moral compass to rise to the top of your profession.

The Black Elite claim the Great White Bigot is the main threat to the black community. That may once have been the case, but now it's more the Great Black Hypocrite that poses the challenge.

Violence Is "Love"

In 1999 football legend Jim Brown faced charges of spousal abuse. Prosecutors said the 63-year-old Brown attacked his 25-year-old wife, Monique, on at least two occasions and told her, "I'm going to kill you by snapping your neck."[71] Jim Brown was in court after Monique called 911 to report that she had fled to a neighbor's house after her husband smashed her car windshield with a shovel. She wanted the police to help her get her things before leaving him.[72]

Brown was eventually convicted of the vandalism charge, but when his wife recanted (as battered women almost always do) the jury acquitted him on the threat charge.

This episode is important on many fronts regarding the death of right and wrong. Jim Brown is someone who has directly positioned himself as a role model for at-risk young black men. In 1988 he founded the Amer-I-Can organization, and he is still its chairman. Amer-I-Can's Web site boasts that its program is designed to raise self-esteem and teach individuals how to turn their lives around and become responsible and productive citizens through self-determination.[73]

Having elected to serve as a role model for young men, Jim Brown has an extra duty to avoid giving them the idea that violence is acceptable. Personal responsibility and self-control are issues at the core of his long-standing activism, and yet his own behavior reveals they are the qualities he lacks the most. Besides sincerity, of course.

In statements before and after his trial and conviction, Brown blamed his predicament on everyone and everything but himself, ranging from the police, to the justice system, to racial injustice, to feminists, to—get this!—his wife's premenstrual syndrome (PMS).

What a role model for young black men everywhere! Brown made the PMS comment during one of the most extraordinary interviews I have ever seen. In August 1999, just a few weeks before the start of his trial, he and Monique appeared together on CNN's *Larry King Live*. Brown explained that he smashed Monique's windshield because of "loving her." He then brought up the subject of PMS. Here's his remarkable comment:

> **J. Brown:** The only time when Monique and I ever have an argument is during that particular period. . . . That's the only time we argue. . . . I haven't made excuses in my life. I talk about the facts. It happens to be a fact in our lives that we have struggled with PMS.[74]

I'm wondering—would that be *her* PMS or *his* PMS? I knew it can make you cranky, but I had no idea it could break windows! Jim Brown, however, admitted to being the one who smashed those windows, because he "loved" Monique.[75]

People who work to help end domestic violence know that destruction of the victim's property is one way a batterer reminds his wife or lover what he's capable of. It's a form of domestic terrorism. Remember, one of O. J. Simpson's encounters with the police prior to his killing Nicole was for smashing *her* car windows.

Even Brown gets it that his behavior influences the young men he is supposed to set a standard for:

> **King:** Have—you've never hit a woman?
>
> **J. Brown:** Of course—not of course I have hit a woman— yes, I've hit a woman in my life, Larry. I have admitted that before. I admitted that in my book. But I have never touched my wife, and since 1988, I have not said a loud word to anyone based upon the work and the people that I am dealing with, because I deal with violent people every day and I must set an example and I must have them believe I'm not a hypocrite or a phony.[76]

His 1999 run-in with the law over domestic violence was not his first. From the *New York Times,* here's the full legal history of this role model for young black men:

- In 1965, an 18-year-old accused Brown of forcing her to have sex after giving her whiskey, but, after a 10-day trial, the jury found him innocent of assault and battery.

- In 1968, in the most famous of his alleged attacks, he was accused of throwing Eva Marie Bohn-Chin, a German model, off a second-story balcony. Brown insists she jumped. In a Spike Lee film about the football star, Bohn-Chin addresses the incident: "I was young, good-looking, a person who loved life. Why would I jump?"[77] Perhaps she was premenstrual. In any case, when she refused to name Brown as her assailant, the charge of assault with intent to murder was dropped.

- In 1969, Brown was acquitted of assaulting a man after a traffic accident.

- In 1971, charges that he battered two women were dropped after they failed to testify at his trial.

- In 1978, he was fined and served a day in jail for beating up a golf partner.

- In 1985, he was charged with rape, sexual battery and assault, but the charges were dropped when the 33-year-old woman gave inconsistent testimony.

- In 1999, he was convicted in Los Angeles of smashing the window of Monique's car, but was acquitted of making terrorist threats against her.[78]

Brown doesn't always use physical violence against women: in one instance he used a legal motion. During the trial for the incident involving Monique, Brown filed a motion attacking the woman judge. In a bizarre and vitriolic statement, Brown accused Judge Dale S. Fischer of "waging a war against all men" and targeting him for disgrace.[79] According to the *Los Angeles Times,* Brown's motion included this accusation: "Fischer is the CEO of a radical and extremist group of white upper-class women who target men of color, including Jim Brown." The motion said, "If Jim Brown does not disclose this, then other men of color, and not of color, will fall victim to this 'hanging' judge."[80] The motion was dismissed by another judge.

You might be asking, What is this radical group of white women who meet to conspire against black men? It's called the American Inns of Court Foundation. American Inns of Court are groups of lawyers, judges, and law students who gather to discuss the legal profession. The current president of the group is a man. Here's how they describe themselves:

American Inns of Court (AIC) are designed to improve the skills, professionalism and ethics of the bench and bar. An American Inn of Court is an amalgam of judges, lawyers, and in some cases, law professors and law students. Each Inn meets approximately once a month both to "break bread" and to hold programs and discussions on matters of ethics, skills and professionalism.[81]

I think it's fair to say the How to Hang Black Men and Especially Jim Brown workshop was never on their docket and never will be.

For malignant narcissists, however, everything *does* revolve around them. Everything awful that happens is someone else's fault. Persecution is unending. Jim Brown's life seems to be made miserable by women who just can't get enough of doing him wrong. Remember what Mike Tyson educated us about: He's miserable and determined to make us share that pain. That window has become invaluable.

> For malignant narcissists, however, everything *does* revolve around them. Everything awful that happens is someone else's fault.

At Brown's sentencing, Fischer ordered him to perform 40 days of community service, to surrender his driver's license for a year, to pay $1,500 to a battered women's shelter, and to attend a year's worth of domestic-abuse counseling. Brown refused to accept that rather lenient sentence. No, he felt that it would require him to "surrender his dignity."[82]

So the judge instead sentenced him to a six-month jail stint. About the sentencing, Brown told Jon Seraceno of *USA Today*: "The last thing I'm going to give up is my manhood."[83] Seraceno reported his further comments:

> "There's no doubt that I'm a political prisoner, but race in America is always under the surface," [Brown] says from a Ventura County jail, where he is locked down 23 hours a day the next five months. "If I were domesticated, I would be accepted racially. I'd have approval if I stayed in my place. The worst thing an African-American man can do is be as free as those more powerful than he is."[84]

Brown would simply be an extraordinarily pathetic man who would deserve our pity if he didn't pose a danger not only to women, but also to young men who sadly still look up to him. Instead of exemplifying personal responsibility, Brown serves as the perfect example of how to revel in the death of right and wrong.

bell hooks unhinged

It almost sounds incredible, but it's not only right and wrong, it's the actual *future* that moral relativists want to kill. They hate themselves, this country, and anyone who actually has a sense of hope. You see, when everything is just awful, you want it to end. When everything is ugly to you, you want to punish it. How better to do that than to kill it? The Left Elite want to kill the future, and in order to do that they need to smash nothing less than your and your children's *hope*.

One doesn't have to look too deep within the Black Elite to find bell hooks (born Gloria Watkins), a radical lesbian feminist socialist social critic and professor who directly attacks the future and proclaims the silliness of our hopes for it. hooks chose the occasion of a commencement speech to project her own hopelessness and hate.

Here is part of what she said to the graduating class at Southwestern University, a liberal-arts college in Georgetown, Texas, on what is supposed to be a day of hope and promise:

> Every imperialist, white supremacist, capitalist, patriarchal nation on the planet teaches its citizens to care more for tomorrow than today. . . . And the moment we do this, we are seduced by the lure of death. . . . To live fixated on the future is to engage in psychological denial. It is a form of psychic violence that prepares us to accept the violence needed to ensure the maintenance of imperialist, future-oriented society.[85]

Welcome to the Black Elite. That's right. bell hooks chastised the audience for caring about tomorrow. And from her point of view, that makes all the sense in the world. In order for moral relativism to infect us, we really must live only for today. If we think about the future, then we have to consider the repercussions of our actions. With no future, there are no repercussions. With no future there is no hope, and suddenly we are all in that Hobbesian reality, animals living only for ourselves and willing to do whatever it takes to get what we want. To hell with everyone else, to hell with judgment and responsibility, because if there is no future there's no reason for either. Responsibility dwells in possibility, in *hope*. That's why it is so threatening to these intellectual Armageddonists.

Ms. hooks refuses, by the way, to capitalize her name because, supposedly, she doesn't want who she is to eclipse what she says. Of course, as she obviously knows, refusing to use capital letters only calls *more* attention to the name itself.

Ultimately, though, not even our compassion can be blamed for the creation of such pond scum as hooks. Her favorite subjects on which to opine, as she did ad nauseam at Southwestern, include how men, capitalism, and the "patriarchy" are responsible for all the evil in the world. Now that you've read this far, you won't be surprised to learn that hooks was not an empty vessel filled with these ideas. Her extraordinary hatred of men and society stems from the most personal of reasons—she had an abusive relationship with a man.[86]

In a terrific analysis of hooks's basic but very serious problems, Jamie Glazov, writing for FrontPageMag.com, tells us that hooks speaks frequently about that relationship. It was after that experience, he writes, that she realized how evil capitalism and patriarchy really were, and became a lesbian feminist.[87]

hooks is a terrific example of the damaged Left Elite and the havoc they are determined to wreak upon our youth in particular, because of their unresolved personal pain. Like so many in the Left Elite, hooks is empowered by victimhood. In order to maintain her pain, she tries to force all her personal rage onto our cultural and political landscape.

This situation simply isn't acceptable. This woman and others like her cannot be the determinant of how your children view the world. Will you, in your compassion, allow those for whom you feel pity to destroy your child's future—and actually perhaps this country's future? I trust not. The first step in rejecting hooks's hopelessness and rage was refreshingly exhibited by some in the audience that commencement day—they booed her. Perhaps there is hope after all!

The New Intellectual?

In addition to encouraging the students at Southwestern to condemn the future because caring about it is a patriarchal capitalist construct, hooks slammed the war on terrorism and equated conservatism with murder. Consider this rubbish from her castigation of the assembly:

> The radical, dissident voices among you have learned here at Southwestern how to form communities of resistance that have helped you find your way in the midst of life-threatening conservatism, loneliness, and the powerful forces of everyday fascism which use the politics of exclusion and ostracism to maintain the status quo. Every terrorist regime in the world uses isolation to break people's spirits.[88]

Ms. hooks needs to take a pill. Unfortunately, she isn't some marginal woman on the fringes only to be heard from when she escapes her cave. No, she plays a major role in deciding what will be taught at universities regarding issues of race, gender, and social construct. She teaches at the City College of New York and tours the country giving speeches specially designed to reach young minds with her gutter message of hate, self-loathing, and hopelessness.

In 1998 bell hooks was named by *The Atlantic Monthly* as one of the New Intellectuals "bringing moral imagination and critical intelligence to bear on the defining American matter of race," and she was included in *The Utne Reader*'s list of "100 Visionaries Who Could Change Your Life." Can you believe this? hooks is *not* a new intellectual. The types of malevolent tantrums she has are as old as the trees—the difference is that moral relativism, hate, and hopelessness are *in*. And so, by default, is Ms. hooks.

While the purveyors of rap music glorify nihilistic violence, bell hooks applies nihilism to the future itself. What a one-two punch for the next generation. Put those two together and who needs Osama bin Laden?

CHAPTER SIX

A Weapon in the Hands of the Left:

The Real Agenda of the Academic Elite

Education is a weapon whose effects depend on who holds it in his hands and at whom it is aimed.

—*Joseph Stalin*

Not everyone who wants to do this country harm is a Radical Islamist armed with a box cutter. Some, like bell hooks, use their academic status to infect students with despair, anger, and hopelessness about this country and even their own future. Moral relativism has become a staple of academic life at the hands of a professorate and staff determined to squeeze the last vestiges of decency and morality out of their young charges.

After September 11, 2001, a horrible date in our history when close to 3,000 people perished, Americans once again came shining through; there was a rejuvenation of the American spirit as we responded with patriotism, anger, and a determination to make sure such an attack would never happen again. We were reminded of every reason why we should be proud and protective of this country. The reaction on our campuses, however, was quite different, with an amazing refusal by both students and professors to recognize right and wrong, good and evil. It gave average Americans a shockingly clear picture of the effects of moral relativism at institutions ranging from the local community college through four-year state colleges to the most prestigious universities.

The American Council of Trustees and Alumni (ACTA), a nonprofit group dedicated to academic freedom, reported on a whole host of extraordinarily revealing comments made by faculty and staff at respected universities across the country. If you're wondering what mentality drives those who have been charged with developing and molding the minds of the next generation, here are some examples:

- "Anybody who can blow up the Pentagon gets my vote." —professor of history, University of New Mexico[1]

- "[W]e should be aware that, whatever its proximate cause, its ultimate cause is the fascism of U.S. foreign policy over the past many decades." —professor of English, Rutgers University[2]

- "[The American flag is] a symbol of terrorism and death and fear and destruction and oppression." —professor of physics, University of Massachusetts–Amherst[3]

- "[I]magine the real suffering and grief of people in other countries. The best way to begin a war on terrorism might be to look in the mirror." —professor of anthropology, Massachusetts Institute of Technology[4]

These comments fairly represent an Intellectual Elite that is completely out of touch with the attitudes and values of the average person in this country. When faced with a monumental tragedy, those in charge of higher learning exposed their moral vacancy by blaming America first.

The Left are no longer able to see the simplest of truths embodied by 9/11: America stands for progress, equity, and freedom. We educate people (both men and women, thank you), help make dreams for the future come true, and create a society in which individuals can thrive. Radical Islamists, as a cultural phenomenon, cut people's throats, destroy buildings, murder huge numbers of people, and condemn the future.

Anti-Americanism persists, in the face of such obvious signs of right and wrong, because it is a requirement of moral relativism. If a student, or anyone else, is to be successfully indoctrinated with the idea that all cultures and ideas are equal, then pride and loyalty to our nation, her past, and our heroes becomes anathema and *must* be eradicated. The special history, achievement, and greatness of America prove, simply by counterpoint, the existence of good and evil, right and wrong. Our history and accomplishments are the antithesis to the moral relativism of which today's professors are so enamored.

> When faced with a monumental tragedy, those in charge of higher learning exposed their moral vacancy by blaming America first.

Where's Sigourney Weaver When You Need Her?

You see, the anti-"Amerika" fanatics from the 1960s may have stopped openly disparaging this nation, but they never stopped hating it. They folded themselves into respected civil-rights organizations, or founded new ones. They went to college (often to avoid the draft), then to law school or graduate school. They realized that the best way to change something, or destroy it, is from the *inside*. I keep thinking of the scene in the film *Alien* where the alien bursts from the man's chest after feeding and growing strong off his body. Yes, the host was killed, but he had served his purpose. In the same way, instead of attacking this country as outsiders, the malignant narcissists from the 1960s *became* the establishment in order to attempt to gut it from the inside. And instead of trying to subvert Americans whose characters were already formed, the Left decided to start from the ground up—by parasitically infesting our nation's secondary schools, colleges, and graduate schools to indoctrinate each generation as it came along. They hate themselves and hate this country, and they are determined to not be alone.

The first step for the Intellectual Elite is to unmake and then remake history itself. Smear the Founding Fathers, cast patriotism as jingoistic, and classify the United States as a genocidal nation bent on terrorism, from its founding to today. On campuses across the country, pride in our country and patriotism are deemed "offensive" and banned. Fewer high schools and colleges are requiring students to take U.S. history courses, and when history is discussed, men like George Washington and Thomas Jefferson are deconstructed and maligned. Someone like Ronald Reagan usually isn't discussed at all, and if he is, it is to complete the vilification. Courses on Western culture and history are attacked as "racist" and often eliminated because the reality of white European men's role in the shaping of world history offends and upsets multiculturalists. Ever since the 1960s, students have been told that everything is relative, judgment is verboten, and if it feels good, do it, while decency and morality are cast as deviant concepts used by the oppressor.

Since it is our universities that turn out the next generation of business leaders, politicians, and lawyers, the Clintons, Enrons, and Global Crossings of the world should come as no surprise. Society's reward for allowing malignant narcissists to take control of our universities is a series of political and business scandals replete with lies, abuse, theft, and the ruination of lives.

Act Gay or Flunk

The message from campus totalitarians to anyone inclined to act on a moral imperative that does not conform to leftist notions is: Do so only at great risk. I'm not talking about receiving a "talking to." There are real repercussions for standing up for what you believe, especially when it comes to morality.

Case in point: Exhibiting the commitment to mind control and conformity, a class at Lakeland Community College in

Ohio—a public institution—required everyone to wear a pink triangle to symbolize homosexual "pride."

Now, as a gay woman, I've always taken offense at the idea that I should be "proud" of my sexuality. I'm proud to be an American, I'm proud to be contributing something to society, but my sexuality, like yours, is a private matter not meant for so-called pride or public display. While ostensibly intended to liberate gay people, the idea of requiring us to strike some kind of public pose about sexuality is revolting enough. To require it of everyone else is at least offensive and on the road to being Stalinistic.

In any case, at Lakeland, one student refused to wear the triangle, citing personal moral issues. Making an effort to work within the system, he approached a school official to ask if he could be given an alternative assignment, and he was rebuffed. He still persisted. As he later told News Channel 5 in Cleveland, "It's a moral issue I have. I pay tuition to come to this school. I shouldn't have to defend my moral issues."[5]

An honors student, he received an F in the class. He actually faced expulsion until the story leaked out of this little community thought-control center.

When a local reporter asked why the young man wasn't allowed to complete an alternative assignment, a morally clueless bureaucrat at Lakeland whined, "I think if the situation were easy, it wouldn't have been part of the curriculum."[6]

Oh, they want difficult situations. I see. With leftism driving the campuses, the more "difficult situation" would have been to have an "Act Straight Day," where all the students would have had to demonstrate heterosexuality in some way so as to show their respect for the heterosexuals on campus. Now *that* would have been tough for Lakeland's harebrained leftists. Can you imagine what the Gay Elite on campus would have done when Heterosexual Pride Day was announced? Boycotts, riots, demands for firings—and what are those drums of tar and feathers doing over there in the cafeteria? Well, the disturbance would probably get GLAAD on the cover of *Time* magazine. At the very least, a(nother) series about homophobia would appear in the *New York Times*.

Don't be fooled. The agenda is not to capture the moral high ground—it is to eradicate yours, so you're left with no place to stand. This isn't even just about propagating a different (nonexistent) sense of morality. The goal is to eradicate everyone else's sense of comfort with their *own* morality, especially that pesky Christian sort. After all, if you're punished for something, it must be wrong, right?

Let's be honest here. The American public, in their generosity and compassion, have accepted homosexuals, despite serious concerns that many Americans have regarding homosexuality and religion, morality, and values. The Lakeland scenario shows that tolerance is no longer enough. Most insulting of all is the fact that this student is told that his morality is now no good. How hypocritical for a group of people who insist that others accept their view of morality to punish a young man who stands by his own. Ultimately, while leftists couch their demands in glowing terms of tolerance and understanding, their actual agenda shows through when they punish those who exhibit a personal commitment to values.

> While leftists couch their demands in glowing terms of tolerance and understanding, their actual agenda shows through when they punish those who exhibit a personal commitment to values.

Alan Charles Kors, codirector and president of the Foundation for Individual Rights in Education (FIRE), writes that he receives letters every day about abuses of liberty. The universities, he reports, "punish individuals without even a semblance of fair procedure."[7] Students, meanwhile, learn "to censor themselves so as not to say or do anything that may possibly bring them trouble." It is critical, he maintains, for the universities to relearn that "[p]ersuasion and moral witness, not repression, are the tools of a free people." When asked how interested observers can help teach the universities this lesson, he answers: Arrange for publicity. "Universities cannot defend in public what they do in private."

The Disgrace of Cornell

"Sept. 11 has made Americans more fearful about the future and more paranoid about the day to day. It has forced Americans to accept a rhetoric of good and evil, and numerous members of ethnic groups have suffered discrimination because of it."[8]

"Forced" Americans to accept a rhetoric of good and evil? This sounds like something that might have come from one of our loopy left-wing special-interest groups, like the ACLU, or possibly even one of the Muslim "civil-rights" organizations (talk about an oxymoron!). But no, this Deep Thought came from Cornell University—to be exact, the editorial staff of the *Cornell Daily Sun,* the university's official student newspaper.

Even today, such a raw exhibition of moral relativism is quite remarkable. Apparently, the slamming of four jumbo jets into buildings and into a field in Pennsylvania—mass murder—isn't all that clearly evil to the intellectual giants at Cornell.

Without something as savage as the attack of September 11th, moral relativism can be a little difficult to point out. It doesn't necessarily expose itself at every turn; it can masquerade as tolerance and understanding. But in a case like this it stands out unmistakably. The *Cornell Daily Sun* had the gall to end its September 11th editorial with this admonition: "[W]e encourage Cornellians to attend one of the many ceremonies Cornell is hosting, to grieve still, to heal a little more and perhaps to learn to be better Americans."

What Cornell's cadre of little journalists offer us here is the epitome of intellectual nihilism. Because there is no right or wrong, we cannot judge. Because there is no right or wrong, the people who died on September 11th can't be divided into murderers and innocent victims. Because there is no good or evil, the attack must have been *provoked,* and so we must "understand" and try to do better, because, after all, we asked for it.

The determination to erase right and wrong doesn't manifest itself only in the student newspaper. If you thought the editorial from the *Cornell Daily Sun* was over the top, take a look at what Cornell's Memorial Convocation on September 11, 2002, ended up promoting. On the first anniversary of the deadliest foreign attack on American soil in our history—outstripping Pearl Harbor by some 500 deaths—this Ivy League institution did not issue a call for patriotism or pride in America; there was no discussion of the evil that Radical Islamists have perpetrated not only on this country, but around the world. Instead, students heard the Reverend Kenneth Clarke, director of Cornell United Religious Work, droning on about how America must "see itself through the eyes of other nations" and how the circumstances we are now facing are similar to those once faced by nations that were victims of our "colonialism and imperialism."[9]

Joseph Sabia of the *Cornell Review,* a conservative student publication, summarized this Day of Disgrace by commenting, "Students were left with the view that Americans were somehow getting what we deserved and that if we respond to national security threats with military force, we would be immoral and hypocritical. Moral relativism, though chic among university-types, is, nonetheless, a disgusting product of intellectual laziness."[10]

Joseph is partly right—the problem here is indeed moral relativism. But in this case it comes about not through intellectual laziness but by design, and it has an extraordinary goal: the destruction of our future and the production of generations who have no commitment, loyalty, or pride in our nation.

One-Trick Professors

For years, David Horowitz, president of the Center for the Study of Popular Culture (CSPC), has decried the disintegration of our university system into a venue for indoctrination by the malevolent Left. Horowitz explains, "[B]eginning in the mid-1960s, the left made a concerted effort to take over our colleges and universities. . . . As they've taken control, they've trampled free speech, virtually banished conservative professors, and turned our schools into little more than huge megaphones for anti-American rhetoric from coast to coast."[11]

Can the professors be so out of touch, so removed from the values and attitudes of the average American? Absolutely they can—just like the rest of their Left Elite tribe. In fact, a study commissioned by the CSPC in 2002 found that more than 80 percent of Ivy League professors who voted in 2000 picked Al Gore and just 9 percent voted for George W. Bush. It gets worse. Who do you suppose was the Ivy League faculty's pick for best president of the past 40 years? That's right—Bill Clinton.[12]

Although these institutions are completely obsessed with the idea of diversity when it comes to skin color and sexuality, they sure don't apply the same standard when it comes to diversity of thought and opinion. The survey asked the professors about their general views, but it also asked them about specific issues. The only question it didn't ask was what planet today's professors come from. Here are some of the findings:[13]

- Asked their party affiliation, 3 percent of the faculty said they were Republicans and 57 percent said they were Democrats. By way of contrast, a recent nationwide survey among the general public showed 37 percent considering themselves Republicans and 34 percent Democrats.

- Forty percent of the professors support slavery reparations for blacks, compared with 11 percent of the general public.

- The professors oppose school vouchers 67 percent to 26 percent, while Americans support vouchers 62 percent to 36 percent.

- The Ivy League faculty strongly oppose (74 percent to 14 percent) a national missile-defense system, while the American public favors such a system by 70 percent to 26 percent.

Frank Luntz of the Luntz Research Companies, which conducted the poll on behalf of the CSPC, commented, "Not only is there an alarming *uniformity* among the guardians of our best and brightest minds, but this group of educators is almost uniformly outside of mainstream, moderate, middle-of-the-road American political thought. So much for diversity."[14]

Berkeley's Shame

Cornell wasn't the only world-renowned American university to give America the finger on the anniversary of September 11th. The University of California–Berkeley was so worried about the display of passionate morality that followed the savage attack on this nation that it decided to ban all patriotic symbols and religious references from its Day of Remembrance on September 11, 2002. For example, the cosponsors of that event—the chancellor's office, the Associated Students of the University of California (the undergraduate student-body government), and the Graduate Assembly—agreed that, instead of the red, white, and blue ribbons distributed most places, student leaders should distribute white ribbons.

Trying to explain the inexplicable, Hazel Wong, chief organizer for the Associated Students, said, "We thought that may be just too political, too patriotic. . . . We didn't want anything too centered on nationalism—anything that is 'Go U.S.A.'"[15]

And consider these little gems from Jessica Quindel, president of the Graduate Assembly:[16]

- "We are trying to stay away from supporting Bush. . . . We don't want to isolate people on this campus who disagree with the reaction to Sept. 11."

- Patriotic songs may exclude and offend people "because there are so many people who don't agree with the songs." For instance, "God Bless America" is "very exclusive" because it mentions God.

- "The flag has become a symbol of U.S. aggression towards other countries. It seems hostile."

Really now, what happened to Ms. Wong and Ms. Quindel to turn them from normal American little girls into confused Berkeley campus organizers? Is it just that their professors were leftists or that these particular young women were rebelling against their parents, or is there something more insidious going on that transforms bright young minds into bug-infested swamp water? The National Association of Scholars (NAS) just may have uncovered the answer.

Teaching Moral Relativism

The NAS is an organization of professors, graduate students, and university administrators and trustees who are committed to excellence in higher education. In early 2001 it commissioned a national survey by Zogby International, which was administered to 401 college seniors between April 9 and April 16, 2001. The results of this survey make one thing quite clear: The growing moral confusion among college students isn't due to some freakish gene that has mutated in the younger generation—it is actually being *taught* to them by the leftists who have commandeered our campuses.

> The growing moral confusion among college students isn't due to some freakish gene that has mutated in the younger generation—it is actually being *taught* to them by the leftists who have commandeered our campuses.

Three-quarters of the seniors polled reported that their professors taught them that what is right and wrong depends on differences in individual values and cultural diversity.[17] Three-quarters of the students also reported being taught that pursuing one or another progressive social policy was a higher priority for corporations than "providing clear and accurate business statements to stockholders and creditors," generally regarded as the bottom line of financial honesty.[18]

Oddly, in a turnabout that could only be provided by the Looking Glass, a huge majority (97 percent) of these same college seniors—our business and political leaders of tomorrow—reported their college studies had prepared them to *behave ethically* in their future work lives. What's remarkable is that these students believe they are being well prepared ethically by professors who, these same students report, are telling them there are no real ethical standards. The modern academic world is the Mad Hatter's oyster. From Bill Clinton to Enron, we have seen the fruits of this belief that the ethical thing is *no ethic,* and it has not been a pretty sight.

Make no mistake about how significant this is. Moral relativism *is* the death of right and wrong. It is the necessary component to the destruction of the very idea of morality and values. Think about it. If everything is relative, then there simply can be no judgment. Without judgment there is no right and wrong. Like God, right and wrong are dead. Within that diseased rubric, perhaps they never existed.

Institutionalizing moral relativism is the coup of the leftist Academic Elite. It is what permits them to brainwash generation after generation into accepting the most base, the most dangerous, the most destructive of behaviors and attitudes. It is designed and is meant to amputate the ability of young people to come to judgment about issues, people, and behavior.

"Tolerating" Ourselves to Death

The NAS findings shed much-needed light on fuzzy-headed college seniors everywhere and certainly help to explain Berkeley's muddled Jessica Quindel. As quoted by the *California Patriot,* the conservative alternative newspaper on the Berkeley campus, Quindel is a gold-plated example of moral relativism: "Quindel, a self avowed hater of the American Flag, the federal government, and the 'Star Spangled Banner,' said she is still patriotic. 'It depends on your definition of patriotism. Everyone has a different definition.'" [19]

There is no solid ground beneath Ms. Quindel and so many others conditioned by the leftists in the academy. There is no sense of pride, guilt, or shame. Everything is relative. Nothing is definitive. Nihilism rules the day. Welcome to the World behind the Looking Glass.

John Leo, in his column for *U.S. News & World Report,* tells how this growing inability to see right and wrong and to judge immoral acts leaves students confused about even the most obvious of depravities. Leo wrote: "Several years ago a college professor in upstate New York reported that 10 percent to 20 percent of his students could not bring themselves to criticize the Nazi extermination of Europe's Jews. Some students expressed personal distaste for what the Nazis did. But they were not willing to say that the Nazis were wrong, since no culture can be judged from the outside and no individual can challenge the moral worldview of another."[20]

Odd, isn't it? These "postmodernists," as Leo terms them, pontificate about how every culture should be taken on its own terms and claim that no judgment can be exercised about terrorists or terrorist nations. They even manifest an inability to condemn one of the most depraved acts of the 20th century—the Holocaust. And yet, these same people, who have been so warped they think Hitler's inner child should be understood, have rallies and marches *condemning the United States*. Of course, the double standard shouldn't be too surprising. Moral relativism acts as a terrific fig leaf for the Left Elite's hatred of this country and desire for its destruction.

We've heard things from "peace" activists essentially demanding that we try to understand bin Laden's (and Arafat's, and every other terrorist's) personal pain and have respect and tolerance for Radical Islamists' frustration at being "oppressed peoples." If this attitude prevails, we will wind up "tolerating" ourselves to death, and will condemn Western civilization—which, it is safe to say, is the most progressive and greatest civilization on Earth—to a very compassionate dustbin.

Rebuking the Decent

It's clear to me why the Intellectual Elite are so panicked about the War on Terror. It makes explicit use of the concepts of good and evil, right and wrong. It is also the ultimate test of what mentality and what *morality* will prevail in this country.

The Academic Elite know this, as they shed their sheep's clothing and punish the few on campus who dare to invoke a moral imperative—who challenge the moral vacuum and stand up to speak the truth. As you can imagine, the stories are not pretty, but they clearly expose the outrageous intolerance of those who carry the banner of "tolerance" in the academy.

One such story belongs to Zewdalem Kebede. On September 22, 2001, just 11 days after the carnage of September 11th, Zewdalem, a political-science major at San Diego State University, was quietly studying in the Reserve Room in Love Library when his attention was caught by a conversation among four Saudi Arabian students sitting nearby. They were talking in Arabic, a language Zewdalem had learned in his native Ethiopia and spoke fluently.

It's clear to me why the Intellectual Elite are so panicked about the War on Terror. It makes explicit use of the concepts of good and evil, right and wrong.

Zewdalem's idle interest was replaced by shock when the Saudis' conversation turned to the September 11 attacks. "They started talking about the Sept. 11 action," Zewdalem recounted. "And with that action they were very pleased. They were happy. And they were regretting of missing the 'Big House.'"[21] He tried to ignore their conversation and continue studying, but he finally decided he had to approach them.

"Guys, what you are talking is unfair. How do you feel happy when those 5 to 6,000 people are buried in two or three buildings?" Zewdalem said. "They are under the rubble or they became ash. . . . And you are talking about the action of bin Laden and his group. You are proud of them. You should have to feel shame."[22]

Zewdalem spoke in Arabic, both to not disturb others in the library and to not embarrass the young men he was speaking to. During the exchange, another Saudi student approached the table and accused Zewdalem of reproaching the others because they were speaking Arabic. The exchange grew heated, with the fifth Saudi intimating that Zewdalem had been threatening his friends. The two sides eventually parted.

I wish I were telling you this story simply to highlight a true American like Zewdalem Kebede. A naturalized citizen, he truly represents the patriotism that built this country and resides in her immigrants as well as her native-born citizens. Unfortunately this story is also an example of how upside-down the academic world has become.

In a scenario only the death of right and wrong could explain, 30 minutes after the exchange, two campus police officers came—for *Zewdalem*. They told him a complaint had been filed against him and wanted his version of the events. On September 25th, according to a report from Accuracy in Academia, Zewdalem received a letter from the university's Center for Student Rights ordering him to respond to his accusers or face sanctions.[23] He had, it was alleged, been "verbally abusive to other students."

The letter elaborated: "[A]ny student of a campus may be expelled, suspended, placed on probation or given a lesser sanction for: Abusive behavior directed toward, or hazing of, a member of the campus community."[24]

Outrageously, the Saudi students are listed as "victims" in the police report, and thus they are protected by not having their names listed. No specific mention was made in the report of what Zewdalem heard them saying.[25]

Jason Foster, a spokesman for the university, told the *New York Times* that the Arab students had complained that Zewdalem approached them in "a threatening manner." According to Foster, the university "believes in the right of students to say what they want, but we also feel we have to protect students from feeling threatened."[26] Hence, Foster said, no disciplinary action had been taken against Zewdalem, but he did receive a letter from a university official warning him, "You are admonished to conduct yourself as a responsible member of the campus community in the future. . . . Consider this letter to be your only warning that future incidents where your involvement is proven will result in you facing serious disciplinary sanctions."[27]

Here, in black and white, is one of the clearest examples I have seen of how the death of right and wrong manifests itself in real people's lives. The university is admonishing a young man to behave "responsibly" in the future when that was exactly what he was doing in the first place! After all, how else can we describe confronting people who were delighting in mass murder? Decency required Zewdalem to confront those young men, and fortunately he was up to the task.

"I'm naturalized American. I have taken an oath to live to protect this country, so that is my part to do—for that I am happy," Zewdalem Kebede said. "I am an honest citizen for this country. I showed those guys that there are people who love America, who defend America. That's what I showed. Is that a crime?"[28] It will be if vacuous campus leftists have their way.

In this case, both Accuracy in Academia and FIRE intervened on Zewdalem's behalf, and they may have had something to do with stopping him from being punished even more harshly. The effort must continue, however, because punishment of those who challenge the leftist status quo rolls on, most of it quietly hidden from public view.

Punishing the Honest

Students aren't the only souls in the academy who face retribution for telling the truth and asking questions that help bring out the truth. Ken Hearlson, an Orange Coast College political-science professor, now knows that all too well. Hearlson was put on paid leave in September 2001 after four Muslim students complained that he had accused them of the hijackings. He was actually barred from stepping foot on the campus—this after teaching there for 18 years.[29]

What Professor Hearlson had done, a week after the attacks, was to ask his class a series of questions relating to the bloodbath. According to the *New York Times,* Hearlson asked his class why Muslim nations had not risen with a single voice to repudiate Osama bin Laden, and why leading Muslim figures seem to deny the Holocaust or, going further, to complain that Hitler did not kill *enough* Jews. Hearlson also referred to flyers that had appeared on campus the previous year, which showed a swastika plastered over a Jewish star. He condemned these as "hate-filled messages" from "Muslim students on this campus." The flyers were signed by a group calling itself Hizb-ul-Haq, or Party of Truth.[30]

One of the students in the class complained to campus authorities about Hearlson's comments and made the claim that Hearlson had accused him *personally* of the terrorism. The student alleged that Hearlson had called him and his friends "terrorists" and "murderers," and that he had told them, "You drove two planes into the World Trade Center. . . . You killed 5,000 people."[31]

Professor Hearlson was well on his way to becoming persona non grata when one student, a young woman who made a habit of tape-recording her classes, came forward with her tape of the lecture in question. Her recording proved that Professor Hearlson, while delivering a passionate message about September 11th, never personally accused the Muslims in his class of being terrorists or murderers. In fact, the claims of any sort of personal attack were exaggerated or completely fabricated.[32]

One would think this would have exonerated Hearlson, but in the morally vacuous hellhole of today's campuses, that was not the case. While he got his job back, he also received a reprimand for allegedly inappropriate behavior.[33]

Hearlson commented to a local reporter about life behind the Looking Glass. "They [the students] lied," he said—and he gets the reprimand? "It doesn't make any sense."[34] The students who made the false allegations that nearly cost this veteran teacher his career and reputation don't seem to have been punished. Certainly no public apology has been made to Mr. Hearlson.

In response to the local reporter's questions, one of the students said he was resentful because Hearlson had "accused us of lying," while another said he just wanted everyone to know "how we were treated unjustly."[35] When asked by the *New York Times* about the tape exonerating Professor Hearlson, the student whined, "[I]f some of the allegations I made were not maybe right, if my memory was shady, this is not the first time anybody brought anything against this teacher." Hearlson, he said, "has a history, and he obviously hasn't learned and he needs to be taught a lesson."[36]

After everything that happened to Professor Hearlson, including some Muslim students calling for his firing and others for actual criminal prosecution for "hate speech," the campus Muslim Student Association (MSA) invited a controversial imam to speak on campus. Mohammad Al-Asi lived up to his reputation of supporting extremist Islamist movements. After a student member of the MSA introducing him compared Israel to Nazi Germany, Al-Asi launched into a tirade about Israeli "war criminals" and characterized evangelical Christians who support Israel as "Zionist, racist, criminal."[37] Double standards are a way of life for the indecent.

Professor Hearlson, by the way, identifies himself as a conservative Christian. I would guess he does indeed have a history—of telling the truth and attempting to impart some modicum of decency and responsibility in his messages about the world. In today's political climate, it is not surprising that there are students who find messages like these offensive. It's time we decide who will teach the "lessons"—people like Professor Hearlson or hypocritical student associations and students who rely on "shady" recollections to punish the decent.

The Tyranny of the Ignorant

One of the symptoms of the oppression of honest intellectuals on campus is the eradication of serious courses meant to educate young people about our intellectual and cultural history. The purging of history courses is no accident. If your goal as a leftist is to instill at the very least an ambivalence and at worst a hatred for America, you don't dare allow legitimate courses about U.S. history into the curriculum.

In fact, the American Council of Trustees and Alumni reports that students can now graduate from 100 percent of the nation's top colleges without taking a single course in American history.[38] As of this writing, the University of Chicago is the latest major college to change its Western civilization course curriculum. Other universities such as Stanford dropped Western civilization courses years ago, after students began protesting them.[39]

Some scholars have admitted the primary reason why Western civilization and American history courses are eliminated is the leftist belief in the "oppressive" nature of the West, and of Christianity in particular. After all, if you teach about the history of this country, or the progress of Europe and the West, you must discuss Christianity and its contribution to civilization, and that is simply too dangerous.

Glenn Ricketts, a University of Chicago alumnus who works for the National Association of Scholars in New Jersey, comments, "It's this idea that Western civilization is responsible for much of what's wrong with the world today. . . . Sure, Western civilization was oppressive at times, but other civilizations didn't produce a bill of rights or a constitution. That's why Western civilization should be taught."[40] Commenting on this dangerous phenomenon, ACTA notes, "As we move forward into the 21st century, our future leaders are graduating with an alarming ignorance of their heritage—a kind of collective amnesia—and a profound historical illiteracy which bodes ill for the future of the republic." I contend this is quite deliberate on the part of the Academic Elite, who realized that it

> If your goal as a leftist is to instill at the very least an ambivalence and at worst a hatred for America, you don't dare allow legitimate courses about U.S. history into the curriculum.

would be easier to infect their students with a moral hopelessness if they had no heroes and no historical benchmark linking decency and greatness. And we can already see the results. In a Zogby poll of American college students taken in January 2002, nearly a third of participants declined to say that they are proud to be Americans.

ACTA, meanwhile, commissioned a survey from the Roper Organization to find out exactly what college seniors did, or did not, know about our historical legacy. The questions were drawn from the basic high-school curriculum, and the students surveyed came from the nation's best colleges and universities as identified by *U.S. News & World Report*'s annual college rankings. The results, compiled in "Losing America's Memory: Historical Illiteracy in the 21st Century," were astounding. You had better sit down.[41]

- Scarcely more than half of the students surveyed knew general information about American democracy and the Constitution, such as the fact that it was the Constitution which established the division of power within the federal government. Over one-third thought the purpose of the Federalist Papers was to win foreign approval for the Revolutionary War or to establish a free press.

- Only 34 percent could identify George Washington as an American general at the battle of Yorktown, the culminating battle of the American Revolution.

- Only 42 percent were able to identify Washington as "First in war, first in peace, and first in the hearts of his countrymen."

- Less than one-quarter (23 percent) correctly identified James Madison as the "father of the Constitution."

A more broadly focused Gallup Poll of college seniors conducted at about the same time yielded similar results:[42]

- Twenty-five percent of college seniors could not place Columbus's voyage within the correct half-century.

- Twenty-five percent could not distinguish Churchill's words from Stalin's, or Karl Marx's ideas from those of the U.S. Constitution.

- Forty percent did not know when the American Civil War occurred.

- Most could not identify certain well-known works as being by Plato, Dante, Shakespeare, or Milton.

Chillingly, ACTA reminds us, "Novelist Milan Kundera once said that, if you want to destroy a country, destroy its memory. If a hostile power wanted to erase America's civic heritage, it could hardly do a better job—short of actually prohibiting the study of American history—than America's elite colleges and universities are doing."[43]

While the scourge of political correctness has dumbed down college teaching and the national discourse generally, there is an even more ominous aspect to these poll results. Judgment requires a knowledge of the *past*. Without the perspective of who we have been, and some understanding of the conscience and character that contributed to the creation of this country and of the Western world, there is no basis for pride and no benchmark by which to compare our country with other peoples and nations.

Think about it. How can we know our place in the world, and embrace the appropriate sense of worth, without understanding the values and morals that shaped the evolution of Western civilization and that compelled the creation of the United States in particular? How is a student to recognize the existence of evil in world affairs without knowing about the words and actions of Joseph Stalin? Where is the judgment of Communism as an immoral and evil failure without the counterpoint of American democracy? How can judgments be made of Karl Marx and Vladimir Lenin without knowing Adam Smith and John Locke? Without studying Columbus, how is a student to truly grasp the role of the Catholic Church in furthering knowledge and literally helping to create the modern world?

You see, the moment you have a complete picture, *judgment naturally follows.*

After all, if a student studied Pol Pot's regime and the work of Winston Churchill and then compared the two, there would be an understanding of evil and good. It's not even something that has to be instilled—universal values are ingrained in us, which is what so threatens the Left and why the concept of values needs to be constantly pushed back.

The complete picture of history obliterates the lies of the Left about the goodness, for all its flaws, of the Western world. Students just might find out that our Founding Fathers were brilliant, *decent* men. That those "dead white European males" like Shakespeare, Plato, Dante, and Milton were indeed remarkable and shaped our dynamic culture—for the better.

The ignorance of the Constitution and American democracy is especially revealing. What do those things have to do with morality? Plenty. This democracy and the documents of our founding embody the principles, the *decency,* that this country represents to the rest of the world. Our integrity—the basic fundamental morality of people like Washington, Jefferson, and

Hamilton—wasn't used simply to defeat a tyrannical imperial regime. Those qualities became embedded in our own great experiment—a country based on faith in God, expecting the best of a virtuous people, and daring to show the world that life could be better.

There is no rhetoric the Left can conjure up that can counter the singular beauty of the Constitution and the Declaration of Independence, which is why leftists in the academy avoid those documents like the plague. Ignorance sustains the moral relativists, and knowledge is to them as water is to the Wicked Witch of the West. I think it's time we invited them to take a swim.

Killing Our Heroes

When courses in U.S. history *are* offered, many times the curriculum has less to do with teaching about America's creation and development than with killing America's heroes. My own experience in a college history class is unfortunately not unique.

I had returned to college in my 30s. Attending the University of Southern California was something that appealed to me because it is a private institution, and so the classes are smaller than what you'd find at an overcrowded public university like UCLA, and professors actually teach their own classes as opposed to relying on teaching assistants. With a minor in history I jumped at a course titled 19th-Century U.S. History. What I experienced in that class was part of what compelled me to write this book.

Being somewhat of a nerd, I was excited at the idea of filling in some of the gaps in my knowledge of 19th-century America. I knew this great country was reshaped by the Civil War, but I wanted to know more about that effort as well as all the other events that shaped the character and built the strength of our nation during the 1800s.

The class was to begin at the beginning of the 19th century, with Thomas Jefferson. I had prided myself on being an autodidact. The things I knew about Jefferson I had read on my own and piecemeal, and I was looking forward to a structured, disciplined look at this man and others who had made my life possible in the greatest country on Earth.

Instead, I sat in disbelief as we were handed a *New York Times* story about Jefferson's supposed relationship with Sally Hemmings. We were then subjected to a rant about the racist Jefferson, the abuser Jefferson, the hypocrite Jefferson. Keep in mind, I was a woman in her 30s sandwiched in with a bunch of wide-eyed, nervous kids from all across the country who were expecting this well-regarded professor to impart his brilliant assessment of American history to them. The thought that this man's tripe was being absorbed as the way to view Jefferson enraged me.

> Ignorance sustains the moral relativists, and knowledge is to them as water is to the Wicked Witch of the West.

Yes, the Louisiana Purchase was discussed, as was Jefferson's writing of the Declaration of Independence, and so on, but all with the undercurrent of what a dreadful man he really was. Always mindful that the professor controlled my grade, I still made a point of speaking up—respectfully (and you know what kind of discipline that took!), but wherever possible challenging his negative attitude.

The professor's stance about George Washington was no better. The first thing out of his mouth in discussing Washington was that he was "not a smart man." The word "moron" was actually used. I piped up when I could, but it was a rare thing indeed for any of the young people in the room to challenge their lecturer. Perhaps they were intimidated, or perhaps concerned about grade repercussions. In any case, the man behind the lectern had a pretty clear field.

Then one day, during a particularly vicious assault by the professor on Washington's intelligence, a young man spoke up. I waited to see if he accepted the idea that our Founding Father was a blithering idiot, or if he would know enough—and have the guts—to challenge it.

The student began in a truly confused but sincere way, "Ah, Professor, I understand what you're saying about Washington, but wasn't he a sort of land surveyor before the war?" Yes, was the answer. The professor crossed his arms. The student continued, "Doesn't that take some kind of intelligence? I mean, how could he be a moron and be a surveyor and do all the things he did?" There was no real answer to that, of course, and so the professor backtracked for a moment and then continued the assault.

What was important and even endearing about this question was that the student wasn't being facetious or deliberately gentle with the professor. He wasn't asking as though he knew and needed to couch his statement as a question (my usual strategy). This young man was truly conflicted by the idea that Washington was just this side of brain-dead, which didn't mesh with the reality of who the man was and what he accomplished. This student had apparently had enough U.S. history in high school to enable him to see the discrepancy. He was also aware enough to realize he was being subjected to a lesson that conflicted with historical reality and moral common sense.

The frightening truth is most students don't have that background and therefore leave those sessions with nothing short of American heroes being morally killed before their eyes.

As the professor described them, the signers of the Declaration of Independence ran the gamut from drunkards to morons to hypocritical slave-owning racists. One of the textbooks we were assigned actually equated the American expansion west with "ethnic cleansing" and described our wars with the Indians as "genocide." The in-class discussion, for the most part, took the same tone.

When we finally got to the Civil War, Lincoln's emancipation of the slaves was couched as an opportunistic ploy because, of course, he also was a hypocrite and, according to the professor, didn't actually care about blacks in this country. No one really did.

You get the picture. It was unrelenting. At no point was one positive, proud, pro-American term used to discuss the men and women who founded this country, built her, and made her great. In this American history class our heroes were killed and our country was cast as arrogant and genocidal.

I eventually complained in private both to the departmental adviser and to the professor himself. Actually, he was a very likable man personally. One thing that troubled me was that he seemed completely oblivious to the fact that what he was teaching could be construed as biased or negative. It was then that I knew this man's style was representative of present-day U.S. history pedagogy. It was nothing strange at all, it was normal, he received awards for teaching, and apparently no one, other than me, was complaining.

Queer Theory

If history is not being taught, *something* is, and it's not what anyone would have predicted 40 years ago. Considering the mentality controlling the university system in this country, however, the following list of courses should not surprise you. Now you'll understand why our future teachers, politicians, and business leaders are apt to know more about 19th-Century Lesbian Writers Who Love Their Cocker Spaniels than about Plato and Shakespeare.

The Young America's Foundation (YAF), the organization that compiled the list, dubs it the "Dirty Dozen." The authors of the report explain:

> The Dirty Dozen highlights the annual Young America's Foundation study *Comedy & Tragedy: College Course Descriptions and [W]hat They Tell Us about Higher Education Today*. The study uses universities' own course descriptions to expose some of the most outlandish and politically biased courses on today's campuses.[44]

Here's a sample of what young people today are being taught:

- Students at Brown University can take Seeing Queerly: Queer Theory, Film, and Video. This course asks, "While Cinema has typically circumscribed vision along (hetro) [*sic*] sexually normative lines, can film also empower viewers to see 'queerly'?"

- Students at Harvard University can take Who Is Black? This course addresses "the social processes through which identities are constructed and changed." The course also discusses "how struggles about who is black take place not only between blacks and whites, but [also between] blacks and other racialized groups, and among blacks themselves."

- Communication students at the University of Minnesota study Language and Sexual Diversity. This class teaches how language is used in "lesbian, gay, bi-sexual, and transgender communities" and the "ways in which sexual diversity affects language use."

- Afro-American Studies at the University of California–Los Angeles offers Cultural History of Rap. In this course, students discuss rap in terms of "musical and verbal qualities, philosophical and political ideologies, gender representation, and influences on cinema and popular culture."

- University of Wisconsin students can study Daytime Serials: Family and Social Roles. In this course, students analyze "the themes and characters that populate television's daytime serials and [investigate] what impact these portrayals have on women's and men's roles in the family and in the work place."

- Vassar College offers Black Marxism. Students learn how "the growth of global racism suggests the symmetry of the expansion of capitalism and globalization of racial hierarchy."

And this is only half of the Dirty Dozen! The replacement of the traditional curriculum with tripe such as this is devastating to the possibility of a serious and consequential higher education in this country. As long as the university is in the hands of the malignant narcissists of the Left, the truth of history will be the enemy, to be suppressed at all costs. History will be rewritten, heroes will be killed, and the truth will be kept dead. The Left Elite know that if the truth of history is unleashed, if Jefferson and Washington were Great Men, if America is the Shining City on a Hill, if morals, values, and character help make dreams come true, then their morally vacant world of victims, anger, and hatred will collapse like the house of cards it really is.

History as Fiction

For the most part, my years at USC were helpful and productive. Most of my political-science and history courses were interesting and educational. I dropped only one course during my time at USC, and that not because of what the professor taught but because I had been literally shouted down by other students in the class. My offense? I had dared to mention the truth about a historical event that didn't conform with the victim-based worldview held by some of my fellow students.

> The Left Elite know that if the truth of history is unleashed, if morals, values, and character help make dreams come true, then their morally vacant world of victims, anger, and hatred will collapse like the house of cards it really is.

It was a class about civil rights and ethics, during which a favorite topic of the Left's came up: Japanese internment during World War II. There were quite a few Asians in the class, and they were taking particular umbrage at the steps our country took 60 years ago in the aftermath of the bloody sneak attack on Pearl Harbor. The comments ranged from America is racist to America is racist, imperialist, racist, unethical, racist, depraved, and, of course, racist. The Japanese had been targeted because of, let's see, oh yeah, racism, and they were interned only because they looked different. This went on and on and on.

So here I was, sitting in a classroom at one of the more respected universities in the nation, and I was waiting for the professor to bring up a fact about the World War II internment that was historically relevant and certainly not a national secret. By the 1990s it was never discussed in the media, but I fully expected it to be in an academic environment, where issues are to be probed more deeply. (I know, I'm naïve!)

I finally raised my hand, "Excuse me, but I think it should be noted that it wasn't just the Japanese who were interned here during the war. Italians and Germans were, too. In fact, they were in the same camps, some integrated and some separated into sections."[45]

The room erupted into a cacophony of chairs moving, students standing to glare at me, gasps, and indignant shouts. It was absolutely amazing. I had assumed some discussion would ensue but this was truly a surprise. A young man of Japanese descent sitting in front of me turned and muttered "Racist bitch."

As you can imagine, I've had a lot said to me in my feminist and civil-rights days, and now in my career as a writer, but even I was taken aback by the rage in this response. I certainly received no help from the professor. He looked dumbfounded. He and the teaching assistants calmed the room down, and the professor actually admonished the class that this was my "opinion" and I had every right to state it. I appreciated his effort, but I reasserted that this wasn't opinion but fact. Students then began to demand "proof," and called me racist (again) and said I was being "disruptive."

The professor, who was as nice as he was clueless, told the class that he, too, had never heard that Germans and Italians had been interned. Very nicely, he asked me if I could bring in material to substantiate my assertion. Of course I could, and did, and then I dropped the class.

The reaction of the Asian students exposed their almost desperate need to deny the truth. Why? If they accepted the reality that people of European ancestry were also displaced and held in camps, that would completely annihilate their certainty that internments of the Japanese were compelled by racism as opposed to national defense. And if that were the case, then their victim-based identity could not survive.

Victimhood keeps people from having to think critically about the complexity of the issues they face. With victimhood there is one pseudo-moral note: "The oppressor hates me." To stop that nonsense would require people to expand their notions of morality and relate to the world on a deeper, more complex level. Seeing the truth of history—like the reality of the internments—makes it possible for young people especially to contemplate the United States as a moral, just society.

In fact, the internments here in the United States during World War II involved everyone with whom we were at war. They had everything to do with national defense, and nothing to do with racism. Which brings us to something that must be faced—the Japanese internment issue perpetually casts the Japanese as *victims* in a war they so brutally started. The internments, plus the bombing of Hiroshima and Nagasaki, were intended to, and did, stop the continuation of that war.

The young man of Japanese descent who muttered the insult at me in class no doubt very much prefers to feel the self-righteousness of victimhood, as opposed to the shame and guilt his grandfather's generation brought to his heritage. With the truth of history I dared to challenge that morally void comfort zone.

The evil nature of the Japanese culture in the first half of the 20th century can be spoken to by all of Japan's neighbors. Flourishing under government patronage and sanctified as the state religion, Shintoism as it was taught at that time held that the Japanese were a divine race, descended from the Sun Goddess, Ama-Terasu. They therefore had the right to do whatever they wanted to the mere humans who surrounded them—and they didn't hesitate. The rape of Nanking; the enslavement of Korea, Singapore, the Philippines; the Bataan Death March—the story of any Japanese conquest of that period includes the wholesale rape of girls and women, bayoneting of children, and beheading of prisoners of war.[46]

A new era dawned in Japan when the emperor, faced with implacable American might, renounced his supposed divinity, and General MacArthur introduced a new Japanese constitution that separated religion and state. However, the period culminating in World War II was one of genocide brutally carried out. *That* Japanese history—which deals with right and wrong, good and evil—is not being taught.

Racism as Virtue

> John and I decided that it was time to launch a journal to document that civil war. The result was *Race Traitor,* whose first issue appeared in the fall of 1992 with the slogan "Treason to blackness is loyalty to humanity" on its cover.. . . The goal of abolishing the black race is on its face so desirable that some may find it hard to believe that it could incur any opposition. . . .

Shocking, isn't it? Would you be even more surprised if I told you this appeared in *Harvard Magazine* and was written by a Harvard academic? Impossible, you're thinking—this is naked racism at its ugliest. Indeed it is, and you'd be right—that paragraph did not appear as I quoted it above. The following is what *Harvard Magazine* actually published in its September/October 2002 issue:

> John and I decided that it was time to launch a journal to document that civil war. The result was *Race Traitor,* whose first issue appeared in the fall of 1992 with the slogan "Treason to whiteness is loyalty to humanity" on its cover.. . . The goal of abolishing the white race is on its face so desirable that some may find it hard to believe that it could incur any opposition. . . .[47]

You see, *this* type of racism is permitted and even applauded at our most prestigious universities. I know it doesn't make sense, but has anything I've described for you in this chapter? That's the whole point—things have indeed become nonsensical, and even unbelievable.

Race Traitor is brought to you by Dr. Noel Ignatiev, a Marxist (of course) and a faculty member at Harvard's W.E.B. DuBois Institute for African-American Research, a leading Black Studies department. I replaced the word "white" with "black" when I first presented Ignatiev's screed in order to get around the conditioning all of us have been subjected to. We have been taught to meekly accept the maniacal ravings of academic black racists as something especially insightful that needs to be seriously considered. We've had it drilled into us that black racism is "pride" or "nationalism" or, in this instance, "loyalty to humanity." Seeing this for what it really is—a dangerous racist polemic—requires a skirting of our conditioning.

Ignatiev, by the way, is white. This is an important point to remember as we watch the Left's malignant narcissists projecting their own issues onto society. Whatever may lie at the root of Ignatiev's hatred of his own race, it clearly runs deep, and he is determined to pass it on to the young people under his care. Yet Harvard not only permits him to keep teaching but showcases him because, like the rest of the prestigious academic world, it is committed to producing white male graduates who believe that they are the "racist, sexist, homophobic oppressor."[48]

Author and columnist Paul Craig Roberts comments, "Dr. Ignatiev has an idea like Hitler. A race is guilty and must go. The communists said it was a guilty class that had to go. If you thought genocide was left behind in the 20th century, be apprised that today genocide has a home in the educational system."[49] In fact, Ignatiev pledges in that essay that his journal will "keep bashing the dead white males, and the live ones, and the females, too, until the social construct known as 'the white race' is destroyed—not 'deconstructed' but destroyed."[50]

You see now even more clearly, I hope, how this environment condemns even the brightest of students. How can a young person cope with the absurdity of it all except by adapting and accepting it? This is *Harvard,* for crying out loud. Kids get sent there believing they've been accepted into a place that represents the best of humanity. If a Great Thinker thinks this, our young people reason, well then, gosh, it must be worth considering.

Lock Up the Babies and Small Animals

If you thought it couldn't get any worse, I will leave you with what represents to me the epitome of the death of right and wrong on our college campuses. When Princeton University appointed bioethicist Peter Singer as DeCamp Professor in the University Center for Human Values, it struck many as simply too absurd. The phrase "Peter Singer, Bioethicist," is truly an oxymoron.

Singer, Australian-born and Oxford-trained, has been advocating moral relativism, euthanasia, and even infanticide for decades now.[51] Sadly, in the true spirit of the Looking Glass, this morally bankrupt individual is perfect for today's morally mangled Ivy League.

If you think there must be some redeeming quality to Mr. Singer's work, think again. Just last year Singer's apparent hatred for himself and humanity sank to new depths in his glowing review[52] of Midas Dekkers's *Dearest Pet: On Bestiality*, for an online sex magazine.

Singer writes that the human taboo on bestiality stems from strong genital similarities between humans and animals, mammals especially, leading to "our desire to differentiate ourselves, erotically and in every other way, from animals." "Who has not," he writes, "been at a social occasion disrupted by the household dog gripping the legs of a visitor and vigorously rubbing its penis against them? The host usually discourages such activities, but in private not everyone objects to being used by her or his dog in this way, and occasionally mutually satisfying activities may develop."[53]

Who has not?! I have not, and you have not, and neither has the vast majority of normal, decent people. And yet students who have been accepted into one of the top colleges in our nation will be taught on issues of *ethics* by a man who takes a romantic view of the potential of a mutually satisfying sexual experience with your poodle, and who also thinks infanticide is not only permissible but sometimes morally obligatory.

If you have been reluctant to believe how degraded our cultural and social institutions have become, listen to some recent comments about Peter Singer. The *New York Times*, in a largely flattering profile, dubbed Singer "perhaps the world's most controversial ethicist."[54] The *New Yorker* declared him to be "the most influential living philosopher."[55] When Princeton president Howard Shapiro appointed Singer to the DeCamp professorship in 1998, he wrote a Letter from the President in which he assures the Princeton community:

> When faculty members . . . conducted a world-wide search for an exceptional teacher and scholar . . . Peter Singer ranked first on their list, and their judgment was strongly endorsed in the letters we solicited from scholars at other universities who also are leaders in this field.[56]

It's inevitable that the moral vacuum that has consumed the primarily leftist campuses in this nation will begin to reproduce itself. The fact that Singer was so highly recommended indicates just how far beyond Princeton this cancer has spread.

Shapiro, in his Ivy-covered cluelessness, wanted Princetonians to know that

> An important part of our purpose as a university is to ask the most difficult and fundamental questions about human existence, however uncomfortable this may be . . . [to] develop both a capacity for independent thought and a set of moral values to guide them through their lives.[57]

Really? With Shapiro advocating "moral values" like Singer's, he has made Princeton unsafe for both your child *and* your beagle.

Is this really good enough? Should we continue to ignore the obvious and defer to those who want nothing but the worst for our children and the future? Clearly not. As the Intercollegiate Studies Institute notes, "Princeton is a trend-setting university with a hallowed history, but when its top ethicist smiles on bestiality, we vote no confidence in its leadership or moral vision."[58]

Are you a Princeton alumnus? Complain. Were you thinking about sending your child to Princeton? Don't. Do you have friends with connections at Princeton? Tell them. Tell Princeton yourself. This isn't some closed society that is not relevant to you. Like it or not, the people Princeton turns out will have an impact on your life.

And you must consider, we only know about the Peter Singer controversy because it made the news. If this is Princeton's standard, if this is the standard for the Ivy League and campuses elsewhere—I contend it is, and Shapiro's letter says it is—we must recognize this as just one small indicator of a much larger problem. As with any cancer, yes, it's there, but it's better you know about it so you can take action. Is dealing with it painful? Sure. Is it easy? No. Will it take a while? Of course. But things *can* be changed.

There are people and organizations who are committed to making a difference on our campuses, but they need your help to do it. Alan Charles Kors and Harvey Silverglate, cofounders of Foundation for Individual Rights in Education; David Horowitz, founder of Center for the Study of Popular Culture; and groups like the National Association of Scholars and the Young America's Foundation, among others, are working tirelessly to make a difference. Check the notes for this chapter, visit the Web sites, make the calls, become involved. Our future depends on it. Literally.

CHAPTER SEVEN

Destruction of the Innocents:

The Left Targets Children

Sex is not harmful to children. It is a vehicle to self-knowledge, love, healing, creativity, adventure, and intense feelings of aliveness. There are many ways even the smallest of children can partake of it.

—*Judith Levine*[1]

Of all the fallout from the Left's assault on our culture and values, the sexualization of children is the most pressing and menacing issue we face. In the name of sexual freedom and individual rights, it is nurtured and supported by academics, the media, and the rest of the Left Elite, primarily the gay and feminist subcultures.

This destruction of innocent youth manifests itself in many different ways. Children are becoming sexually active at younger and younger ages[2]; child molestation is on the rise[3]; children and adolescents are increasingly engaging in sexual activity with each other.[4] At the same time, the suicide rate among adolescents is skyrocketing. In fact, from 1952 to 1995 the incidence of suicide among children and young adults nearly tripled. From 1980 to 1997 the rate of suicide among persons aged 15 to 19 years increased by 11 percent and among persons aged 10 to 14 years by an astonishing *109 percent.*[5] What is compelling our children, as young as *10 years old,* to kill themselves?

As a starting point, take another look at the epigraph at the beginning of this chapter. Do you see what it means? The author is saying, literally, that sex is not only not harmful, it is a **good** thing for children—even the "smallest." Who is this promoting an argument that endangers toddlers, destroys lives, and empowers child molesters?

If right and wrong were alive and well, this bizarre statement could only come from some pedophile trying to rationalize his actions. Instead, it was expressed by author and journalist Judith Levine in a discussion of her book *Harmful to Minors: The Perils of Protecting Children from Sex.* Levine, frighteningly, is a respected part of the Left Elite, highly regarded in academia and in the gay and lesbian establishment. She gives an accurate picture of what the Left Elite have in store for you and your children.

> The Left Elite only pretend to be concerned about what's best for everyone else because it is the most effective way to manipulate you and your children into their abyss.

Most Americans probably think the sexualization of children is an awful *but unintentional* side effect of the general increase in sexual freedom. Reality belies this. I contend it is actually a specific and conscious part of the agenda of the malignant narcissists in charge of our culture. David Spiegel, associate chairman of the department of psychiatry and behavioral sciences at Stanford University, agrees. "There is a movement," he says, "to normalize sexual relationships between adults and children. It is wrong, empirically, morally, ethically, and it's illegal."[6]

Think about it. The gay and feminist movements of the 1960s were based in sexual liberation. To many people at the time, this was a noble effort, especially with its links to individualism. As the years went by, these movements basked in growing acceptance of their sexual message—tolerance for gays and lesbians, reproductive freedom for women, sexual freedom for women. At that point, however, the Left's damaged leadership could not stop. Both personally and politically the stakes became higher and higher. Each success, instead of an end, became a means to another end, another envelope to push, more rules to break, more tradition to skewer.

Ultimately, the message from the Left was that "no rules" was the rule. Ideas about morality cramped one's lifestyle; personal responsibility implied archaic moral standards; decency and virtue were code words for oppression and meant to ruin your life. As we've seen, for malignant narcissists, everything *is* about them. The Left Elite only pretend to be concerned about what's best for everyone else because it is the most effective way to manipulate you and your children into their abyss.

Why sexualize children? There are a number of reasons.

- Making sex with children "normal" furthers the needs of malignant narcissists (often damaged themselves by physical and/or emotional abuse in childhood, or by sexual molestation), by forcing society to assimilate with *them.*

- Increased sexual compulsion among children spreads sexually transmitted diseases, thus making both compulsion and STDs "normal" and thereby eliminating the stigma attached to aberrant and deviant behaviors.

- Conditioning children into sex addiction *guarantees* the Left Elite control of your culture for generations. It also promises sex-addicted future consumers on which the porn industry relies. By destroying those lives, they strike the final blow to family, faith, tradition, decency, and judgment.

Most leftists don't actually molest children, of course, but the commitment to "sexual freedom" has in fact developed into an inability to criticize or limit "sexual expression," including with adolescents. It has been a natural progression for damaged people who have no boundaries and whose identities are tied to sexuality.

The Fallout

The Left Elite crow about the beneficial effects of the increase in "sexual freedom" during the past four decades. One thing they leave out is the fact that the suicide rate among children and teens has been increasing along with the increase in sexual activity among children and in the number of children afflicted with STDs.

Polls taken in the mid-1950s indicate that fewer than 25 percent of girls under 19 were sexually active. In 1982, 47 percent of female teenagers polled reported having had sexual intercourse, and by 1990, that figure had increased to 55 percent. In 1995, 61 percent of black female teenagers reported having had sexual intercourse.[7]

Judith Levine insists that sex "is not ipso facto harmful to minors; and America's drive to protect kids from sex is protecting them from nothing. Instead, often it is harming them."[8] This is exposed as the lie it is by Dr. Meg Meeker in her powerful and important book *Epidemic: How Teen Sex Is Killing Our Kids*.[9] What she reveals is as shocking as it is deadly.

- Nearly one in four sexually active teens is living with a sexually transmitted disease.

- Nearly 50 percent of black teenagers have genital herpes.

- One in five children over age 12 tests positive for herpes type 2.

- Although teenagers make up just 10 percent of the population, they acquire between 20 and 25 percent of all STDs.

- Fifteen percent of all boys will be infected with the herpes virus by the time they're 18.

Every day, Meeker reports, 8,000 teens become infected with a new STD.[10] What is she speaking of? Herpes, a lifelong disease with no cure, causes painful genital ulcers. The human papilloma virus (HPV) doesn't just cause genital warts, it is the one virus we actually know causes cancer. It is responsible for 99.7 percent of cervical cancers and the deaths of 5,000 women annually. Boys and men aren't off the hook either. HPV is linked to penile and anal cancer, and may have a role in head and neck cancers. As with herpes, there is no treatment for this virus.[11]

In addition to herpes and HPV, the most common STDs are chlamydia (symptomless but can cause infertility), hepatitis B, gonorrhea, syphilis, HIV/AIDS, trichomoniasis, and chancroid. Penicillin is no more the simple cure—these pathogens have had decades to become resistant to antibiotics, requiring much more complex treatment. When there's treatment at all.

So, courtesy of the Left's insistence that children have some natural inalienable right to sex, a frightening percentage of teens will grow up living their lives infected with chronic, debilitating diseases. These diseases will at the least inhibit intimacy; at the worst, they can cause infertility, cancer, and in some cases a premature, painful death. Unless, of course, the young people who are afflicted kill themselves first.

It becomes clear, when you look at the reality of the numbers, that the Left Elite's "sexual liberation" and "freedom" are nothing less than death and destruction for our children.

And yet we still see the Left in academia, Levine and others, continuing to bang the drum that sex between and with children is a *good thing*. These Serious Thinkers portray their fixation on remaking children in their own sick image as a sexual revolution for children. In reality it is destroying lives, and with it, our future. Literally.

Definition Is Everything

Lobotomizing Americans into accepting the destruction of children's lives, while normalizing sexually predatory behavior, is the ultimate coup and, I believe, the last blow in the death of right and wrong. After all, if the last frontier in indecency— using children for sex—becomes acceptable in the name of civil rights, there is truly no hope for the future. And when nothing matters, when the moral vacuum is complete, actual evil will have won the day.

There is nothing less than that at stake here.

One of the things Judith Levine does is implement the most subtle of culture-change tactics. Throughout her book, the term "child-adult sex" replaces the term "pedophilia." Do you see the intent here? Definition is everything. The word "pedophilia" carries with it a whole load of negative baggage. It immediately and appropriately says that sexual abuse of children is wrong. It is a word that stigmatizes the subject it refers to.

The term "child-adult sex," however, says something *very* different. First, by definition, it says "sex" is possible between a child and an adult. Let's be honest here. Sex is no more a part of child sex abuse than it is a part of rape. Both are acts of violence and control. Yet the news coverage and reviews of Levine's book repeat her outlandish euphemism for child abuse. Definition is, in fact, everything, and changing reality is the order of the day for our moral relativists.

Levine isn't the only one pushing funny terminology. One of the more shocking things I came across while doing research for this chapter was the new term for girls: "adolescent women." Notice what's happening here. By defining girls as "women" the moral relativists are attempting to condition us into believing girls have "women's rights," deserving of everything that comes under that banner.

The Web site of the notoriously leftist Alan Guttmacher Institute (AGI) was the first place I came across this absurd, and dangerous, term, and I have since seen it used in a Centers for Disease Control (CDC) report about sexual activity among girls.

Founded in 1968, AGI describes its mission as "to protect the reproductive choices of all women and men in the United States and throughout the world."[12] Alan Guttmacher himself, we should remember, was president of the Planned Parenthood Federation of America and a leader in the International Planned Parenthood Federation in the 1960s and early 1970s.

Here's just one snippet from an AGI paper that exposes the organization's developing agenda of eliminating parental authority in the lives of children:

On the one hand, it seems eminently reasonable that parents should have the right and responsibility to make health care decisions for their minor child. On the other hand, it may be more important for a young person to have access to confidential medical services than it is to require that parents be informed of their child's condition.[13]

Gee, isn't it nice that people in a think tank are deciding these things for you? Obviously, the AGI agenda goes a bit beyond choices for "women." In reality it is representative of the Left establishment's efforts to normalize the sexualization of children at virtually any cost.

Erasing terminology like "girl," "boy," and even "teenager"—which remind us we're dealing with children—is of paramount importance if sexualized children are to become the norm. It's one way past our walls, brainwashing us to slide into the Left's sick and desperate pit. Essentially, with the death of right and wrong, girls are no more. Forget even the use of the term "female." No, all human females are now Women, with the right to sexual freedom—freedom from parents, freedom from right and wrong, freedom from a decent, healthy childhood and future life.

> I for one will not silently watch this destruction of children in the name of women's rights and sexual freedom.

As a feminist, I strongly object to this denigration of the efforts of authentic feminism. How awful, how unforgivable it would be if today's feminists allowed their concern for women's rights to be used to destroy the lives of little girls, to make girls into sex objects, whereas authentic feminists have been fighting against the objectification of women for ages. I for one will not silently watch this destruction of children in the name of women's rights and sexual freedom.

It really must be acknowledged that the Left's commitment to so-called sexual freedom and reproductive choice has veered out of control. I am pro-choice and always will be, but I do not view abortion as some fun thing for a woman (or girl, whether or not she's termed an "adolescent woman") to do during her lunch hour. The reality is it's a surgical procedure, and I hope very few women and no girls need to act on their right to abortion.

Part of slowing the abortion rate is to acknowledge that abstinence is not some freakish, unnatural idea. And yet, the Left Elite, while admitting the STD epidemic in their own literature, steadfastly refuse to discuss or emphasize the fact that something seems to have gone terribly wrong with their sexually "free" (actually anarchic) society. What is the Left's response to rising suicide rates among children and youth, and the epidemic of incurable and sometimes fatal STDs? The only thing discussed in research paper after research paper, monograph after monograph, report after report, is how to get children to use condoms, or how successful Norplant is, or the benefits of oral sex versus sexual intercourse, yadda, yadda, yadda. "Safe sex" is the mantra. Do you actually think any school sex ed curriculum discusses the fact that sex can cause cancer? That sex, courtesy of the sexual revolution, can kill you? Of course not. The presumption is sex is good, children want it, so children are told all you have to do is have "safe sex." Which, of course, doesn't exist.

Never discussed is a values-based framework geared to having girls and boys wait before becoming sexually active. It is presumed that they *will* act, that they are sexual creatures who need expression, and the Left is eager to help them find it. The Left Elite are determined to make sure the idea of restraint and personal responsibility is eradicated in the world of children, just as it is in theirs.

Smoke and Mirrors

Judith Levine *does* believe there is a sex-related danger to children out there. Not surprisingly for this confused woman, the danger she perceives comes from the "conservative religious agenda that would deny minors all sexual information and sexual expression."[14] What she's referring to is "abstinence-only education. . . . These so-called protections are more harmful to minors than sex itself." How dare she. I'd like Levine to find me a 12-year-old who has gonorrhea or who killed herself because of abstinence.

Is it possible to be more completely behind the Looking Glass?

Levine's book was not published by some off-the-wall fringe publisher sometime back in the 1960s when certain segments of the Left were literally confused with drugs. No, it comes to you freshly published in 2002, courtesy of our academic establishment, specifically the University of Minnesota Press. Is it possible that I misunderstood the intent of her book? Consider this from the cover flap: "Sex is a wonderful, crucial part of growing up, and children and teens can enjoy the pleasures of the body."[15] Really? At what point did sex become a wonderful, crucial part of *your* 12-year-old's life?

A favorite tool of apologists for sexual predators is to point to the Dutch age-of-consent law. Levine does just that in her book, calling it a "good model."[16] Just what is this new standard that would be a "good model" for our society? It permits sex between an adult and a child aged 12 to 16. I remember when I was 12 years old. I couldn't be trusted to make a decent decision about what to have for dinner, let alone "consent" to sex. The safety of children rests with adults who know enough to protect them from the perverse sexual obsessions of adults and the predatory tendencies of teens slightly older than themselves. It's the least we owe the next generation in an increasingly complex world.

In a Newhouse News Service interview about the book, Levine exposes just how unsound her sense of right and wrong really is. When the interview turned to the Catholic Church's sex-abuse scandal, she said a sexual relationship between a priest and a youth "conceivably" could be positive.[17]

When challenged, she immediately retreated, asserting in the same interview that she disapproves of sex between a child and an authority figure. Talk about splitting hairs—*all* adults are authority figures to children! And her retreat was merely tactical. According to a report from the Associated Press, Levine "believes teen-agers deserve more respect for the choices they make in consensual affairs, and suggests that America's age-of-consent laws can sometimes lead to excessive punishment."[18] In other words, it's not the molester who's wrong, it's the age-of-consent laws.

By the way, Levine's publicist wants the world to know she has written about "sex, gender and families" for two decades. She is one of the founders of the feminist group No More Nice Girls and the author of *My Enemy, My Love: Women, Men, and the Dilemmas of Gender.* Her articles include "The Dykes Next Door,"[19] published in *Ms.* magazine.

One thing not included in Levine's press materials is an admission she made in an interview: that as a minor she had a sexual encounter with an adult that was, as she put it, "on the balance" a "perfectly good experience."[20] Remember the origins of malignant narcissism: Those who work to change our culture, our lives, and the lives of our nation's children are seeing the world through their own lenses. Many of the activists, "scholars," politicians, and talking heads on the Left who promote the destruction of values are re-creating their own original youthful trauma and projecting it into other people's lives with the hope of mastering it.[21] Of course, this is done at everyone else's expense, culturally and personally.

Open Season on Children

The academic assault on children isn't limited to Levine. She is not, in fact, some anomaly struggling all on her own. She is but one foot soldier of many. It would be a mistake to think an idea as repugnant as children having the "right" to be sexually molested is some esoteric notion circulating only among isolated swamp-brained leftist intellectuals. Any solace we may take from the fact that Levine's book will mercifully not be read by most people will unfortunately be short-lived. In fact, her message is being frantically ushered along by mainstream media into the homes and minds of millions.

The publisher's Web site crows about the stories that have appeared about Levine and the book. *Time* magazine: "Child Sexuality: Challenging the Taboos."[22] Challenging the taboos?!

The Nation: "[K]ids have a right not just to safety and knowledge but to pleasure too."[23] *Philadelphia Daily News:* "A fresh taste of truth."[24] *USA Today:* "Experts debate impact, gray areas, of adult-child sex."[25]

Note that even in *USA Today,* the word "pedophilia" has been replaced by the euphemism adult-child sex, as though such a thing actually exists. The legitimizing of the term gains extraordinary ground when *USA Today* uses it. And whether the writers and editors intended to move Levine's message, that's what they do every time they publish an uncritical account of the book.

Other coverage included CNN: "Levine's book has sizzle." ABC News posted its story online[26] with segment headers such as "A Model of Consent," "Hysteria Overshadows Other Messages," and "Savaged for Ideas," this last referring to critical reactions to the book by people like Dr. Laura Schlessinger. It now does not matter how many people read *Harmful to Minors.* The news coverage of this tripe is at least as useful in furthering the message, because it brings it into the national bloodstream.

Even an obscure study can play a large role in legitimizing each further step in targeting children. As an example, in 1998 the American Psychological Association published in its *Psychological Bulletin* a study which asserted that some sexual liaisons between children and adults could actually be beneficial to children and should not be termed "child abuse."[27]

This study, known as the Rind Report, was read by comparatively few people. However, four years later it was used by Levine to justify her position and was referred to in many of the news stories as evidence that Levine is correct and her critics are, as *The Nation* gleefully termed them, "bombastic."[28] While Dr. Laura Schlessinger—who besides being a radio host is a certified family and marriage therapist—led a campaign against the Rind Report, resulting in congressional condemnation of it, it has already been used to defend child molesters in at least three court cases.[29]

At about the same time as the Rind Report was making the rounds, helping intellectual pedophiles to legitimize their corrupt sexual interest in children, Harris Mirkin, a political-science professor at the University of Missouri–Kansas City, opened up another front in this battle. Mirkin understands very well what is at stake. As he once wrote, "children are the last bastion of the old sexual morality."[30]

In 1999, in the *Journal of Homosexuality* (by this time, you shouldn't be surprised by the nature of this journal), Mirkin wrote that not all sex with children should be put into the same category. "According to the dominant formulas," he writes, "the youths are always seduced. They are never considered partners or initiators or willing participants even if they are hustlers."[31] (Those wretched little hustlers—they never take enough of the responsibility!) "Though Americans consider intergenerational sex to be evil," he continues, "it has been permissible or obligatory in many cultures and periods of history."[32] What another nice new term: "intergenerational sex." That "pedophilia" label *must* go—it's just so darn . . . stigmatizing. And, gee, I guess since other cultures think sex with kids is okay, we'd better get with the program. But that also means we should worship the cow, cut the hands off thieves, make women wear burqas, and set women on fire if they "dishonor" their husbands. Yeah, those other cultures seem just dandy.

Robert Stacy McCain of the *Washington Times* has written one of the more important stories on the issue. In his exposé "Endorsement of Adult-Child Sex on the Rise,"[33] McCain offers a frightening litany of academic arguments for "consensual sex with children," including:

- In 2000, the Institute for Advanced Study of Human Sexuality in San Francisco published an article, "Sexual Rights of Children," saying there is "considerable evidence" that there is no "inherent harm in sexual expression in childhood."

- San Francisco State University professor Gilbert Herdt, coauthor of the 1996 book *Children of Horizons: How Gay and Lesbian Teens Are Leading a New Way Out of the Closet,* said in an interview with the Dutch pedophilia journal *Paidika* that "the category 'child' is a rhetorical device for inflaming what is really an irrational set of attitudes" against sex with children.

- A 1998 "meta-analytic" study [McCain is referring to the Rind Report] . . . argued, among other things, that "value-neutral" language such as "adult-child sex" should be used to describe child molestation if it was a "willing encounter."

Here you see the continuing and intensive effort to change definitions and push "value-neutral" language, even to the point of eliminating the word "child" from the discussion. Value-neutral thoughts require value-neutral language. Of course, it's only the spread of moral relativism that makes these rank arguments intellectually possible. Such arguments cannot thrive unless normal people throughout society have lost the ability to come to judgment. Only then can moral terrorists like Levine and Mirkin get published and be taken seriously.

Remember, whenever one of these members of the Left Elite presses the value-neutral case, it provides a stepping-stone helping to legitimize the next book or monograph or paper that challenges the "taboo" on child sexual abuse while "arguing against the 'moral panic' over child sexuality,"[34] as Mirkin has whined. Like a game of Connect the Dots, the deeply damaged individuals of the Left Elite constantly refer to each other and give their published work to sympathetic friends in the news media who obligingly pass their ideas along. It is like the Wizard of Oz pulling the strings and hoping we won't notice. Their success relies on the average American being brainwashed enough to swallow whole the most dangerous and grotesque of lies—that destroying children will save them.

> Their success relies on the average American being brainwashed enough to swallow whole the most dangerous and grotesque of lies—that destroying children will save them.

All you have to do is pull back the curtain and say no.

The End of Innocence

As you can see, the *idea* of normalizing the sexualization of children in the minds of the public is of great importance to leftist thinkers. But this disgrace goes beyond rhetoric. Gaining acceptance for this concept is only one step toward the actual endgame—the literal destruction of children in the name of the sexual revolution. After all, it is the only way malignant narcissists will ever feel normal, healthy, and acceptable: by remaking society—children—in their image.

That remaking has now taken root in the sex-education programs within our public schools. We saw some of this in the discussion of the Gay, Lesbian and Straight Education Network in chapter 4, but it's by no means confined to gays.

A statement made in response to a speech I gave at Penn State reveals a great deal about the ignorance of leftist activists today. I was speaking about my first book, *The New Thought Police*. During the question period, a student offered the observation that the Right is in control of our culture. His main example? The *limits* of sex education in schools.

In an effort to not embarrass him I refrained from asking what time machine he had used to get from 1962 to 2002. I think he won the contest for Most Ignorant Statement by a College Student. Coming in a close second was the young woman at UC Davis Law School who insisted that the media were controlled by the Right. When I pressed her for an example, she offered "Ted Turner."

At any rate, the young man at Penn State insisted that sex education in public schools did not go *far enough*. The Right, he passionately declared, had kept sex education dumbed down, limited, and restricted to simple "sperm meets egg" biology. This is always the argument, by the way, of leftists as they try to explain the epidemic of STDs, HIV and AIDS, and teen suicide. They rant about the lack of information and lack of support for children who are naturally going to act out sexually.

Of course, reality is the opposite of what my interrogator at Penn State argued. Here is the shocking reality: "Sex education" has become, literally, "*sexuality* education," right down into elementary school. No more is it about biology. Now children as young as five years old learn about masturbation, homosexuality, and anal intercourse, among other things.

Founded in 1964, the Sexuality Information and Education Council of the United States (SIECUS)[35] has gradually become the main dispenser of sex-education guidelines to America's public school systems. In fact, the Division of Adolescent and School Health of the Centers for Disease Control recently entered into a five-year agreement with SIECUS, allowing the organization to do even more outreach through its School Health Project.[36]

How is it that, with SIECUS promoting sexual "health" for decades, this nation has seen a correlating epidemic of sexually transmitted diseases afflicting our children? Take a look at what SIECUS offers in its "Guidelines for Comprehensive Sexuality Education: Kindergarten–12th Grade."[37] This document tells teachers and school administrators what they should be instructing the children under their care. Here is a sampling of the "Developmental Messages" the guidelines suggest are appropriate to the various age groups:

Children Ages 5–8

- "Both girls and boys have body parts that feel good when touched."

- "Vaginal intercourse occurs when a man and a woman place the penis inside the vagina."

- "Some men and women are homosexual, which means they will be attracted to and fall in love with someone of the same gender."

- "Bodies can feel good when touched."

- "Touching and rubbing one's own genitals to feel good is called masturbation."

- "Masturbation should be done in a private place."

Children Ages 9–12

- "Sexual intercourse provides pleasure."

- "A bisexual person is attracted to both men and women."

- "Homosexual and bisexual people are often mistreated, called hurtful names, or denied their rights because of their sexual orientation."

- "All people are sexual beings."

- "Many boys and girls begin to masturbate for sexual pleasure during puberty."

- "Human beings have a natural physical response to sexual stimulation."

Children Ages 12–15

- "Understanding one's sexual orientation can be difficult."

- "Talking openly about sexuality enhances relationships."

- "Masturbation, either alone or with a partner, is one way a person can enjoy and express their sexuality without risking pregnancy or an STD/HIV."

- "When two people express their sexual feelings together, they usually give and receive pleasure."

- "Orgasm is an intense pleasurable release of sexual feelings or tension experienced at the peak of sexual arousal."

- "Young people can buy some contraceptives in a drug store, grocery market, or convenience store without a doctor's prescription."

- "Many religions today acknowledge that human beings were created as sexual beings and that their sexuality is good."

Children Ages 15–18

- "Gender identity is determined by a person's feelings of maleness or femaleness."

- "The telephone number of the gay and lesbian center in this community is _____ (fill in)."

- "Having values different from one's family can be difficult."

- "Some sexual behaviors shared by partners include kissing, touching, talking, caressing, massaging, sharing erotic literature or art, bathing/showering together, and oral, vaginal or anal intercourse."

- "Some people continue to respect their religious teachings and traditions but believe that some views are not personally relevant."

- "Some sexual fantasies involve mysterious or forbidden things."

Perhaps some of you as parents think these messages are helpful, and that's fine. For *you*. My beef here is that *any* message to children about sexuality belongs in the hands of parents, *not* of strangers in positions of authority, frankly, like teachers. Certainly, we at least owe youngsters a childhood protected from the valueless machinations of troubled adults. This is not about whether or not to teach the reproduction process in school—this is about whether or not you, as a parent or guardian, will be the one to choose when, how, and if your child is "taught" about masturbation, sex for pleasure, and homosexuality.

Make no mistake, SIECUS has been working diligently for years to cut you out of the process of instructing your children on such matters. The or-

> Any message to children about sexuality belongs in the hands of parents, *not* of strangers in positions of authority, frankly, like teachers.

ganization, *which receives our tax dollars* through its partnership with the CDC, has a mandate to instruct and influence public-school teachers about what to teach your children. Its Web site boasts:

Since they [the "Guidelines for Comprehensive Sexuality Education"] were first published in 1991, they have become the most widely recognized and implemented framework for comprehensive sexuality education across the country. . . . They have been used by local communities to plan new programs, evaluate existing programs, train teachers, educate parents, conduct research, develop peer programs, and write new materials. They are being used by schools, community agencies, and churches and synagogues to educate young people about these important topics.[38]

With apologies to Martha Stewart, this is *not* a good thing.

When Numbers Lie

SIECUS notes on its Web site, "In the latest Gallup opinion poll, 87 percent of parents support school-based sexuality education, up from 76 percent just ten years ago."[39]

Let's get real now. How many of those polled, when asked about sex ed, still think we're dealing with "sex education" appropriately involving the technicalities of reproduction or even the specifics of STDs in a health class for 15-year-olds? Probably most of the 87 percent.

We don't get to see the wording of the question asked in the Gallup Poll, but I betcha it didn't include asking parents if "sex ed" should include their 5 year-olds being told that touching and rubbing their own genitals feels good; or their 9-year-olds being told how it's "natural" to respond to sexual stimulation. Lessons like these only aid and abet monsters like those who kidnapped, raped, and murdered 7-year-old Danielle van Dam and 5-year-old Samantha Runnion in 2002. Do you think the Gallup researchers asked parents if it would be a good idea to tell their 12-year-olds that masturbating their "partner" is a good way to "express their sexuality"? I think not.

I have a feeling many parents have no idea what exactly is being taught to their children, until the day they catch their 10-year-old masturbating or engaging in a sex act with his little 9-year-old friend. Or the day they overhear their 12-year-old talking about oral sex, or find condoms in their 14-year-old's dresser drawer. They then may chalk it up to a different generation's sensibilities, when in fact their children are being *programmed* to behave in a way that is harmful and not natural for them.

As Dr. Meeker notes:

> In many ways our efforts as a society . . . to understand [children's] sexual freedoms, have backfired. Many parents were taught that one cannot judge youngsters who choose early sexual activity because to do so would violate some inalienable personal right.[40]

Dr. Meeker rightly posits that the end result is families and society facing "deadly diseases spawned by unrestrained and premature sexual activity." While she's on target there, an important point is missing. After all, *nothing* good could have come from the false concept that "children's sexuality" needs to be "understood." We were in serious trouble the moment that insult became even somewhat legitimized, giving the malignant narcissists of the Left a powerful weapon in their war on children.

It shouldn't come as a surprise that organizations determined to sexualize children have enemies lists. SIECUS has one on its Web site. Termed "Opponents of Comprehensive Sexuality Education,"[41] it lists various conservative and family organizations. The main criterion that gets you on the list is if you advocate sexual abstinence for children and teens. Groups such as True Love Waits, Friends First, and Respect, Inc. are termed "fear-based" abstinence groups.

Last time I checked, it was *good* for children to be afraid of incurable STDs, HIV, depression, and suicide. But the call to normalize and promote sexual activity among children has made advocacy for abstinence the deviant position.

She Won't Be Bullied

There is no better illustration of this than the censorship of Erika Harold, Miss America 2003. During a press conference a few weeks after her crowning, Ms. Harold told reporters that she had been ordered by pageant officials to not speak publicly about sexual abstinence, the issue that was most important to her and was her platform when she won the Miss Illinois contest.

Even then, state pageant officials had advised her to adopt "teen violence prevention" as her Miss America platform because, they argued, it was more "pertinent." At the press conference, Ms. Harold was described as "furious" about the gag order. She told a *Washington Times* reporter, "Quite frankly, and I'm not going to be specific, there are pressures from some sides to not promote [abstinence]."[42] Even more forcefully, Ms. Harold said she would "not be bullied," as pageant officials tried to stop reporters from even asking her about her abstinence message.

Ms. Harold's interest in this issue is not new. She has advocated teen sexual abstinence for years as a representative of Project Reality, a Chicago-based nonprofit organization that has been a pioneer in the field of abstinence education. The *Washington Times* quoted Ms. Harold as saying that after she won the Miss America crown, a young girl from an inner-city Chicago school sent her an e-mail asking her to continue the abstinence campaign. "She said, 'You changed my life because of what you said, and now I made the decision to be abstinent because of what you said. And I really hope that as Miss America you continue to share that because it changed my life and I think it can change lots of others.'"[43]

Said Ms. Harold: "And I would hate to think that there are kids all over the country who now wonder, you know, 'Did I make the right decision in making that commitment, if this person who inspired me to do it no longer is willing to share that commitment on the national stage?' And so I would feel a hypocrite if I did not."[44]

How revealing that an organization which has raised the ire of the feminist establishment because of its "traditional outlook" now finds the issue of abstinence too hot. Some apologists have countered that the Miss America organization shouldn't be a "political platform," while others suggest that sexual messages have never been acceptable as platforms.

In addition to being wrong, these arguments are just plain silly. During the competition, Miss Nevada's performance piece was a reading of Matthew Shepard's father's statement in the 1999 trial of his son's murderers.[45] To say nothing of Kate Shindle, Miss America 1998, and her platform of AIDS prevention. In addition to so-called "safe sex," Ms. Shindle advocated publicly funded condom distribution in public schools and government-funded needle exchanges for drug users.[46] A couple of doozies for an organization that doesn't want "political" or "sexual" messages.

The discrepancy does serve as a perfect illustration of where our culture is headed. Discussion of AIDS, condom distribution, and needle exchanges for drug users is deemed more than appropriate, while abstinence for teens is simply too controversial. Pageant officials eventually reversed themselves on the issue, but only because of concerted criticism and public pressure, brought about in great part by the *Washington Times* coverage. Sandy Rios, president of Concerned Women for America, told the *Times,* "They are attacking Erika Harold's values. . . . In an age when beauty queens are regularly disqualified for inappropriate behavior, who would have thought that a virtuous one would be silenced for her virtue?"[47]

When you think about it, if the Left were truly concerned about the welfare of children, there would be no reason to reject messages about sexual abstinence. After all, such messages can only help. Abstinence is the only truly safe sex, to say nothing of the fact that children are not sexual creatures, despite what the degenerate Left Elite want you to believe.

Planned Destruction of Children

The folks at Planned Parenthood (PP) also have an enemies list on their Web site. They call it their "profile" fact sheet.[48] What gets you onto PP's enemies list? The common factors are being antiabortion (of course) and being supportive of abstinence until marriage.

In its effort to make sex appealing to children, Planned Parenthood likes to call sexual behavior "sex play." That does make it sound like a fun pastime to engage in—an alternative to, say, tetherball or dodgeball during recess, dontcha think? Sex, to them, is *play*, after all. Nothing to be afraid of, nothing really to take seriously. Like SIECUS, PP attacks abstinence programs as "dangerous fear- and shame-based curricula, prescribing abstinence as the only solution to preventing pregnancy and sexually transmitted infections including HIV/AIDS."[49] And? Did I miss some other new miracle solution that absolutely prevents those things? Of course not. Abstinence *is* the only way to be sure of preventing pregnancy and STDs, and Planned Parenthood knows it.

This is particularly ironic for an organization that was founded to help women manage their reproductive lives. PP's current obsession with demonizing abstinence clearly reveals that this is not about individual freedom—it's about breaking down traditional ideas concerning appropriate sexual activity.

Even with children and adolescents facing the obscenity of an epidemic of STDs, AIDS, and suicide, Planned Parenthood has the gall to call abstinence education "dangerous and irresponsible."[50] In fact, visit PP's Web site at http://www.plannedparenthood.org and type in "abstinence" in the search box. You'll retrieve 100+ documents decrying the horrors of abstinence.

Exposing the organization's schizophrenia and perhaps even malevolence, the same search brings up a "Safer Sex" fact sheet from Planned Parenthood of Central Oklahoma. This document confirms that "teens in the U.S. are becoming infected with HIV at an average of more than one an hour, every hour, every day."[51] That's a pretty sobering statistic. Surely Planned Parenthood should do something about it? Unfortunately, it did: The very same fact sheet recommends *anal sex* as a "safer" form of sex for people to consider!

I know it's unbelievable. Here is the segment from the fact sheet itself, and the entire "Safer Sex" suggestion list:

> Want to free yourself of worries about getting an STI [sexually transmitted infection], perhaps even an STI that has no cure? Then read on. . . .

Safer sex includes:
- masturbation
- mutual masturbation
- erotic massage
- kissing
- body rubbing
- *vaginal, anal, or oral intercourse* [emphasis mine] using a barrier, such as a male latex or plastic condom, a female condom, or a dental dam
- shared erotic fantasies or role play
- sex toys that aren't shared

Look at that opening sentence. The euphemistic STI is bad enough. More importantly, PP does more than suggest, it *tells* every reader, including any child or adolescent directed to that fact sheet, that he or she can be "free" of "worries" about contracting a deadly disease, while remaining sexually active.

PP then horrifically includes anal sex on the list of "safer" practices. Oh, sure, it says to use a condom or other "barrier," but let's get real here. *The most dangerous* sexual practice in terms of passing along the AIDS virus and other STDs is included as being on a par for safety with masturbation. With what we know today, to recommend or even suggest anal sex to teens or anyone else as something to consider engaging in, even with a condom, is one of the most irresponsible and inexplicable things I've ever seen.

Making matters worse, on the same "fact" sheet, PP warns, "The effectiveness of condoms decreases if you don't use them properly or if you don't use them every time." The effectiveness *decreases* if you don't use them every time?! Wow.

PP's own material admits that most children and adolescents who have been infected have no clue they're harboring STDs. PP announces that a teen can contract HIV and not show symptoms for 10 years. It also cautions young people that others will lie about a contagious condition in order to get them to have sex. It admits STDs (like herpes and HPV, both viruses you can never get rid of, *not* mere "infections") can be passed orally, and yet it also recommends oral intercourse—which it terms an "outercourse," furthering the newspeak to make kids more comfortable engaging in risky sex acts.

In the face of these incurable, torturous, and often deadly diseases, reason demands an effort to encourage children to refrain from sex, plain and simple. To advocate otherwise indicates a blind devotion to sex without rules, regardless of the cost, even to children's lives. PP's willingness to sacrifice children to the God of Sexual Freedom and Liberation is appalling, and anyone associated with Planned Parenthood these days should be ashamed.

> In the face of these incurable, torturous, and often deadly diseases, reason demands an effort to encourage children to refrain from sex, plain and simple.

But a sense of shame, for the people running these groups and for the Left Elite in general, has been destroyed, along with any sense of values. Feeling shame is one surefire way of knowing you're doing something wrong. Kill shame, and an unobstructed path has been opened for the wrong to become right. Do teenage single mothers feel shame anymore? Do statutory rapists feel shame anymore? I argue that they do not because of the malignant narcissistic culture that has put a stranglehold on our society.

Hand in hand with shame goes a sense of fear, which helps, or at least used to help, delineate right from wrong. Wrongdoing brings unpleasant consequences. Fear of unpleasant consequences promotes rightdoing. Kill the fear, and the path to an amoral wasteland is made wide and straight. And so Planned Parenthood goes to work, complaining, for example, that

> right-wing ideologues who want to institute sexual abstinence until marriage . . . threatened to inspire public doubt about condom use and unnecessary alarm among the many sexually active women and men—as many as three out of four—who have been infected with this extremely common, and most often harmless, infection [HPV].[52]

With extraordinary disregard for the seriousness of the one virus we *know* causes cancer, PP insists HPV is "usually benign" and goes on to assure us that "while a handful of sexually trans-mitted HPVs can cause a variety of conditions that can lead to dangerous cancers if they remain untreated, it is a gross and dangerous exaggeration to typify HPV as a 'dreaded virus.'"[53]

Perhaps PP could explain to us—why should a virus that causes cancer *not* be dreaded? Oops, there I go with that silly fear thing again. Funny, I just don't want to die a slow horrible death. But that's just me.

PP's own material acknowledges that HPV is the most com-mon STD—three out of four sexually active men and women are infected, it says—and yet no one need worry. Because it's common; because almost everyone already has it anyway!

With messages like this to children, no wonder they're con-tracting STDs at epidemic rates. No wonder everyone has HPV, when PP's guidelines for children recommend anal and oral in-tercourse as "safer" sex play.

Teenwire.com: The Modern Volcano for Child Sacrifice

I have supported Planned Parenthood in the past, but like many donors and activists, I focused on the one issue that I felt most passionate about—reproductive freedom. Only when I began to look into the Left's agenda of sexualizing children did I realize the breadth of that agenda and how morally bankrupt the organization has become.

If you think I'm stretching it when I tell you PP is targeting children to become more sexual, take a look at its Web site for teens. If you click on a box on PP's homepage that says "Young people speak out," it will link you to Teenwire.com. The sec-tion for "parents and health professionals" admonishes, "Please remember that this Web site is for teens. This is their place. Take a look around the site if you like, but please do not register on the site."[54] What is it Planned Parenthood doesn't want parents to find out?

Designed to look hip and easy, Teenwire.com bills itself as "Sexuality and relationship info you can trust from Planned

Parenthood Federation of America." Among the "info" parents just might object to is this little gem: "Having sexual curiosity about a member of one's family is fairly normal."

A box on the home page offers a "Sextionary." The day I visited the site, the Sextionary addressed the question "What is performance anxiety?" There is also a box labeled "Today's Question," where Teenwire.com's constituents can ask for advice on whatever has been troubling them. That day, the question was accompanied by a photo of a boy who looks about 15 years old (obviously to appeal to the target audience). He asks:

> Dear Experts,
>   Say you have AIDS but you don't want to tell nobody but you still have sex with somebody and there's the possibility that you give it to that person.

What is Planned Parenthood's response? You'd better sit down. After describing technically what AIDS is, PP offers that someone who's infected "needs to be cautious" about telling other people, and that a person is "honor bound" to tell their sex partner they may have infected them with AIDS, so they can then find out if they're infected and "protect" themselves.[55] Honor has a role—but it's not after the fact. And do you see the other false message here? We're told that people who are infected with AIDS can still "protect themselves." Once you're infected there is no protection! PP knows this, and yet still uses this language. The goal can only be to make adolescents feel comfortable with the most dreaded of repercussions.

The decent, moral message to that boy who has AIDS (and to every other child who might visit the Web site) is an adamant "Don't have sex!" or "Having sex while infected with AIDS is incredibly irresponsible and dangerous. It can be fatal to the other person if transmitted." PP also might have thought of admonishing him that he should be ashamed of himself, and should feel wracked with guilt if he has in fact infected his sex partner.

Instead, Planned Parenthood cutely agrees that caution in telling other people is reasonable, then offers some helpful advice about how to have sex despite being infected with a fatal disease, like "Don't touch sores or growths that are caused by sexually transmitted infections." Gee, thanks.

And gosh, fella, you'd better tell your probably 14- or 15-year-old girlfriend that she might have acquired the disease, which will condemn her, like you, to a slow and awful death. But hey! Make sure you continue to have sex, and remember, "the body fluids to be most careful about are blood, *cum, precum* [emphasis theirs—they actually link terms to a pop-up glossary, revealing that they *know* they're telling things about sex to kids who have no clue even what the words mean!], vaginal fluids, and the discharge from sores caused by sexually transmitted infections."[56] But don't let those sores stop you—just don't forget that condom!

Dear Experts: How Can I Destroy My Life?

How young are the kids who are using this site, and how much is Planned Parenthood contributing to the destruction of children's lives? Here are some other questions posted by children on Teenwire.com, along with the astonishing answers from the Planned Parenthood "experts":

Dear Experts,
What does S&M mean? I heard some people talking about it and I was too embarrassed to ask them what it meant. Thanks.

Answer:
"S&M," or sadomasochistic sex play, is mutually agreed upon sexual stimulation that incorporates domination and/or pain in sex play. It uses fantasy scenarios that explore dominance and submission and sometimes includes bondage—tying people up. Mutual consent is what makes S&M different from abuse and assault. . . . Hope this information helps!

Isn't that nice? PP hopes the info helps. The experts then describe various S&M techniques, like "safe words," "scenes," and so on. Boy, am I glad that little girl now understands that she can consent to pain and physical abuse! Thanks, Planned Parenthood!

> Dear Experts,
> Okay I had a sex dream once. I had a dream that I had sex with my best friend who is a girl. Does that mean I am a lesbian?

> Answer:
> . . . So many people, young and older, have questions about their sexual orientation. . . . No one knows for sure what makes men and women lesbian or gay, bisexual or heterosexual. Sexual orientation develops naturally—perhaps even before birth. . . .

No one knows for sure what makes people *heterosexual?* Newsflash for Planned Parenthood: It's called "nature." To suggest to this girl that heterosexuality is as unknown a dynamic as homosexuality is extraordinary to me. The responsible answer to a girl asking this kind of question is that more than 90 percent of the population is heterosexual, which means the odds are astronomical that she is straight, that her dream was just a dream, and that if some night she dreams about being a cocker spaniel, she won't become that either.

If a teen who identifies herself as a lesbian confessed that she had a sexual dream about a man, would Planned Parenthood suggest that she might in fact be "questioning" her homosexuality and be a closet heterosexual? I think not. Nope, the prescription for that girl would be more "gay pride."

So, if someone challenges you about Planned Parenthood's role within the movement to sexualize and pervert children, just suggest a visit to Teenwire.com. A few minutes online should clear up any misunderstanding.

The Real World

Children having sex with children is disastrous enough, but that isn't the only real-world repercussion of the Left's vile agenda. As I explained earlier, a major goal of this perverted movement is to normalize child abuse as "child-adult sex." Sexualizing children is meant to warp the way all adults view children and confuse our understanding of what children are truly ready for.

While sexual predators have always blamed the victim, there is a new spate of adults molesting children while claiming the relationships are "consensual," or asserting that the child was the aggressor and in charge. What else could we expect in a culture that is now, courtesy of the Left Elite, saying the same thing with such gusto? What else could have come from the Intellectual Elite's insistence that children are sexual beings, want to act on it, and *will* act on it?

> There is a new spate of adults molesting children while claiming the relationships are "consensual," or asserting that the child was the aggressor and in charge.

Unless, of course, adults act on it for them.

Remember the 1997 Mary Kay Letourneau scandal? Everyone was shocked by the revelation that the 35-year-old schoolteacher, a married mother of four, had engaged in a sexual relationship with a 13-year-old student. She had first met her victim when he was in her second-grade class in a suburban Seattle elementary school. She was his teacher again in the sixth grade, and the relationship became sexual the following year.[57] By the time she was arrested, she was pregnant by her former student.

Despite her betrayal of her position of power and trust as a teacher, the destruction of her own family (her husband divorced her), and what must be extraordinary damage done to her children from that marriage, Letourneau received a good deal of sympathy. The judge in her case, Judge Linda Lau, gave her an 89-month jail sentence but suspended most of the sentence; Letourneau wound up serving only six months.

Why? Because both the victim and his mother said he didn't feel like a victim, and he claimed the relationship was "real love." In a normal world, where children weren't obscenely sexualized at every turn, adults in trusted positions would realize that a 13-year-old's perception of "real love" doesn't count.

At the sentencing hearing, Letourneau, on the edge of tears, said she was sorry and it would never happen again. Judge Lau believed her but ordered her never to see the boy again. If she did, Judge Lau warned, she would have to serve out the balance of her seven-year sentence.

Letourneau was freed in January 1998, and then it happened again. Despite the court order, the relationship was promptly renewed. When it was discovered, Letourneau was sent back to prison. She was also pregnant again. And she insisted that she was in no way a sexual aggressor. "He dominated me in the most masculine way that any man, any leader, could do," she said. "I trusted him and believed in him and in our future."[58]

And what happened to the boy? Vili Fualaau, the boy who claimed he was madly in love and not the victim of a molester, and who was a father of two at the age of 15, would slip into drug abuse, crime, and depression. In 2000 he and his mother sued the school district and the town of Des Moines, Washington, for failing to protect him from Letourneau, whom he now does consider his abuser.[59] Now that he's older.

The Pink Elephant

When it comes to child molesters who wear collars, there is a deliberate public relations effort by the gay activist establishment to keep the news media from pointing out that there is a rather large elephant in the room—a pink elephant, and it's wearing a boa.

"Pedophile priests." We hear it over and over again, and there is a reason why this is the phrase the Left wants us to focus on. Labeling the abusive priests as "pedophiles" allows the Gay Elite to self-righteously assert that the vast majority of gay men aren't pedophiles, which is true. At the same time, as I explained in the discussion of ephebophilia in chapter 4, we're being lied to about the problem itself.

Some of my Catholic friends believe that the majority of boys abused are indeed under 12 years old, which would make this a situation of pedophiles running wild. That's just not the situation. While there are two high-profile cases (and probably more to come) of actual pedophile priests, the reality is that the victims are overwhelmingly teenage boys. David Kupelian of WorldNetDaily.com reports that Stephen Rubino, a lawyer who has represented over 300 alleged victims of abuse by priests, estimates 85 percent of the victims have been teenage boys.[60] Catholic psychiatrist Dr. Richard Fitzgibbons, who has treated many victims and offending priests, agrees with that figure, noting that 90 percent of his patients are either abused teenage males or their priest abusers.[61]

"This is chiefly a scandal about unchaste or criminal homosexuals in the Catholic priesthood," sums up *National Review* senior writer Rod Dreher. "For Catholics, to start asking questions about homosexuality in the priesthood is to risk finding out more than many Church members prefer to know. For journalists, to confront the issue is to risk touching the electrified third rail of American popular culture: the dark side of homosexuality."[62]

The Molester Among Us

Dreher makes an important point, frankly one that GLAAD and the entire Gay Elite should also be making. While it is true that it is gay men in the priesthood who are victimizing boys, this is clearly a *subgroup* of gay men who have been attracted to a unique environment within which they are not getting the help they need to control their urges. The response of the Gay Elite has been "It's not us!" Instead, they should admit the root cause of the problem, state the fact that this is not representative of who gay people are, and then immediately join the call for removing from the priesthood men, gay or straight, who cannot be true to their vows.

That would be the normal, decent, moral thing to do. When you can't even manage that where *children* are involved, it indicates how dead the concepts of right and wrong really are for today's Gay Elite.

I know the people, and the types of people, who run the special-interest groups that are supposed to make life better for women and gays and lesbians. Most of those people have made a noble commitment based in an idealism that asserts that every American deserves to have the same rights as every other American. But when your advocacy becomes protection for the sick and perverted among you, you have a serious problem.

Despite the efforts by the Gay Establishment to obscure the reality that the sex abuse by priests stems from the homosexual subculture in the church, more and more evidence is coming to the fore which confirms the link. In his book *Goodbye, Good Men,* investigative reporter Michael Rose does an extraordinary job of documenting the homosexual infiltration of the American Catholic hierarchy and the subsequent destruction of foundational values and core teachings.

One does have to wonder, Why are priests suddenly obsessed with—and rejecting—the church's sexual teachings? Doesn't this focus seem odd to you? Come on now. For more than 1,500 years, the Roman Catholic Church has made it clear that celibacy is part of the program—that when you seek to become a priest you agree to cease all sexual activity. It's called "abstinence."

After all, celibacy is something that many human beings have been able to adopt without turning into freakish child molesters. While there are tragic reports of girls being abused as well, why don't we see the same flood of heterosexual priests going batty and jumping on 14-year-old girls? Could the problem be the swamping of the church with sexually compulsive gay men?

Why have these damaged gay men joined the priesthood, only to betray their vows to God and to society? How have they dared to destroy the lives of children in their selfish effort to obtain sexual satisfaction? The answer lies partly with them and partly with our society, since these malignant narcissists have been brought up and developed by our rotting culture. And, like their compadres in the secular world, they now cannot help themselves from trying to destroy the world around them—to smash it into submission. The abuse of children by Catholic priests, I contend, is the most perfectly clear microcosm of the conscious and subconscious agenda of the Left to make society—all of it—look like them. In this instance, it is gay men, and the Gay Establishment, using the church for their gratification while simultaneously blaming the church for what certain gay men have inflicted.

Of course, this can only succeed if we allow it to. As a gay woman, I refuse to have this be my legacy, and I know untold numbers of decent gay people are as appalled as I.

The Rumor Confirmed

While Michael Rose's assertion that the church has essentially been overrun by gays has been brushed aside as hearsay by the establishment, it has recently been confirmed by a survey commissioned by the American bishops and conducted for the Council of the National Federation of Priests. This survey of 1,200 Roman Catholic priests did not ask them if they were homosexual themselves, but asked them for their impressions of their environment. According to the *Washington Post,* more than half of all the priests surveyed identified a "homosexual subculture" in their diocese or seminary.[63]

The *Post* adds, "The survey also showed a growing generation gap overall between priests ordained in the '60s and '70s right after the Second Vatican Council and the much more orthodox younger generation of priests. The two groups differed radically on their views of the status of a priest and on the Church's sexual teachings." It is indeed the attitudes we fostered as a society in the 1960s and 1970s that are now coming back to haunt us. As the American church and her priests adapted to the left-wing demand that they blend with society, we now have to face the ugliest part of that society having infiltrated the last bastion of peace, safety, and decency.

After the survey, one 37-year-old priest told a focus group about the atmosphere at his seminary: "It was extremely corrosive. . . . There were many who had homosexual orientation but were perfectly fine and reasonable human beings. . . . But there was a homosexual lifestyle subculture which . . . ran the seminary practically."[64]

I have to tell you, I laugh every time an establishment feminist rants that the child sex-abuse tragedy would be solved if priests were allowed to marry. The priests we're talking about would only be subdued, *maybe,* if they were allowed to marry other men—or pubescent boys.

The main thing that needs to be done in order to attract more straight men into the priesthood is to eliminate the homosexually charged environment in the seminaries. Rose documents that what the priest quoted above told the focus group is far from an isolated case. At many seminaries, those who do not conform to and accept the gay lifestyle are directly and indirectly punished.[65] Rose reports that some orthodox men left the seminary after suffering sexual harassment by homosexual faculty and students, while others were drummed out as "too rigid" because they admitted to being against homosexuality. So, let's make it clear: It's not the priesthood or sexual abstinence that causes men to sexually abuse adolescent boys. *It's sexual compulsion among gay men.*

The suggestion that allowing priests to marry would attract more heterosexual men to the priesthood is also silly from another point of view. It presupposes that sex *must* be part of a priest's life, because, of course, sex *must* be a part of everyone's life. The projection here is mind-boggling.

If the strict rules of the church were the cause of the problem, we would logically expect to see either a consistent number or an increasing number of priests throughout the centuries victimizing boys and young men. And wouldn't *at least* a simple majority of priests have succumbed to this supposed sinister result of celibacy? In fact, a *New York Times* survey[66] found the opposite is true.

In the most comprehensive analysis of the tragedy to date, the *Times* survey covered cases of 1,205 accused priests through December 31, 2002, and 4,268 people who have claimed publicly or in lawsuits to have been abused by priests. The *Times* found that most of the abuse occurred in the 1970s and 1980s, with those ordained in 1970 and 1975 representing the highest percentage of priests accused of abuse. Most known offenders were in fact ordained in the 1970s, more than in any other decade.[67]

The *Times* also confirms that 1.8 percent of American Catholic priests have been accused of abuse, and four out of five victims of priests are male. That is nearly the opposite of the figure for those victimized by nonpriests, nearly two-thirds of whom are girls and women.[68]

So let's get serious here. With this reality, critics of the church are asking us to believe that centuries of strict teachings requiring celibacy suddenly converged mysteriously on the seminary classes of 1970 and 1975, causing the particular men ordained in those years to explode and become serial homosexual child molesters. To say nothing of the fact that 98.2 percent of men serving under the same conditions have somehow managed to escape that inevitable demon.

Of course, thinking people cannot deny the eerie coincidence of the emergence of active homosexuals in the priesthood from the classes that sprang from the most transformative time for the Left in America's history, a time when the black, gay, and feminist civil-right movements made tremendous advances. This horror inflicted on children is the diseased flower of that incredibly important time. Like any dramatically powerful and life-changing idea, Radical Individualism can be used for great good or great harm. The greatness of the American character lies in this idea and its realization, and we have every duty to condemn its abuse. For the Gay Elite especially to pass the buck is shameful.

Shifting the Blame

Cathy Renna of GLAAD had this to offer about the sex abuse scandal: "People often get their views from their religions, so we don't want the pulpit saying that being gay is wrong. But mostly this is about the Catholic leadership refusing to accept the blame, and shifting it over to us."[69]

Isn't that interesting? GLAAD is deciding what is and is not okay for the church to teach. I have to remind Ms. Renna of a simple fact: It is time for the *gay establishment* to stop shifting the blame to someone else. It is time for the sexually compulsive gay men in the priesthood to accept blame. It is time for the Gay Elite to admit that it is a sexually predatory group of gay men who have perpetrated this horrific debacle on who knows how many innocent boys and their families.

After all, the vast majority of priests *have* maintained their commitment to celibacy—both priests who identified themselves as homosexual and priests who identified themselves as heterosexual prior to entering the priesthood. The problem is with the cadre of men who, whatever their other reasons for being attracted to the priesthood, were attracted by the prospect of unsupervised access to boys (and sometimes other men). We discussed the Boy Scouts' dilemma in dealing with gay men who are compelled to be near boys. The only solution in both instances is to not let anyone with *any* sexual agenda infiltrate entities that give them access and power over adolescents.

Is the church hierarchy somewhat responsible for what has happened? Of course. The moving around of abusive priests and covering up of molestation are things for which many bishops and cardinals have come under fire. As of this writing, Cardinal Law of Boston has finally, and appropriately, resigned.

Meanwhile, groups like GLAAD and others of the Gay Elite are doing a pathetic dance around the real problem some gay men face, trying to get you to not notice the elephant wearing the tutu. That dance is a slap in the face of every decent gay and lesbian person in this country. Pedophilia and ephebophilia are not part of the lifestyle of the decent individual, gay or straight. It is time for the gay community to reject excuses for those sexual compulsives who are gay or simply identify themselves as gay out of convenience, and for the activist leadership that continues to enable the indecent to define the community.

Unless gays and feminists wake up, the right to molest children will be the legacy of their civil-rights movements. Support of that will destroy the compassion and understanding Americans have felt for those struggling for greater personal freedom. And understandably so.

CHAPTER EIGHT

Trashing the Public Trust:

Media's Destruction of Culture

It is not enough to show people how to live better:
There is a mandate for any group with enormous powers of
communication to show people how to be better.

—*Marya Mannes*

I go to films for the same reasons most people do—to escape, mostly, but also hopefully to learn something and to be inspired. The opening scene of *American Beauty* disabused me of any notion that this film was going to be either escapist or inspirational. But I did learn something.

From the outset I didn't like it. I wasn't quite sure why at first, but it gnawed at me until I realized the message of the film was in direct contradiction to everything I found important in life. Its message was that tradition was useless, everything was meaningless. And what happens if everything is meaningless? Of course, there is no right or wrong, no good or evil. *American Beauty* perfectly represents the cynicism and nihilism that drive the Left Elite.

According to the dictionary, nihilism is "the viewpoint that traditional values and beliefs are unfounded and that existence is senseless and useless . . . a doctrine that denies any objective ground of truth and especially of moral truths."[1] It denies beauty, justice, and, essentially, our very existence.

I sat and watched this film as it hammered home the idea that there are no values, no morality, nothing virtuous to strive for. In *American Beauty,* the concepts of right and wrong are simply obstacles to finding one's true self. In the opening scene, Kevin Spacey's character tells the audience that he's going to be dead in a year but it really doesn't matter, because he's dead already.

His traditional marriage and his home in the suburbs are holding him back, making him miserable. He is sexually frustrated, hates his job, hates his wife's obsession with status. His existence, for all its traditional symbols of success and normality, is hopeless. The most sympathetic character in the film is the young drug dealer next door, who falls for Spacey's miserable and morose teenage daughter.

Of course, the drug-dealing kid's father is an abusive ex-Marine, who has driven his wife to a quiet madness. He collects Nazi memorabilia and beats his son, constantly cautioning him against becoming a "fag." Very predictably, the "homophobe" is living a lie, and eventually gets a crush on the Spacey character.

Meanwhile, our hero's life changes when he sees a friend of his daughter's, a high-school cheerleader blonde. He becomes obsessed with this girl, quitting his job and abandoning his wife and daughter. He takes up bodybuilding, buys the car he always wanted, and finds a resource in the neighbor boy, smoking pot at every opportunity.

His liberation lies in reverting to a juvenile world of girls, cars, and drugs, where there are no responsibilities, no meaning, no right and wrong. He finally finds himself when he rejects everything that means anything. In the world of the film, happiness is possible only when all values—marriage, family, work, fidelity, integrity—are obliterated.

I had gone to see this film with a friend. She didn't like it either, but her initial sense was that the film was "an attack on heterosexuality." Actually, it was an attack on *everything* traditional—in fact, all the choices decent people make in their lives. From the filmmakers' point of view there is no evil other than the idea of good and evil itself. There is no judgment—the son who is regularly beaten by his father still considers him a "good man." The destruction of marriage, work, and family is not only not bad, it is imperative. These were all obstacles to our hero's personal truth.

As for the ex-Marine, his life is in every sense a lie. As a Marine, he represents very basic values of import to most people in this nation—patriotism, a commitment to preserving our freedom and individual rights. To smear those values, the film associates them with homophobia, domestic violence, abuse, lying, and even mental illness. Not too subtle a message there.

And when the homophobe makes advances to the Spacey character and is spurned, he kills the object of his crush and himself. Evil here is as banal as good. Neither man's life means anything. Nothing they've done matters.

What message are you supposed to take away from this? Your traditional beliefs, your commitment to our country, your opinions about homosexuality or anything else are crazy. Your values are worthless, and even a lie. In fact, tradition, beauty, hope are all false. They mean nothing, and so you mean nothing.

The film had good performances; it was nicely shot and technically well directed. It was nominated for eight Academy Awards and won five, including Best Actor for Spacey, Best Picture, and Best Screenplay. Yes, the folks in Hollywood loved this story, and they should. It is perfectly representative of the hopelessness that pervades so much of their product and, courtesy of them, infiltrates so many of our lives.

This is what our Entertainment Elite are feeding us. A cynicism, I contend, whose impact is on a par with the effect of the violence that disfigures so much of our film and television. After all, if nothing means anything, what's the use of striving to lead a decent life? Why work hard and make commitments if the future is a lie? *That* is the sense of pointlessness we've seen grip the last couple of generations. Regardless of how many films celebrate humanity, a film like *American Beauty,* with the acclaim it has enjoyed, counteracts any social good that can come from our creative community.

There have been many discussions of the impact of gratuitous sex and violence in film. I think we should be as concerned—if not even more so—about the impact of nihilism and cynicism. I believe it is this—the message that everything is meaningless—that allows the other base, destructive material to seep into our culture without much protest. Once we have accepted the meaninglessness of life and the uselessness of religion or any system of values, and have become cynics ourselves, why complain?

> Why work hard and make commitments if the future is a lie? *That* is the sense of pointlessness we've seen grip the last couple of generations.

Stephen Farber, former film critic for *California* magazine, said it well: "It has become chic to praise a movie for being nihilistic, macabre, unsentimental. . . . When did critics get the lunatic idea that the greatest movies were the cold-blooded dissections of human venality and depravity?"[2]

This may be the idea of filmmakers and critics, but it certainly is not ours, and we must say so.

Beyond TV Land

The mass media are among the most important foot soldiers for the Left Elite. After all, if the leftists are to succeed in their agenda of changing our culture, their ideas must be disseminated to as many people as possible. Television and film are our culture's standard, supposedly representing who, and how, we are. That permits them to play the pivotal role in conditioning us to accept the death of right and wrong. Television news and entertainment, the film industry, and even theater all present, day after day, night after night, material that reinforces moral relativism, the death of tradition, and the destruction of values.

For most of us, it's pretty obvious that the general nature of our popular culture is crashing and burning. Violence, promiscuity, and drug use are all standard fare in today's film and television. As syndicated radio host and former film critic Michael

Medved has tirelessly pointed out, the entertainment industry has broken faith with the public.

The good thing is that the problem is so obvious, we have noticed it. I contend, however, that the extreme violence and sex promoted in our cultural media are just the obvious symptom of a much more insidious problem. It's the less obvious examples that interest me.

Whenever I bring up the decline of film and television with my liberal friends there is an automatic presumption that any critique of entertainment is simply a pretext for suggesting censorship of some sort. That's just silly. However, the fear of being labeled "intolerant" or against freedom of expression keeps many people from even considering challenging the direction of the mass media.

As I noted earlier, my first book was about the importance of freedom of expression. This book, about the concomitant responsibilities that come with that freedom, is indeed Part 2. It emphasizes the fact that the rights we are blessed with are only worthwhile when they're applied with personal responsibility and consideration of other people. Freedom of expression does not mean we have a duty to acquiesce to chaos in our culture. Not at all. Our responsibility is to discuss, debate, and even demand something better. We are the marketplace for which the usual garbage is produced. The responsibility to praise or criticize is on our shoulders. If we do nothing, then we become part of the problem.

The reality, though, is that this is not a simple subject. As I discussed in *The New Thought Police*,[3] film and television should challenge us. The fact that some of us will be offended by some material is not the issue here. That's inevitable. There's no way we could, nor should we want to, homogenize everything in the creative world to be acceptable to everyone. Keep in mind, the things that can make us better are not necessarily always pleasant or simple. Humanity is complex, and so should be our entertainment. But it is also not too much to ask that the challenges we face should make us better people; that the gatekeepers of our culture should ask themselves if what they're doing is right or wrong in the larger scheme of things.

I chose the quote from journalist and poet Marya Mannes for the epigraph of this chapter to emphasize that those in control of the mass media have a responsibility to show us how we can be better. The general failure of the Entertainment Elite to do this is seen in almost all of their product. Are there decent films and television shows? Sure. In fact I can't tell you how many times I've had the title *Touched by an Angel* literally shouted at me by friends as the proof that TV isn't all that bad. The problem is, that's the only example they can come up with.

I, like you, do know of a few more, but the reality is that it's more than difficult these days to turn on the television if you have children. You know we're in trouble when a chip has to be placed in your television to block programs that will harm the psyche not only of your child, but of your whole family. I don't know about you, but I'd like to watch something other than the cable channel TV Land every now and then.

The Home Front

We are at no loss for ideas and images meant to numb our minds and push us along the path to an irreversible cultural moral relativism, where judgment, decency, and good sense are archaic notions, relics of the past. I'll go into details later, but here are some of the highlights of our current cultural scene. A drug- and alcohol-addled man and his seriously dysfunctional family are lauded as the new adorable model for the American family; television programming glorifies incarcerated murderers by presenting them as rock stars behind bars; news magazines and television news programming portray Palestinian homicide bombers and other terrorists as sympathetic freedom fighters; a prominent *New York Times* columnist alternates between savagely attacking the president of the United States and singing the praises of a rapper who encourages violence against women and minorities; a theater production becomes world renowned and is applauded by so-called feminists everywhere despite (or because of?) the portrayal of the molestation of a girl by a 24-year-old woman as a liberating experience—for the victim!

From the subtle to the extreme, our culture and our values are under unrelenting attack from the media. And the media, in all their forms, are fundamentally important because, by definition, they *are* our common culture. By default, each new assault on decency and morality through these media automatically changes the standards in our culture.

One of the things on my mind as I began this chapter will give you a hint of how deeply brainwashed we all are when it comes to culture. I kept asking myself, How can I prove I'm not a prude? I see so much around us deserving of criticism but, like you, I have endured accusations, name-calling, mockery, and derision when I point out the moral void of the mass media. For those of you who may think criticism of Ozzy Osbourne, for example, is somehow passé, think again. The effects of that man and people like him are only just starting to become apparent in our cultural and moral fabric.

> From the subtle to the extreme, our culture and our values are under unrelenting attack from the media.

It's funny—knowing my history as you do by now, and who I am, I think you would agree that I haven't been sheltered, nor am I somehow "repressed," sexually or otherwise. Some of you, in fact, may think I need to pull in the reins! That said, it's important for you to know that even I still struggle to loose the restraints our leftist cultural controls have placed on my critical mind. I know you do, too.

I will remind you what I remind myself constantly: To expect some level of morality and decency in one's life does *not* make one a prude or an unhip relic. It's understandable, however, that we are confused about our expectations given what the media continue to jam down our throats. We're told, in the august pages of the *New York Times,* no less, that a hate-mongering rapper who rhapsodizes about murdering gays and lesbians, assaulting pregnant women, and killing his mother is just like Elvis—criticized only by those who cling to an antiquated idea of values and morality.

The media are so integrally important in our lives. They encapsulate the best and worst of who we are and what we have to offer as a culture. Unfortunately, the worst seems to be winning the battle. There are also many fronts in this war. It's not just the entertainment side of television programming, for example, that has become shockingly violent and indecent. Today's news programming and the rhetoric it subjects us to also does its best to move us further toward the moral void.

Murphy and Dan

Let's take a look at exactly how much things really have changed and how much harm has been done to the concepts of right and wrong in the last 10 years alone on an issue as important as the meaning of family.

We live now in a milieu that tells us anything goes, everything is okay, and all ideas and behaviors have merit. That's hogwash, and you know it. It's understandable to be intimidated, however, when even decent political leaders on the Right seem to have given up.

Flashback to May 1992, when then–Vice-President Dan Quayle issued his famous rebuke of Candice Bergen's character, Murphy Brown, in the television sitcom of the same name. Quayle complained that Murphy Brown's decision to have a baby out of wedlock undercut traditional family values and dismissed the importance of fathers. He also pointed out the link between out-of-wedlock childbearing and rising levels of poverty among women and children. Quayle added that it "didn't help" when Hollywood glamorized such behavior.

As a feminist, I feel this was, and still is, the right message. My authentic feminism is based on the principle that women should be allowed to make their own individual choices about how to lead their lives. There are also circumstances where one parent is better than two, especially if the absent parent was abusive. But let's be honest here. There is a place for encouragement of decent decisions and discouragement of attitudes that perpetuate poverty among women and children in the real world. The Hollywood Elite evidently decided it was their social and political duty to promote single motherhood. Unfortunately, like many on the Left, the producers and writers were thinking only of themselves and their own lives. Their children, like Murphy Brown's baby, were not going to be facing a life on welfare, but the people watching the show are mostly not in their income bracket. If the producers and writers thought beyond their own isolated, privileged lives, they might become aware of the fact that growing up in a single-parent household dramatically increases a child's likelihood of poverty[4] and welfare dependency.[5] Moreover, children of single parents are more likely to turn to crime later in life.[6]

> We live now in a milieu that tells us anything goes, everything is okay, and all ideas and behaviors have merit. That's hogwash, and you know it.

Quayle was hammered incessantly for his remarks, but he had acutely spotted a harbinger of cultural change on the horizon. Years later, when asked by a reporter about the incident, even Candice Bergen agreed that Quayle's comments were "the right theme to hammer home . . . family values . . . and I agreed with all of it except his reference to the show . . . the body of the speech was completely sound."[7] Bergen had the courage to add that, in retrospect, she "didn't think it [her show] was a good message to be sending out."[8]

Quayle's concern was indeed legitimate, but who can forget the fits of contempt and self-righteousness that the media worked themselves into at the time? Every day brought more columns, cartoons, and late-night TV jokes, and at the end of it the vice president was no longer, in the public mind, a likable, commonsensical guy—he had become stupid, hopelessly archaic, and an Enemy of Women.

Quayle never recovered politically from the concerted attacks by the Left. And at the same time, a message was sent to everyone else in public life: No matter how hostile to our common values the Hollywood Elite might be, with the media in their control it is far too dangerous to challenge their worldview.

Ozzy and George

In the 10 years that have passed since Dan Quayle met Murphy Brown, there has been the kind of "progress" one can see only through the Looking Glass. *Murphy Brown* is long gone, but every week, more than 6 million viewers tune in to MTV to watch *The Osbournes,* as the train wreck of moral relativism rolls on.

The Osbournes is a sort of family reality show. Ozzy Osbourne, his wife, and their two seriously dysfunctional children agreed to allow MTV to film their every move for six months—a commitment that has now expanded into three television seasons. The show is well known for the number of "bleeps" the censors have to use to cover the Osbournes' foul mouths. And yet media commentary on the show spins Osbourne as an eccentric but lovable guy who has simply done a few too many drugs in his life.

In fact, many of us remember Osbourne as the leader of a heavy-metal rock band called Black Sabbath, known for the depravity of its lyrics. The song "Sabbath Bloody Sabbath" includes these lines: "God knows as your dog knows.../ Living just for dying/ Dying just for you."[9] In "Suicide Solution," Osbourne urges, "Wine is fine but whiskey's quicker / Suicide is slow with liquor / Take a bottle drain your sorrows." Some of his more revolting antics during the heyday of his career included biting off the head of a bat during a concert and the head of a dove during a meeting with record executives.[10]

And yet, you've probably heard the present-day Osbourne praised as a "family values man." And not just by the usual suspects on the Left. President George W. Bush felt it was appropriate to single out and applaud Osbourne at a White House Correspondents Dinner. Dan Quayle, meanwhile, almost 10 years to the day after his *Murphy Brown* comments, praised the "family values" of Daddy Osbourne. "You have to get beyond the sort of dysfunctional aspect," Quayle said about the vulgar Osbournes. The show, according to Quayle, features two "loving parents . . . an intact family . . . involved with their children." In fact, he added, "There are some positive things you can get out of this crazy family." After all, unlike Murphy Brown, the Osbournes are *still married*.[11] Talk about lowered expectations!

The Osbournes' 17-year-old daughter, Kelly, complains that she was once late for her 2:30 A.M. curfew because her 16-year-old brother, Jack, was drunk.[12] Jack complains that "My mom has a tendency of flashing. My friend was over the house one time, sitting in the kitchen. She comes [in], lifts up her shirt and goes, 'Hey, do you think I'm sexy?'"[13] These comments were not revealed by some tabloid in an effort to undercut the show with its fans. No, they were showcased on MTV's Web site for the program and were meant to encourage viewership and further solidify the family's position within the new Cultural Elite.

Why is today's TV Ozzy so lax when it comes to discipline—so unlike the TV Ozzie of 50 years ago? Osbourne explains, "For instance, a week ago on a Thursday I said to Kelly, 'You have to come home by sunset tonight because you have tutoring tomorrow.' It turns out she doesn't come back [until] God knows how late. [I said], 'I'm gonna ground you.' What does she do? She sneaks out and gets crazy drunk and she's going to OD on alcohol!"[14]

Mama Sharon, it's true, takes sterner measures to impose some standards on the children. As an example, after discovering a half-consumed whiskey bottle in her daughter's room, Sharon expresses her disapproval by attempting to urinate into the bottle in order to discourage further consumption.

Through it all, the press coverage and popular discussion led by the media casts this out-of-control family as lovable, goofy, and daring in allowing America to see their dysfunction.

People magazine, for instance, proclaimed the Osbournes "2002's most inspirational couple," while in the same article mentioning that Ozzy at one point attempted to murder Sharon during a fight.[15] Not to be outdone, *Time* magazine, supposedly one of our more trustworthy news providers, describes Osbourne as a "dear, lumbering, Dad," and comments, "TV thrives on facile distinctions between 'functional' and 'dysfunctional,' but this family is delightfully functional in its own bleeping-mad way."[16] For such fare, according to television critics, we should be thankful.

When this lesbian feminist is more outraged than the president of the United States and the former critic of *Murphy Brown,* you know we're in a lot of trouble!

No One's Immune

Satanism. Drug abuse. Sexual acting-out. Domestic violence. Possibly alcoholic children. This is apparently America's new lovable family standard.

What happened here? A few things. First, Quayle and, I dare say, many others of the Right Elite, considering how they're embracing the mess of the Osbournes, learned their lesson from the *Murphy Brown* battle. One does not criticize the entertainment industry and expect to flourish as a politician. It is simply too powerful an entity. And so you bend to the culture the Left sees fit to create. You adapt, or you are cast out. None of us are immune from the powerful influence of America's entertainment and mass-media establishment.

> Things are monstrously pathetic when even the stalwarts of the Right, those we can usually rely on to say something of import about our disintegrating culture, not only do not criticize but join in the chorus of praise.

Secondly, no one in politics is immune from the spreading moral relativism of our culture, courtesy of the Left. If you can't beat 'em, join 'em. Things are monstrously pathetic when even the stalwarts of the Right, those we can usually rely on to say something of import about our disintegrating culture, not only do not criticize but join in the chorus of praise.

Does it matter what message *The Osbournes* sends? Absolutely. MTV's target audience is young people. Young men and women today are particularly influenced by the images they see on television. In this instance, not only do they see alcoholism and general depravity glorified on television, but national leaders lionize those who represent the antithesis of what is important to the vast majority of Americans.

Some commentators have opined that our traditional moral conservatives have not chosen to speak out on this issue because having too many targets can weaken one's credibility.[17] Also, being swamped with problems can distract or overwhelm even the best among us. Lawyers call it drowning your opposition in paper. In the case of our culture, the Left is drowning us in decay.

Osbourne, of course, has every right to do whatever he pleases. The challenge here is how we respond, as individuals. Our first responsibility is to recognize that the Osbourne situation is not a fluke but a microcosm of our disintegrating culture. And just because politicians we trusted to express our outrage for us have succumbed, it does not mean that, somehow, you're wrong about what's important. The bigger issue is whether or not you retreat—what becomes of your relationship with your own family.

The Increasingly Repulsive Global Village

It doesn't end there. By the time *The Osbournes*' current contract with MTV runs out, the family will have netted more than $20 million. MTV is owned by the global media megalith Viacom, whose other media outlets include publishing giant Simon & Schuster.[18] Now guess who signed the Osbournes to a $3 million book deal that will tie into the television show? Carolyn Reidy, the president of Simon & Schuster Adult Publishing Group, assures us, "The Osbournes are a popular phenomenon of the first magnitude. Their appeal is multi-generational and covers the entire political and cultural spectrum. We're bleeping delighted to publish them at Simon & Schuster."[19]

When it comes to cultural control, it's important to know how interconnected are the corporations that run the show. Using the variety of media outlets they control, the people at Viacom are throwing acid on the fabric of our culture, furthering the death of right and wrong. And they're bleeping delighted about it.

Of course, 6 million viewers for *The Osbournes* is impressive, but it is far from the whole of America. One crime here is that American media have allowed a miserable figure like Osbourne to *arrive,* and make his own contribution to the death of right and wrong. One thing you can do immediately, of course, is to cancel the part of your cable service that carries MTV and its sister station, VH1. I'm serious. It's a simple action, but it will enable you to make a statement about what's important to you and your family without hindering anyone else's freedom of expression.

Whenever public discussion takes place about the garbage on television, whether it be *The Osbournes, The Anna Nicole Show* (it's amazing how the bottom of the barrel keeps getting deeper, isn't it?), *Joe Millionaire,* or even the Victoria's Secret "fashion" specials, we inevitably hear from a supposed First Amendment activist who argues that people who don't like what's on television should simply turn off the set. That's an interesting message to those of us who are concerned about what's being pumped into the mainstream of our culture.

First of all, this is not an issue of being personally offended. What leftists have difficulty comprehending is that most people actually think beyond themselves. We have a responsibility to our society and our civilization as a whole. It's the least we owe to our children and the generations to come. What the leftists are saying to us with their suggestion that if we don't like what we see, we should turn away, is that *we're* out of step, *we* do not belong, and so we have no right to say anything. After all, it's the people who *watch* television who affect the decisions about what will air and what will not.

This is indeed one of the biggest problems for those of us who reject what television and film are doing to the quality of life in this country. The fact that millions of people are watching *Joe Millionaire*—or another huge cable success, *The Sopranos*—is what's pointed to. What's not discussed is the fact that 280 million Americans are *not* watching. Or are *not* buying movie tickets. Or are sick of the way the *New York Times* and CBS/NBC/ABC spin the news. The supermajority of us are in effect allowing the sickest among us to shape our culture. If decent Americans who reject the direction film and television are taking—all 280 million of us—accept the lie that we have no say, the Left Elite will continue to have their way by default.

While it may be tempting to dismiss this perverted "pushing of the envelope" in television (as the producer of *Joe Millionaire*, a program that serves only to humiliate women, termed it),[20] Britain provides a serious caution against apathy. The United Kingdom's Channel 4 aired a documentary in January 2003 called *Beijing Swings,* which featured "performance artist" Zhu Yu eating the corpse of a dead baby.[21]

Shocking? Absolutely, but is it so far removed from NBC's *Fear Factor,* where contestants must do hideous things for victory and money? One episode that aired around the time of this writing required the contestants to eat the bowels of a horse.[22]

The issue here, as I've said, is not whether you or I are *offended* by material like this, or whether or not we choose to watch it. I'm not offended—I'm *angered* at the destruction of my culture, which continues whether or not I watch it happen. Young women and men who are not watching this tripe have to deal with its impact on the scads of their peers who *are.*

While American TV has so far stopped short of anything as horrifying as cannibalizing a dead infant, *The Osbournes, Joe Millionaire,* and other so-called reality programming are an important warning sign. As long as our culture is shaped by a gang of irresponsible and indecent people sitting around trying to figure out how to make television more and more extreme, Zhu Yu can't be far off.

In the meantime, as our news and entertainment outlets become more uncivilized and base, so does the audience. Then, having cultivated a certain type of audience, the media conglomerates can argue that because their audience is addicted to sex and violence and the perverted, they are entirely right to provide more sex and violence and perversion. It is the epitome of the vicious circle. The malignant narcissists have welcomed their few brethren as the audience, and together they are to control the culture. And if we don't like it, as far as they're concerned, we can just shut up.

Killer as Hero, Part II

The Left Elite's glorification of their Ideal Man—the grotesque murderer—doesn't end with Mumia Abu-Jamal. In fact, this sick romance continues to impose itself on our culture, week by week, courtesy of Big Business.

Besides MTV Networks and Simon & Schuster, the properties of Viacom include CBS Television, BET, Showtime Networks, Infinity, Viacom Outdoor, Paramount Pictures, Paramount Television, Paramount Parks, UPN, Blockbuster, and theatrical exhibition operations in North America and abroad. You can see how unrestrained media mergers have created a virtual monster, with tremendous leverage over our culture.

It appears Viacom isn't satisfied using MTV to glorify alcoholic drug addicts. No, on one of its other television networks, VH1, glorifying savages is the order of the day.

Thanks to the vigilance of Fox News Channel's Bill O'Reilly and his snappy staff, it was brought to America's attention that VH1 produces a series called *Music Behind Bars.* No, this isn't a special where Wayne Newton sashays into Attica to entertain the denizens in striped jammies; this is a series that showcases the convicts themselves as "musicians" and features them in rock concerts. And you thought prison was supposed to punish people!

America has always been entranced by its celebrities, and being on television immediately gives one an air of authority, of superiority. Fame, regardless of how it is achieved, is seductive and impressive. The people who program television know this, which makes the immorality of the decision makers at VH1 crystal clear.

The "band members" their show lionizes aren't in prison for writing bad checks or shoplifting. They are the scum of the Earth, murderers and other hard-core criminals who have forever and irretrievably ruined other people's lives. As O'Reilly reported, in 1982, 18-year-old Lisa Mosbrook was stabbed to death by Tony Morrison, who was sentenced to life in prison in West Virginia. In 1995, 21-year-old Michael Hart was shot in the back by Jason Henthorne, also in West Virginia. Hart died, and Henthorne was given a sentence of 15 years to life.[23]

Now consider VH1's promotion for the episode featuring these monsters: "Tony and Jason are two inmates serving life sentences for murder. Tony's R&B band Midnight Love and Jason's country band Dakota are among the fourteen musical groups at the Mount Olive Correctional Complex in West Virginia. In this episode, the two men must get along and combine styles when the musical director asks them to collaborate and create a song for an [VH1's] upcoming concert."[24]

Isn't that nice? Lisa and Michael are dead. Forever. The families they left behind are without them. Forever. So what do these two killers get? Musical directors, bands, "style," and a TV show. This is simply not normal. It is moral depravity beyond measure. And yet, because national TV producers put it on, our critical minds slow down a bit as we wonder, Are we the ones who are out of step? No, we are not. We're making a critical judgment about right and wrong, and this is just plain wrong.

> So what do these two killers get? Musical directors, bands, "style," and a TV show. This is simply not normal. It is moral depravity beyond measure.

In the episode from Graterford Penitentiary in Pennsylvania, the band featured was Dark Mischief. Its lead singer is 25-year-old Christopher Bissey, who as a drug dealer back in 1995 gunned down 15-year-old Mary Orlando and 17-year-old Jennifer Grider near Lehigh University.[25] Bissey is in a rock band and on television instead of having gone to the electric chair because one juror in the penalty phase of his trial didn't have the guts to do the right thing.[26] Bissey was therefore sentenced to life in prison without possibility of parole. Instead of watching his execution, Mary's and Jennifer's families and friends are condemned to watching him become a star.

Evil as Interesting and Cooperative

If you're wondering what kind of mentality thinks up this stuff and then decides it's a good idea to put it on television, well, it's a mentality consumed with moral relativism. The *Music Behind Bars'* Web site declares, "For many prison inmates, making music is the only taste of freedom they'll ever get." And we want that? I don't suppose the families of Lisa and Michael want their murderers to have a "taste of freedom," but we can be sure VH1 didn't ask them.

Consider these comments about making the program, from "Jay," a producer:

> What truly surprised me about the air [inside a prison] was something more visceral. . . .
>
> Floating in the air, palpable and just out of reach was the unmistakable stench of evil.
>
> . . . The people who had killed, raped, stolen, bludgeoned etc., they were all living behind the imposing cement wall that surround[s] Graterford prison. . . . All this said, we got along with everyone really well. The guys in the band that we spoke to were all cooperative, interesting, and yes, human.[27]

VH1 sees evil as cooperative, interesting, and human. That is the message it is sending to society, and especially the target audience of adolescents and young men. It is assuring its audience that killing someone not only is no roadblock to becoming a rock star, it can actually help. Beyond the pale, however, is the re-victimization of victims, as family members are faced with the men who killed their loved ones having a good time and being featured on television.

While we're all familiar with the leftist claims that terrorists, murderers, and other malevolent pond scum need to be understood and helped, this is not a complicated issue. It is one on which decent people have reached a consensus: Evil people need to be punished. Murderers should not be praised and glorified. A cold-blooded killer is not a hero. And yet, even after a national television exposé resulted in tens of thousands of angry e-mails and letters, VH1's programmers and producers don't seem to care that they've been caught making money on the backs of murder victims while slugging away at the foundations of our culture.

VH1's commitment to this atrocity becomes all the more enlightening when you remember that it was a Viacom property, Paramount Television, that never really gave Dr. Laura Schlessinger's television program a chance. The Gay Elite complained that her morality-based message was "offensive,"[28] and Paramount executives were so afraid of offending various leftist subcultures that they eventually pulled the plug on her show.

Dr. Laura's message of respect, decency, and morality, while embraced by mainstream America, was too controversial for a morally corrupt left-wing special-interest group, so Paramount acted to silence her. Viacom then produces, through another property, a program that glorifies murderers, and mainstream America makes it clear they're offended. Yet no one apologizes, nothing is stopped. In fact, VH1 and Viacom give the decent in America the finger.

Revealing, isn't it?

Suspension of Disbelief

Make no mistake about Viacom's diversified but solidly leftist plan for the expanse of culture it controls. Do you remember Paul McCartney's October 20, 2001, Concert for New York City at Madison Square Garden? I certainly do. Aired on VH1, it was a benefit for the victims of the September 11 attack, and the audience was full of New York City firefighters and police officers, and of family members holding up pictures of fallen loved ones.

Then Hillary Clinton walked onstage and the most remarkable thing happened—the heroes of 9/11 started booing. The audience exploded with shouts of "Get off the stage! We don't want you here!" After about 20 seconds of this, she left.[29]

While the reaction of New York's Finest and Bravest is in itself enlightening, what VH1 did to that segment is even more so. For the rerun of that program on Christmas Day 2001, VH1 *digitally erased* the boos and catcalls aimed at Hillary Clinton and replaced them with cheers and applause.[30] This altered version was used for the DVD commemorating the event, cementing into the historical record a version of reality altered to fit Viacom's preferred worldview.

It's worth remembering, as we pull ourselves out of this muck for a moment, which publishing house it was that wrote an $8 million check to Hillary Clinton for her memoirs: Viacom's Simon & Schuster. I think it's safe to say that Hillary's tome will exhibit the same kind of historical revisionism she enjoyed courtesy of the VH1 editors.

Zippergate

The unique and ubiquitous power of television is not confined to the actual news and entertainment programming. It also extends to commercials and even promotional spots.

I remember one of the times I had the pleasure of being a guest on Fox News Channel's *The O'Reilly Factor*. I had been asked to come on the show to discuss a promotional ad CNN had run for Paula Zahn's new program, *American Morning*. How did CNN decide to introduce Ms. Zahn? A male announcer asked, "Where can you find a morning news anchor who's provocative, super-smart, oh yeah, and just a little sexy?" There were quick shots of Zahn's profile and lips, the word "sexy" was flashed on the screen, and the sound of a zipper being unzipped was heard in the background.[31]

While it may seem trivial, I argued on *The Factor* that an ad so sexualized would, and was meant to, affect how Zahn was viewed by her audience. Bill energetically disagreed, but I reminded him that corporate advertisers spend thousands to purchase a 30- or 60-second spot on *his* television program specifically because they know how much influence the televised image has, even if it lasts for a minute or less.

An ad like the one for *American Morning* is meant to lure a demographic segment of the population more inclined to watch wrestling, and so dumbing down and sexing up Ms. Zahn was the order of the day. There were many complaints—including from Zahn herself and from CNN Chairman and CEO Walter Isaacson—and the 15-second ad was pulled after running about 10 times.

You and I do not necessarily need to worry about Paula Zahn's image, but this is important for what it tells us about the mentality that drives one of the most powerful news networks in the world. The suggestion that zippers should be in action while Zahn delivers the news is not only humiliating to women but also an extraordinary insult to smart, decent people. Yet it should no longer be surprising.

In spring 2001 AOL Time Warner merged its television operations, which include the WB Network as well as all the Turner Broadcasting assets, among them TBS, CNN, and the Cartoon Network. At that time, the head of the WB Network, Mr. Jaime Kellner—who had developed programming like *Buffy the Vampire Slayer*—was appointed the top executive of the merged television operations. In his new role of deciding how to best bring the news to you,[32] one of the first decisions this man made was to bring on actress-model Andrea Thompson, best known for appearing seminude on *NYPD Blue,* to anchor news segments for *Headline News.* Thompson lasted less than a year.

Again, this may seem of secondary importance, but you must remember there was a point in a boardroom when grown men and women in charge of a portion of our culture, led by Kellner, decided it would be a good idea to turn CNN's news programming into sexualized entertainment geared for 18-to-24-year-old males.

Coming as I do from public relations with some involvement in network television, I can tell you that promotional campaigns are just that—campaigns. They aren't thrown together by a group of interns in between trips to fetch coffee for men like Kellner. They're designed by top executives with much thought and with a target audience in mind. After the zipper promo ran, CNN executives, including Kellner, claimed they had no idea such an ad would be running.[33] I find that hard to believe, and so should you.

On their own, perhaps these incidents wouldn't cause much concern, but I submit they provide the perfect little window into the state of mind of those who control our culture. It's not just entertainment programming that is being trashed up and dumbed down, it's also news programming. And, in fact, we view news programming with a significantly more open mind than we do entertainment programming—because we're watching supposedly to learn something. That's why, when you connect the dots, this becomes so revealing.

The only reason we're not seeing Paula Zahn delivering the news in a bikini is that she has integrity and enough power to say no. And because the rest of us haven't been completely lobotomized. Not yet.

The Moral Schizophrenia of PBS

In 1989, in celebration of my successful campaign for the presidency of Los Angeles NOW, I was given a book, Bill Moyers's *A World of Ideas,* by a feminist friend. I would later realize how ironic that title is for a man who cannot stand ideas other than his own.

Moyers currently hosts a program on the Public Broadcasting System (PBS) called *Now.* As you know, PBS, just like National Public Radio (NPR), is funded in great part with our tax dollars. The programming on both of these networks caters to leftists, making a mockery of their being representative of some kind of public trust. If you're anywhere right of center (which most of us now are, since the only thing missing from the American Left these days is black shirts), listening to either network makes you feel as out of place as a polar bear in Palm Springs.

On November 8, 2002, Moyers delivered the following remarkable diatribe:

> The entire federal government—the Congress, the executive, the courts—is united behind a right-wing agenda for which George W. Bush believes he now has a mandate. That agenda includes the power of the state to force pregnant women to surrender control over their own lives. It includes using the taxing power to transfer wealth from working people to the rich. It includes giving corporations a free hand to eviscerate the environment and control the regulatory agencies meant to hold them accountable. And it includes secrecy on a scale you cannot imagine.
>
> . . . And if you like God in government, get ready for the Rapture. . . .

Republicans out-raised Democrats by $184 million and they came up with the big prize: monopoly control of the American government and the power of the state to turn their radical ideology into the law of the land. Quite a bargain at any price.[34]

Terrifying, isn't it? Women losing control of their bodies, evisceration of the environment, big scary secrecy, and of course the dreaded Rapture. Even I, as a pro-choice feminist, am outraged by Moyers's exploitation of issues that are important to many Americans, using them to inflict his own paranoid end-of-the-world hysteria on the rest of us. I betcha Bill also has some headless chickens running around somewhere.

Using our tax dollars to spew this drivel, Moyers concludes by telling us that our vote, our decision-making process about who will lead this country, not only didn't count, it doesn't exist. We're really nothing more than prostitutes—bought and paid for. His rant is meant to incite fear and distrust of the government and of the men and women working with the weight of the world on their shoulders trying to keep this nation free and safe.

In a world where right and wrong were alive and well, we wouldn't have to worry about what someone like Bill Moyers thinks. But the fact that he's on television, and taxpayer-supported television to boot, makes his message sound legitimate.

Oh, by the way, we're also paying the salary of PBS president and CEO Pat Mitchell. In case you were wondering whether Ms. Mitchell, who was named to those positions in March 2000, might be working to make PBS representative of Americans in general as opposed to just leftists, don't hold your breath. A profile of her in *Electronic Media* magazine reported that she knows "how to make all kinds of television (she has been a network correspondent, a syndicated talk show host and a documentary maker) and all kinds of friends (actor Robert Redford, former boss Ted Turner and former Soviet leader Mikhail Gorbachev are among the members of her fan club)."[35]

Well, at least only one of them is an *official* Communist.

To give you a point/counterpoint illustration of the agenda of those who handle programming for PBS, while Moyers's antireligious, anti-Republican, fear-based message gets a full airing, Charlie Daniels was not permitted to sing his patriotic song paying tribute to the heroes of 9/11 on PBS's annual Fourth of July special because, according to the producers, the song wasn't "upbeat enough."

The *New York Post* reported that Daniels has been performing the song, called "The Last Fallen Hero," in concerts since the winter of 2001. The song deals with the 9/11 terrorist attacks and makes a plea for national unity in the war on terror.[36] The lyrics include these lines: "Oh, the cowards came by morning and attacked without warning, leaving flames and death and chaos in our streets. In the middle of this fiery hell, brave heroes fell."

Reached by phone after PBS decided to cut the song, Daniels spoke to the *Post*'s Adam Buckman. "The song is a tribute to the people of 9/11," Daniels said, "and I thought it was the absolute perfect Fourth of July song. . . . I refuse to be a part of anything that goes on the Fourth of July that we have to ignore our fighting men and women, that we have to ignore the victims of 9/11. I just don't think it's right."[37]

Even standing on its own, the decision not to let him sing "The Last Fallen Hero" was a slap in the face not only of Daniels, but of all of us who love our country and honor the brave men and women who have died for it. For those of us who do not think Castro's Cuba is a paradise, Palestinians are victims, and Radical Islamists are freedom fighters, it is intolerable. Let's be frank. Putting a friend of Ted Turner and of the last official Communist in charge of PBS or anything else involving the "public trust" is indecent and irresponsible.

The "Good" Rape

The Vagina Monologues is an award-winning "feminist" play. It is also a bestselling book. Supposedly it is a "celebration" of female sexuality, and yet there is one vignette where a teenage girl is fed alcohol by a 24-year-old woman and then raped.

This is not a matter of interpretation. It has been reported that early performances of the play at colleges had the girl at

13 years old (she is presented as 16 years old in the book) say-ing, "Now people say it was a kind of rape. . . . Well, I say if it was rape, it was a good rape."[38] A good rape? In this case it took conservatives to call attention to what feminists have for years defined and decried as rape.

After complaints, the reference in the play to the "good rape" has been removed. In the book of the play, however, in the vignette titled "The Little Coochi Snorcher That Could" (a reference to what the drunken teen calls her genitalia), it is still undeniably what feminists would term rape if the older person had been a man. The story offers a disturbing picture of a mo-lestation presented as a romantic, empowering experience. Consider this "feminist" scenario:

> One day she invites me into her car . . . she kisses me and tells me to relax . . . and the pretty lady makes me a drink. . . . The alcohol has gone to my head and I'm loose and ready . . . she gently and slowly lays me out on the bed.[39]

After concluding that she now will "never have to rely on a man," she then says of her molester, "I realized later she was my surprising, unexpected politically incorrect salvation." [40]

So, the liberating message of this modern feminist clarion call is that rape, when committed by a woman, is not only okay, it's "salvation" for the victim. This kind of hypocrisy is why I rejected establishment feminism in 1996. Even then, however, I could never have guessed how deeply nihilism would come to infect the modern feminist agenda. And yet here it is, and we see it most clearly through modes of entertain-ment. It's not even just the depravity of Eve Ensler, the creator of this material—it's the fact that it has been embraced by women in both the feminist and entertainment establishments. Call me silly, but I thought one of the goals of the feminist movement was to *stop* women being looked at as sex objects.

Or as body parts. And yet, here is Ms. Ensler's own account of several incidents that I suppose are meant to inspire us in our womanhood. At a performance of *Vagina Monologues*, ac-tress Glenn Close "gets 2500 people to stand and chant the word *cunt* [emphasis Ensler's]. . . . A woman brings her uterus to the theatre to have me sign it. . . . A young man makes and serves me a vagina salad for dinner with his parents in Atlanta, Georgia. Bean sprouts are the pubic hair."[41]

When the singer Madonna was at her height, there were myriad feminist claims that she, too, was an example of how successful feminism was. I said then and I'll say now, feminism wasn't about creating an environment where Madonna could feel comfortable masturbating onstage. Nor was it about making thousands of people comfortable shouting the word "cunt"—an extraordinarily derogatory word used to degrade and humiliate women for centuries.

Heck, once the feminist and creative establishments are done making "cunt" an "empowering" word, why don't they take back "whore"?

In addition to illustrating my point about moral relativism, where nothing matters and there is no right or wrong, I'm hoping to show you that when you reject this kind of thing, it's not authentic feminism that repulses you—it's nihilism. This play, in both its staged and its book versions, makes a mockery of the respect women have been looking for since before the modern feminist movement began.

In my world, dignity, self-respect, and feminism are not contradictory terms. Unfortunately, for Eve Ensler and her buddies, they absolutely are.

Rewarding the Worst

I wrote in chapter 5 about the Left's agenda of integrating degenerate and violent rap singers into mainstream culture. This integration has as its goal making the most vile among us into heroes for the next generation, and forcing those who know better into silence lest we be labeled "censors" or enemies of "freedom of expression." Manipulating pop culture is the Left Elite's surefire way of forcing society to bend to their depraved view of themselves and this country. The elevation of rap singers to pop star status is the cultural equivalent of an armed invasion of your home.

No discussion of the disintegration of our values would be complete without noting the astonishing acceptance of loathsome rapper Eminem. I noted in *The New Thought Police* the nature of this man's work, which includes lyrics that rhapsodize about kicking his pregnant wife in the stomach and this little gem, from the song "Kill You," about murdering gays and lesbians: "Kill you, you faggots keep egging me on / Till I have you at knife point then you beg me to stop."[42]

How did this cultural terrorist become an acceptable member of our pop culture? Courtesy of the Left Elite's foot soldiers in the media, of course. First, as I outlined in chapter 5, rappers such as Ice-T (really, it's absurd even having to write such a name) get movie and television deals. They are moderately sanitized by pretending to be other people as they take hostage the American standard for entertainment.

Ice Cube followed the same path. In his little ditty "Natural Born Killaz," he contributed the following to the cultural landscape: "Barrel one touches your motherfuckin flesh / Barrel two shoots your fuckin heart out your chest / . . . decapitatin I aint hesitatin ..."[43]

What is Ice Cube's reward? He has been given starring roles in films such as *Three Kings*, with George Clooney, and *Dangerous Ground*, with Michelle

> Manipulating pop culture is the Left Elite's surefire way of forcing society to bend to their depraved view of themselves and this country.

Pfeiffer. For his latest film, his biography says, "[A]n actor, screenwriter, director, producer, rapper, and music producer, Ice Cube has become a modern day Renaissance man positioning himself as an influential force within the entertainment industry and one of his generation's cultural icons."[44]

Eminem is being ushered through those same doors with his first (and I say first because there will be more) major motion picture. *8 Mile* has been lauded by the critics, as has its star's performance. Costarring Kim Basinger, the film is meant to transform Eminem into another "cultural icon," just like Ice-T and Ice Cube.

The Fall of the New York Times

The *New York Times* is doing its bit to make sure this cultural hijacking succeeds. In a *New York Times Magazine* cover story about Eminem titled "Mr. Ambassador," *Times* columnist (and former theater critic) Frank Rich offers nothing less than an orgiastic love fest. He portrays Eminem as an Everyman with a "happy" audience that reminds him of churchgoers. Describing an Eminem concert, Rich writes:

> At its climax he [Eminem] vows to urinate on the White House lawn and hurls expletives at Lynne Cheney and Tipper Gore. But the roaring throng of 16,000 at the Palace of Auburn Hills is not angry. There is barely a whiff of pot in the air, let alone violence. It's a happy crowd, mixed in race and sex, that might just as well have congregated . . . at a megachurch or a mall.[45]

This is how the brainwashing starts, and the marginalization of the decent people who make up the majority in this country. Most Americans don't have to struggle with the question whether to go to church or to an Eminem concert, but Frank Rich wants us to think that our contemporaries like this garbage—that *we* are the odd ones out. Things have changed, the culture is moving ahead, and you'd better get with the program. Normal people *like* Eminem, so if you don't, something is wrong with *you*.

The effort is to construct a false front for a cultural movement that the vast majority of Americans reject but are afraid to publicly condemn.

Rich does understand the need to address the extraordinary violence promoted by Eminem. His take?

> That Eminem is also showing Elvis-esque potential to bust out of the youth market is not entirely a surprise. Any listener with open ears and some affinity for the musical vocabulary of hip-hop can easily become hooked on his music . . . the mayhem is so calculatedly over the top that

it seems no more or less offensive than typical multiplex Grand Guignol.[46]

I see. The worse the violence, the less attention we should pay. What a terrific prescription for today's world: Don't counter violence, ignore it. And clearly, if you don't like the garbage Eminem is pouring into our culture, *your ears aren't open*. It's natural and understandable, in Rich's world, to become hooked on music where women are "whores" and "bitches" to be kicked and beaten, and gay people are "faggots" to be murdered.

We've all been raised to view the *New York Times* as the Newspaper of Record—a media outlet that reports the news without bias and with great journalistic ethics. If it's in the *Times,* it must be true.

If that was ever the case, it must have been before my time. Nowadays, we should regard the *New York Times* as we would the *National Enquirer*. It may be interesting to read, but you wouldn't want to view the world through its prism. It's funny—I used to read the *Times* to find out what was happening in the world. Now I read it to stay on top of what the current leftist agenda is in this nation. That such a venerated American icon has declined so terribly is tragic, and a great loss for everyone.

The Fall, Part II

Frank Rich is not some anomalous wretch wandering the esteemed halls of the *Times*. He is a symbol of its alienated and bitter agenda. Increasingly stymied by Americans' rejection of the Left's cynical worldview, people like Rich and fellow columnist Maureen Dowd perfectly represent the fallen daily's hatred of America.

Dowd's columns have been must-reading for many people for a long time. She even won a Pulitzer Prize in 1999 for her columns about the Clinton-Lewinsky scandal. But something has happened to Ms. Dowd. No longer informative and clever, her writing has become childish and vindictive. The silver lining of Dowd's having regular access to the pages of the *Times* is that she exposes what moral relativism really is, and how far gone she and her compadres really are.[47]

No doubt to the joy of anti-Semites everywhere, her column for October 6, 2002, blamed a supposed Jewish cabal in the Bush administration for pushing the war on Iraq. Dowd asserts, "Influential Jewish conservatives, inside and outside the administration, have been fierce in supporting a war on Saddam, thinking it could help Israel by scrambling the Middle East map."[48] In the same column she refers to the then-Republican leadership in the Senate—Trent Lott, Tom DeLay, Dennis Hastert, and Don Nickles—as the Four Horsemen of the Apocalypse.

Just two weeks after castigating her imagined Jewish cabal, Dowd wrote a column portraying the president as some buffoonish character from the *Beverly Hillbillies*. In one of the most astonishingly insulting and vindictive things I've ever read, Dowd referred to the president as "boy" no fewer than 10 times. Here's a snippet, reflective of exactly how morally bankrupt Dowd has become:

> The Boy Emperor picked up the morning paper and, stunned, dropped his Juicy Juice box with the little straw attached. "Oh, man," he wailed. "North Korea's got nukes." . . . "Get me Condi!" the boy yelled. "And a peanut butter and jelly sandwich."[49]

Dowd also is unkind, shall we say, to one of those Jews she complains about:

> "I am the chairman of your Defense Policy Board," an amused Richard Perle replied. "I am an adviser to Rumsfeld, a friend of Wolfowitz's and a thorn in Powell's medals. . . . I'm killing time trying to get your foreign policy to rise. I'm known as the Prince of Darkness."

Delightful, isn't it?

Move Over, Elvis

Whom *does* Dowd like? Take a wild guess . . . you have two more seconds . . . that's right! Eminem! Maureen Dowd, in polemics that give new meaning to Orwell's Newspeak, declares that those who are doing their best to keep the world from being annihilated are pushing us toward Armageddon, while she coos that Eminem, a man who glamorizes violence and nihilism, is the "Boomers' Crooner":

> A gaggle of my girlfriends are surreptitiously smitten with Eminem. They buy his posters on eBay. They play him on their Walkmen at the gym. . . . It doesn't feel quite so rebellious to like The Most Evil Rapper Alive . . . if your mom is rapping along when he describes how he'd like to rape and kill his mom.[50]

What is it we're supposed to believe has made the Girlfriends of Maureen so enthralled with Eminem? With what lyrics have they been smitten? Could it be these from "Kill You": "Put your hands down, bitch, I ain't gon' shoot you / I'ma pull YOU to this bullet and put it through you"? Or these from "Kim," dedicated to his wife: "Don't you get it bitch, no one can hear you? / Now shut the fuck up and get what's comin to you"? Or these from "Bitch Please II": "Bitch, please—you must have a mental disease / Assume the position and get back down on your knees—c'mon"?

Dowd's extraordinary irresponsibility in saying that women *enjoy* and essentially fall in love with a man chanting about raping, torturing, and murdering them is repulsive and sick. In her stunning exhibition of deadly nihilism, courtesy of the *New York Times,* the message is sent once again that women *like* to be abused and want to be raped.

Dowd's destructive and arrogant mind-set reminds me of *New Yorker* film critic Pauline Kael's reaction to Richard Nixon's landslide victory over George McGovern in 1972: "How can that be? No one I know voted for Nixon."[51] Dowd and her "gaggle of girlfriends" are as out of touch as was Kael in her cloistered world. Leftists like Kael and Dowd and Rich are not only removed from the American mainstream, they are removed from the values and common decency that are at the heart of every one of us.

Their moral relativism born of nihilism is indeed a cancer, but this is one disease that we do not have to allow to metastasize into our lives. We know what causes it—our own acquiescence to the Left's bankrupt rhetoric. All we have to do is say no.

CHAPTER NINE

The Injustice System:
Putting the Decent in Danger

Injustice anywhere is a threat to justice everywhere.

—*Martin Luther King, Jr.*

On May 26, 2000, the last day of the school year at Lake Worth Middle School in West Palm Beach, Florida, 13-year-old Nathaniel Brazill shot his English teacher, Barry Grunow, to death with a .25 caliber handgun he had stolen from a family friend. In this case, the American justice system worked, up to a point. The perpetrator was caught, tried, and convicted. Young Brazill, tried as an adult, was convicted of second-rather than first-degree murder for this deliberate killing, and thus was sentenced to 28 years in prison rather than death. But that's better than nothing from a system that more often than not releases the guilty back onto the streets because of lawyer gamesmanship and absurd technicalities.[1]

So, hooray for the good guys, and thank God our judicial system works the way it ought to, right? Wrong. Fast forward to November 2002. In a related civil suit, the court awarded Pam

Grunow, Barry's widow, $24 million—$10.8 million from the family friend who was the victim of Brazill's theft; $12 million from the school board, for failing to prevent Brazill from returning to school that day; and $1.2 million from Valor Corp., the distributor of the gun. This was the first time in the United States that a gun seller was found partly responsible for a murder. And the civil jury placed none of the responsibility for the crime on Brazill, despite his conviction on the criminal charges.

Brazill's actions and statements that day leave no doubt that he had murder on his mind. He had been sent home early after a water-balloon fight. He walked part of the way with a classmate, whom he told that he was going to kill the guidance counselor who had disciplined him. Arriving at his home, he picked up the gun he had stolen several days before, bicycled back to school, snuck in the back way to avoid security, returned to Barry Grunow's classroom, stood in front of his teacher for 11 seconds pointing the gun at his face, and then shot him in the head.[2] In the nihilistic world of our justice system, a bunch of lawyers managed to convince the civil jury that the person who actually pulled the trigger was not responsible.

Of course, the absurdity of this is palpable. Only in a world where right and wrong have been murdered would a jury feel comfortable finding an inanimate object partly responsible for a very human crime. If Brazill, in all his pathetic self-centeredness, hadn't shot Barry Grunow, Grunow wouldn't be dead. The weapon Brazill chose is incidental. A gun, like a knife or an automobile, can be used for a variety of things. Whether its use is for good or for evil depends on what the person in control of the object intends. But this is a fact that we are being conditioned to reject.

Did Pam Grunow just wake up one morning and decide to pursue this civil suit? Apparently not. In fact, it was the Brady Center to Prevent Gun Violence (formerly Handgun Control Inc.) that filed the suit on her behalf. Their lawyers' premise for including Valor Corp. in the suit? The firearm was "defective" because it didn't have a "built-in lock," and it was "unreasonably dangerous" because it was small and inexpensive. Oh, so I guess an AK-47 isn't unreasonably dangerous because

it's really big? Here's some insight for the Brady Center to consider: There was a defective and unreasonably dangerous
element in the killing of Barry Grunow—and his name is
Nathaniel Brazill. With their reasoning, all Chihuahuas are
going to have to be confiscated because they, too, have no
locks and are small and inexpensive.

While the jury rejected the major claims that the gun was
defective and unreasonably dangerous, it, oddly, still found
Valor negligent for failing to supply "feasible safety measures."[3] Let's be honest—the only "safety measure" that could
have stopped this crime would have been if Nathaniel Brazill
had not been raised in a world shaped by the malignant narcissists of the Left Elite.[4]

Valor Corp. did not place the gun in Brazill's hand, did not
whisper "murder" in his ear, did not drive him to school and
place his finger on the trigger. And yet, in this Looking-Glass
world, it is now held partly responsible for Grunow's death.

Interestingly, the lead attorney in the suit, Bob Montgomery, was best known as one of the driving forces behind the
lawsuits against the tobacco companies. Now that he has
proved it's possible to find gun companies responsible for murder, it won't be long before the gun-control hounds unleash a
similar flood of cases on the courts. Meanwhile, thugs in court-
rooms from Los Angeles to New York City will chorus, "The
gun company made me do it."

The Truly Guilty

One thing among many of which Americans should be proud is
our justice system. We have a history of fairness and justice second to none. After all, many of our ancestors came from places
where neither usually operated. They knew what it was like to
be railroaded, falsely accused, and maliciously prosecuted. Our
system is one that was designed to make sure that the innocent
were protected while the guilty were identified and punished. It
was designed to be a mechanism for the search for truth because the Founding Fathers knew what it was like to be subjected to a system that was capricious, unethical, and immoral.

I fear that is exactly what our justice system today is becoming.

Unfortunately, no agency, no segment of our society is immune from the moral relativism fostered by the Left. The integrity of our justice system depends on the officers of the court—lawyers and judges—being honest, decent men and women. All too often, however, we see moral ambiguity ruling the day—making a mockery of the search for the truth and prosecution of the guilty. Trials are no longer about freeing the innocent, punishing the guilty, and making restitution to the injured. They have devolved into a contest over who will *win*. Defense attorneys are guilty of this "win" mentality, prosecutors are guilty, and even judges are guilty.

We have seen the results throughout this book—with judges or juries failing to impose death sentences on cop killers, dropping charges against a woman who murdered her own child, freeing violent men on parole, taking a lenient and sometimes even sympathetic view of child molesters, giving more rights to convicts than to law-abiding citizens, and, now, holding a man whose property was stolen and the company that had sold the stolen property responsible for the use the thief made of it.

> Trials are no longer about freeing the innocent, punishing the guilty, and making restitution to the injured. They have devolved into a contest over who will *win*.

Defense attorneys tend to bear the brunt of criticism in our society, and with good reason. Today's defense attorneys have done more to smear the courts' reputation than any other party. Of course, no matter how deeply we believe that defense attorneys must be held responsible for their actions, we usually retreat when we hear one of the familiar refrains—"Everyone has a right to a defense" or "I'm a defense attorney because I believe in the system."

Obviously, none of us disagree with the notion that everyone accused of a crime deserves a vigorous defense. Americans understand and embrace the concept of fairness to the accused, which our founders thought so important that it is enshrined in no fewer than five of the first ten Amendments to the Constitution. What disgusts us is a generation of lawyers and judges who are dedicated foot soldiers in the war against our country's principles.

The majority of lawyers and judges today are first- or second-generation products of the 1960s. As we know, the homegrown Marxists and radical leftists of that period didn't move to Hanoi—they stayed here and became politicians, journalists, and special-interest-group flacks. They also became professors at law schools, and their progeny, indoctrinated with leftism, became today's lawyers and judges.

I've exposed for you throughout this book how the moral relativism and nihilism that control the leftist subcultures in this country have been vigorously attacking our cultural moral fabric. Of course, the law and its administration is a special front in this war.

One fact that those on the Left do their best to forget is that our legal system stems from a long European tradition that began with the Bible. The details of the biblical prescriptions have mostly been dropped over time, but our laws still have a basis in morality that many on the Left oppose.

Most of us view our laws and how they're applied as an indication of what's right and wrong. Or, in fact, of whether or not there is a right and wrong. Consigning one of our most important morally based systems to a nihilistic void would complete the transformation of our society from a Shining City on a Hill to an empty, meaningless wilderness. I say "would" because although we see too many symptoms of the failure of our justice system, the slide can still be stopped.

In order for the malignant narcissists to advance their agenda, they must remove morality from the law, or replace it with false morality. An important example of false morality is hate-crime legislation.

In *The New Thought Police* I wrote about the extraordinary danger the whole concept of "hate crimes" poses to civil liberties and the very people it's meant to protect.[5] Of course, it is already illegal to kill, maim, beat, stab, or otherwise torment another human being. What hate-crime legislation says is that it's *more* wrong to kill, maim, beat, stab, or torment someone of color or of a different sexual persuasion. When we say, "It's more wrong to kill some people than others," *that* is false morality.

Conditioned by their time and educated by the leftists who had wrested control of the academy, many of today's lawyers and judges are unable or unwilling to allow true morality and ethics to guide their actions and decision-making processes. This is one way to transform the system from within: to make morality irrelevant simply by abandoning it. This is not so difficult for many of these people. Keep in mind how morally vacuous malignant narcissists really are. It's just silly to expect them to advance concepts that benefit society as a whole (like decency and fairness), ahead of their debased agenda of making society mirror their own immorality.

The Sixth Amendment to the Constitution details the rights of anyone accused of a crime, including the right to the "assistance of counsel for his defense." What does that translate to in a system filled with people who refuse to distinguish between right and wrong? Today, a "vigorous defense" includes lying. It includes deliberately misleading juries. It includes not just defending a client but doing everything possible to get him released—even when the lawyer knows the client is guilty.

Freeing the Monster

You remember five-year-old Samantha Runnion—and your memory will have to serve, because she's dead, and the immorality of defense attorneys just may have contributed to her torturous death.

In July 2002, in one of the unfortunately many high-profile child kidnappings of that year, a man grabbed Samantha from outside her apartment complex in Southern California as she played with a friend. Her naked body was found the next day along a nearby highway. She had been raped and then asphyxiated.[6] The sick bastard who did this had then posed the little girl's body in what police described as a "provocative" position.

Erin Runnion, Samantha's mother, had taken care in telling her daughter what to do if a stranger ever tried to take her away. The little girl, called "Mantha" by her mom, was taught to scream for help or yell "Fire!" if anyone forced her into a car. She would reassure her mom that she would always be able to get away because "she could run really fast and was as strong as Hercules."[7]

What Erin couldn't protect her daughter from was a legal system that had freed the man police believe committed this crime. Two years before Samantha's kidnapping, Alejandro Avila was charged with child molestation. John Pozza, Avila's attorney in that case, persuaded the jury to disbelieve the two main witnesses against his client—two 9-year-old girls, who testified in graphic detail about the abuse they said he had inflicted upon them.

The mother of one of the girls was a school custodian who worked evenings; she would sometimes ask her then-boyfriend, Avila, to baby-sit while she was working. Interestingly, her apartment was in the same complex as the Runnions'.

According to her little daughter as reported by the *Los Angeles Times*, "When my mom went to work, he would take me into the room and he would do those things to me."[8] Typically, he would order her to take off her clothes. Then he would remove his own clothing. "Then he would start touching me and then making his private part touch mine," she said.[9]

Pozza battered away at the girls' credibility and told the jury that Avila's ex-girlfriend had encouraged them to make up their story. Pozza did this although he knew his client had *failed a lie-detector test* about the accusations.[10]

Despite the girls' dramatic and detailed testimony, John Pozza convinced the jury that they just couldn't be believed. You may be thinking that's his job—to create reasonable doubt. But at any cost, and when he knew his client was at best not telling the truth, and at worst guilty? Call me old-fashioned, but I contend that assisting a client with a defense should not include lying to a judge or fabricating scenarios to mislead a jury.

At any rate, Avila was out on the street again, thanks in part to what Pozza callously touts on his Web site as his track record of "wins."[11] Who "won" in the acquittal of Avila on those charges of child molestation? Certainly not the two 9-year-old girls, whose tormentor never received the punishment he deserved, and definitely not Samantha Runnion. In fact, society as a whole lost. That, I contend, is an absolutely unethical abuse of our justice system.

Of course, parasitic defense attorneys like Pozza will wail that they're just doing their job. Are they really? Their job is to be faithful to the system, to society. They, no less than prosecutors and judges, are officers of the court. They are to give assistance to the accused. Nowhere is it written that this assistance is a free pass to deceive the court in order to get your client acquitted, no matter what.

In fact, the system itself includes reminders to defense attorneys that there are higher values than "winning," and allows for lawyers with a moral conscience to remove themselves from a case. The American Bar Association has a rule, Rule 1.16 (b.3), which states that a lawyer has the right to withdraw from any case "when the client insists on taking action the lawyer finds repugnant."[12] I think most of us would find freeing a child molester morally repugnant.

Despite his airy use of sports terminology, Pozza can't dismiss the seriousness of his "win" for Avila. If he had found the thought of a child molester being set free morally repugnant and had withdrawn from the case, or at least provided only the basic assistance called for (which does not include telling a jury two young witnesses are essentially *lying*), Samantha Runnion might still be alive today.

Whenever you hear defense attorneys say they have "no choice" as they try to explain why they're going to extraordinary lengths to free a fiend, remember that moral relativism is their friend, and misleading people their stock in trade.

Of course, her killer is the one who is ultimately responsible. But men who do that kind of thing to little girls don't just have a bad night, flip out, and decide to, just once, molest a child. Child molesters are almost all serial criminals. The U.S. Department of Justice, along with every other expert on the issue, confirms that child molestation is part of a long-term persistent pattern of behavior.[13] In fact, when the FBI joined the search for Samantha Runnion, their profile "painted a portrait of a man with a history of kidnapping and sexually assaulting children."[14] Lawyers know this, including lawyers who defend these sickest and most dangerous perverts.

Whenever you hear defense attorneys say they have "no choice" as they try to explain why they're going to extraordinary lengths to free a fiend, remember that moral relativism is their friend, and misleading people their stock in trade.

Defending the Indefensible

Of course, there are legitimate defense attorneys out there, and, as I've pointed out, our right to a defense is enshrined in our Constitution. It's one of the things that separate our country from most others, and I would never want to lose that. My point is that we should be able to rely on defense attorneys who are decent people. One doesn't need to be morally bankrupt to defend the accused. We all want this system to work, but somehow too many of us have bought the notion that lawyers have to be pond scum in order for that to happen.

For an attorney, to know your client is guilty but go into a courtroom and lie to a jury in order to gain an acquittal is simply and clearly wrong. The same goes for prosecutors who know a defendant is innocent, but try to pin a conviction on him anyway. The problem is that except for the occasional censure from the bench, attorneys are not held personally responsible for unethical tactics used to set a felon free.

The very least we can do is call attention to those who insult our understanding of right and wrong. Unfortunately, we're dealing with more than being insulted here—we're dealing with people who put all of society at risk because of their narcissistic inability to see beyond themselves and their obsession with "winning."

Doing the Devil's Bidding

Consider Steven Feldman, the lead defense attorney for David Westerfield. Westerfield is the now-convicted kidnapper/murderer of seven-year-old Danielle van Dam. On February 2,

2002, he slithered into the van Dam home and abducted young Danielle. Her body was found 25 days later, dumped, as the prosecutor would put it, "like trash" along a rural road.[15] The body was so badly decomposed the authorities were never able to determine exactly what the fiend Westerfield had done to Danielle. Considering he was a heavy consumer of child pornography, we can assume her final hours were hell on Earth.

The jury found Westerfield guilty of possession of child pornography, kidnapping, and murder. The jury also recommended that Westerfield be executed. At that point in the trial, one of his lawyers turned to him and said, "I'm so sorry." Really? I hope that lawyer is the only person alive who's "so sorry" for Westerfield. Decent people are sorry for Danielle and her family.

Of course, even Westerfield, in all his depravity, deserved a defense. That's not the issue here. What has rightly shocked many people is the revelation that Westerfield's lawyers apparently knew for a fact their client was guilty of this unspeakable crime.

The *San Diego Union-Tribune* reported that minutes before Danielle's body was found under a bush along a desert highway, Feldman and his colleague Robert Boyce were brokering a deal with the prosecutors. "He would tell police where he dumped the 7-year-old girl's body; they would not seek the death penalty," law-enforcement sources told the *Union-Tribune*. "[D]efense attorneys Steven Feldman and Robert Boyce were negotiating for a life sentence for the 50-year-old design engineer. . . . The deal they were discussing would have allowed Westerfield to plead guilty to murder and be sentenced to life in prison without the possibility of parole."[16]

While prosecutors were seriously considering the plea bargain, Danielle's body was discovered by some of the scores of volunteers who had been searching the area ever since her abduction. "The deal was just minutes away," one of the newspaper's sources said.

Of course, as soon as the body was found, Feldman and Boyce had lost their bargaining chip. The case was going to trial, and they knew their client had only a slim chance of not being convicted and given the death penalty. So they did every-thing possible not just to *assist* their client, but to try to get him found *not guilty*. Believing a person deserves a defense is not the same as doing everything in your power to get him off scot-free.

I'll say this again: Feldman and Boyce had to have known their client was guilty. And yet they sought experts willing to testify that bugs found under the little girl's body indicated a timeline of death that exonerated Westerfield. Danielle was dumped, the defense claimed, at a time when Westerfield was already under police surveillance, making it impossible for him to be the culprit.[17]

The indecency of this assertion is absolutely astounding. Here was Feldman, not just countering the prosecution's case, but presenting a scenario to the judge and jury that appears he *knew* was false. It's interesting, isn't it? If a witness lies in the courtroom, it's perjury, a serious crime. When it comes to de-fense attorneys, however, it seems there are no rules.

In the Westerfield case, thank God, the jury didn't buy it. Even clever and unscrupulous defense lawyers couldn't obscure the fact that Danielle's blood was found on Westerfield's jacket. In the end, it was the physical evidence—fingerprints, blood, hair, and fibers—that convinced the jurors. One of them told the *San Diego Union-Tribune* they had disregarded the bug "hired guns." Juror No. 6 described the bug experts as "just not trustworthy."[18] Westerfield was convicted and sentenced to death.

> Believing a person deserves a defense is not the same as doing everything in your power to get him off scot-free.

We must ask ourselves, When did defending the accused before a jury devolve into at-tempting to deceive the jury on behalf of the accused? When did the right to a defense turn into a sport where lawyers count "wins," where getting a client off, regardless of guilt, became the goal? It is with the death of right and wrong that these be-came paramount and eclipsed fairness and justice itself.

There is one more twist to this story. After the trial was over, Westerfield's lawyers asked for and received a hearing to plead that his sentence should be changed from death to life in prison without possibility of parole. Why? Because two police detectives attempted to visit Westerfield in jail after he had obtained a lawyer. The defense argued that the police were trying to violate their client's constitutional rights, and that this justified reducing Westerfield's sentence "as a means of punishing" the San Diego Police Department. Why were the detectives going to see Westerfield? To tell him they had found Danielle's body.[19]

Judge Mudd eventually rejected the motions for a reduction in sentence, but the fact remains that the van Dams were forced to go months longer without closure so these boys could play their little technicality games. The pain and suffering of the victims continued, courtesy of our injustice system.

"I Don't Care"

Not surprisingly, there are indications that Feldman is the classic malignant narcissist. In the one interview he gave after the Westerfield verdict, he revealed his moral bankruptcy by refusing to acknowledge the implications of his actions. Saying he had no regrets, Feldman commented, "Whether or not an individual is guilty or not guilty is not my issue. I don't care. My job is to evaluate the case and assist the person as best as I possibly can. That is the ethical requirement of the criminal defense lawyer."[20]

This is perfect Orwellian Newspeak—describing any-means-necessary actions like Feldman's as ethically *required*. We've heard this tripe for far too long. It's time we reject those excuses and call them what they are—self-indulgent, immoral, and outrageous. Here's a newsflash for Feldman: Our justice system does *not* require a moral void among defense attorneys, nor does it require them to be dead at heart.

At one point, this man who was presenting to a jury scenarios that it seems he knew to be completely false actually had the gall to say it was his job to keep the *prosecution* honest! The *Union-Tribune* reporter asked Feldman whether he had ever secretly regretted seeing one of his clients acquitted of a criminal charge. "No," Feldman responded. "It's always the right decision. It's the right decision because it means the prosecutor messed up, it means the police cheated, it means somebody messed something up."[21]

No regrets, no shame, no guilt. No responsibility. No conscience? Feldman manages to ignore the implications of his own egregious behavior by claiming that if it works and a fiend is let out onto the streets to kidnap, rape, and murder another little girl, it's because someone else "messed up." If Westerfield had been found not guilty, that's exactly how Feldman would have explained the "win," to borrow Pozza's term.

While the Westerfield guilty verdict and death sentence is a gift to society, lawyers like Pozza, Feldman, and Boyce are still out there working for monsters and condemning families like the Runnions and van Dams to reap what lawyers like them sow.

Destructive Confluence

What happens when morally vacuous judges, moral relativism, and the sexualization of children coincide? The most ugly of events. We've all been conditioned to believe that somehow the judge sitting up there on the bench knows more about Important Things than the average person. We believe that person possesses something that allows him or her to understand and see clearly the issues we face when our social pact to treat each other decently falls apart.

A judge is supposed to be above it all, unbiased, able to discern, at the very least, right from wrong. He or she is supposed to be the supervisor, the final arbiter, the insurer that all that goes on in a courtroom will be *fair.*

Unfortunately, what many people forget is that judges are just lawyers in robes. A little disheartening, isn't it? I squirm every time I remind myself of the little fact that money and power can get you elected or appointed to the bench. That's all it takes. If Feldman and Pozza become rich and powerful enough, they, too, can become judges.

And so the death of right and wrong afflicts judges, too. They can be as jaded, as warped, as morally bankrupt as their shark brethren swimming beneath them in the courtroom. The damage a judge is in a position to do, however, can be even more serious to individual lives, and to our society as a whole, when that judge is captivated and controlled by the Left's corrupt agenda.

The "Sexual Needs" of a Child

Pamela Diehl-Moore, a 43-year-old teacher in Lyndhurst, New Jersey, began a sexual "relationship" with a 13-year-old boy just after he finished her seventh-grade class. Diehl-Moore, a divorced mother of two—including a girl just two years younger than the boy she molested—pled guilty to sexual assault under a deal that would have sent her to prison for three years. Obviously, the impact on the boy cannot be reversed, but in terms of justice, so far so good.

"We are talking about a sexual assault of a little boy," prosecutor Martin Delaney said at the sentencing hearing. "We need to send a message to these people that this is unacceptable and you will pay with your liberty."[22]

Enter Superior Court Judge Bruce A. Gaeta. Upon hearing of the plea bargaining between Delaney and the molester's attorney, Judge Gaeta rejected the proposed deal. Gaeta described the sexual encounters as "just something between two people that clicked beyond the student-teacher relationship."[23]

I suppose, then, that the molestation of a 13-year-old boy by a priest is just something that "clicks" between two people, too? That, of course, is the argument of leftists who no doubt are thrilled when their depraved premise finds legitimacy in the eyes of a trial judge—er, in the eyes of a lawyer with a robe on.

Judge Gaeta wasn't through, however. Revealing his own sick view of the appropriateness of adults using children for sex, he proclaimed, "I don't really see the harm that was done and certainly society doesn't need to be worried." He added, "Maybe it was a way for him, once this happened, to satisfy his sexual needs."[24]

If you wondered how the dangerous nonsense I described for you in chapter 7 affects regular people's lives, and destroys the lives of children, here you have it. Gaeta, representative of the Left's success in classifying children as sexual beings with "sexual needs," then sentenced Diehl-Moore to five years' *probation.*

As we've seen, there are still decent people who are rightly furious with this kind of outrage. In this case, county prosecutor John L. Molinelli appealed the sentence, and a New Jersey assemblywoman, Republican Rose Heck, called for Judge Gaeta's enforced retirement. "Does that mean that he believes there should be no law against adults having sex with minors?" Heck asked. "If so, I would suggest it is time for this judge to be removed from the bench."[25]

> Unfortunately, what many people forget is that judges are just lawyers in robes. They can be as jaded, as warped, as morally bankrupt as their shark brethren swimming beneath them in the courtroom.

Heck's advocacy for fairness and decency, in reminding people that sexual assault against a boy should not be treated any differently in court from sexual assault against a girl, was met with derision by—you guessed it—a criminal defense attorney. "These politicians ought to stay the hell out of our judiciary," spewed Robert Galantucci. "When they make these outrageous political statements, it shows they have no understanding of what our constitutional system provides."[26]

Welcome to our Looking-Glass world, where advocacy for the safety of children and for fairness in a courtroom is considered the "outrageous" statement. Perhaps it's not clear to Mr. Galantucci, but Representative Heck, like most everyone else, *is* getting a clear view of what the system is providing these days—and we don't like it very much. Legitimizing the sexual abuse of children and freeing child molesters is not something we will willingly put up with.

The battle in New Jersey provides the best microcosm yet of the monumental struggle we face. On one hand, we have lawyers furthering the shameful destruction of children's lives for the pleasure of sick deviants. On the other hand, we have a lawyer and a politician fighting it. Only one side can win.

In this case, the good guys have at least won a round. Prosecutor Molinelli succeeded in his appeal of Gaeta's shocking sentencing decision. A higher court agreed that jail time was indeed appropriate and sentenced Diehl-Moore to three years.[27]

In the meantime, however, the leftist agenda of brainwashing us all into sacrificing the nation's children continues. And Judge Gaeta still sits on the bench, handing down decisions. Even if he is eventually removed, the battle will not be over. Make no mistake here—Gaeta isn't some freak who slipped through. There are plenty more like him, no doubt to the delight of leftists everywhere.

Those Damn Flirty 11-Year-Olds

In August of 2000, an 11-year-old girl leaving a baseball game at Philadelphia's Veterans Stadium lost sight of her aunt. Intercepted by three 16-year-old boys offering help, she was taken to a trash enclosure and gang-raped.[28]

The three were arrested and put on trial before Family Court Judge Abram Frank Reynolds. Judge Reynolds enraged many in the community with comments that further victimized the little girl by attempting to pass some of the blame to her. At one point during the trial he opined, "She wanted their attention"[29] as if that mitigated the horror of the boys' crime! That wasn't enough for Judge Reynolds, however. He also characterized the child as "flirty and flighty."

One of the three was acquitted; the other two, John Scaruzzi and Michael Ibbetson, were convicted. However, citing the need for "mercy," for the rapists, Reynolds sentenced these predators to juvenile "treatment" centers, not jail, and for just a few months. And not before Christmas, of course. The judge allowed these animals to spend the holiday at home before beginning their sentence.

Judge Reynolds doesn't seem to understand that common decency in the normal world requires showing mercy to the victim, not the gang-rapists.

The prosecutor did oppose Reynolds's extraordinary decision. "The reason I objected is the serious nature of the charges and what I thought was the strength of the case I had," Assistant District Attorney Dan McGravey said. "I thought they might be a threat to the community."[30]

Uh, ding-ding-ding goes that trolley.

In an editorial on the case, the *Philadelphia Daily News* got it right:

> Try to imagine how a 5 foot 2, 60-pound, underdeveloped child could be so "flighty and flirty" that a 6 foot 1, 180-pound man couldn't resist her.
>
> For the rest of her life, this child may carry some unwarranted guilt as if her actions justified theirs. If she does, it will be in large part because Judge Reynolds seemed to care less about her healing than he did about theirs.[31]

While we wade through Judge Reynolds's indecency, there are heroes to this story. Ministers and others in the community held press conferences. Activists gathered 3,000 signatures and filed a complaint against the judge with the Pennsylvania Judicial Conduct Board, asking that Reynolds not be assigned to future sexual assault cases.[32]

The results of the Judicial Conduct Board's investigation, unfortunately, were predictable in a system where moral relativism has burrowed deeply. The board not only concluded that Reynolds handled the case properly but added, "The record was thoroughly reviewed for any type of derogatory comment regarding the young victim and nothing of the sort was found."

You must keep in mind, every new action, every new case, every new immoral stand taken by a judge and accepted by our society *resets the standard.* Consequently, referring to an 11-year-old gang-rape victim as "flirty and flighty" is no longer considered derogatory.

"We just wanted justice, and I think the judicial conduct here is just terrible," said organizer Sacaree Rhodes. She added that the victim's family was angered by the board's findings. "He treated the victim like she was responsible for what took place," Rhodes said.[33]

In a letter justifying the findings, the chairman of the Judicial Conduct Board, John W. Morris, said, "Pleasing everyone is impossible and, as I now consider it, the best judges are those who do not strive to please anyone, but who simply call each case to the best of his or her ability."

That's interesting. Shouldn't some modicum of morality, decency, fairness, and concern for the victim be a part of that "best ability"? Messrs. Morris and Reynolds should be aware that we as a society also have standards. It says volumes when a judicial conduct board considers comments like Reynolds's appropriate. And we should say in volumes that they are not.

It was remarked at the time that Reynolds is black, as was the victim. The two convicted rapists are white. Some in the black community decried what they saw as racism on Reynolds's part. While some reverse racism may have played a role, what this case really demonstrates is that moral ruin is an equal-opportunity affliction.

Ultimately, Reynolds kept Scaruzzi in residential sex-offender treatment for nearly seven months, followed by six months of house arrest. Accomplice Ibbetson spent nearly a year in a separate residential treatment facility.[34] Both are now free. According to reports, the victim still has nightmares and is frightened by the fact that her tormentors have been released.[35]

And Judge Reynolds? Three days after the Judicial Conduct Board released its report, he was promoted to Supervising Judge.

Smelling the Coffee

Judge Durke G. Thompson gives Judge Reynolds a run for his money when it comes to outrageous decisions. A judge in Montgomery County, Maryland, Thompson has made a series of decisions and comments that have infuriated decent people.

In one instance, during the sentencing hearing for a man convicted of molesting an 11-year-old girl, Thompson told the girl and her family that "it takes two to tango." Thompson later said the comment was taken out of context,[36] but exactly what context could excuse the use of that phrase when addressing the family of a victim of molestation? Thompson eventually apologized, and in an interview with the *Washington Post* he said he regretted not using the phrase "wake up and smell the coffee" instead, to chastise the victim's family.[37]

In another case where Thompson presided, a man pled guilty to molesting his 15-year-old stepdaughter. Sidney R. Richardson had actually begun sexually abusing the girl when she was just 9 years old. At that time, he was convicted, spent some time in jail, and was ordered not to return to the home where his stepdaughter lived.

At 15 the same girl was pregnant—by Richardson. How did this happen? Judge Thompson, over the objections of the prosecutor, the probation officer, and Richardson's therapist, had allowed him back into the home.[38]

When interviewed about the case, Thompson whined to the *Washington Post*'s Phuong Ly, "I'm not responsible for people committing crimes. . . . What do you want me to say, that I'm omniscient and I know what's going to happen in every situation? People violate probation all the time."[39]

What planet has Thompson been living on? It doesn't take psychic powers to know that child molesters don't stop. But it does take an enormous moral void to ignore that reality.

It's ironic when a judge, the person who is supposed to represent and attempt to enforce society's rules about personal responsibility, refuses to recognize or take responsibility for his own actions. At this point, though, none of us should be surprised.

A *Washington Post* editorial put it best:

> Judge Thompson wants Mr. Richardson held responsible for his conduct, and he should be. But the judge had a responsibility too, to protect a child who had no other recourse, and if the facts alleged in this case are true, he failed miserably.[40]

Perhaps it is Judge Thompson who should "wake up and smell the coffee."

Not Brain Surgery

In 2002 the Washington State Supreme Court unanimously overturned the convictions of two men who had been charged under the state's voyeurism law. The jurists ruled that photographing or filming up a girl's or woman's skirt without her permission *is not against the law.*[41]

The men had been arrested in separate incidents. Sean Glas was arrested for taking photographs up women's skirts at a mall in Union Gap, near Yakima, and Richard Sorrells was nabbed for doing the same thing with a video camera at the Bite of Seattle community festival. Several witnesses at that event told police they also saw Sorrells videotaping under the dresses of *little girls.* A woman at the festival, her boyfriend, and several others chased Sorrells down and handed him over to the police.

Glas admitted he was taking the photographs to sell to Internet pornography "fetish" sites, which post such images and sell them for a fee. Sorrells claimed the photos he took were for "private use."[42] The police later examined Sorrells's camera and found there images taken up women's as well as girls' skirts—which in a normal world would make him guilty of child pornography, too.

In one of the more remarkable comments about what our standards are these days, Sorrells was most disturbed by the fact that one of the women at the festival thought he was trying to steal something from her purse. With righteous indignation he told police, "I did not have my hand in her purse. I was holding my camera so I could videotape up her dress. . . . I'm not a thief—I'm a Peeping Tom."[43]

I see. He's not a pickpocket. He's just a pervert. Whew!

A Flaw in the Judges

Police Captain Neil Low, who handles voyeurism cases in Seattle, said something needs to be done, but he missed the point. "I'm still outraged but not at the judges," he said when the State Supreme Court overturned the convictions. "I'm outraged that there's a flaw in the system we need to fix."[44]

Why *not* be outraged at the judges? What is the system but people? In fact, this decision precisely revealed a flaw in the people interpreting the law. And yet Low is not alone in his reluctance to hold them responsible. We have been conditioned to believe that somehow jurists, especially at a Supreme Court level, are like the pope in one special way—they're all infallible. It is the one branch of our government that has been presented as untouchable.

Regular people are told they don't have the right to criticize a ruling such as this, and yet it provides the perfect opportunity to remind ourselves that judges are just people—again, just lawyers in robes. I contend we have a duty to watch, and listen, and complain and critique and demand change when judges' decisions conflict with our sense of what's right and decent. This is one of those instances.

The grounds on which the two miscreants, Glas and Sorrells, were initially convicted were pretty clear. The voyeurism law states, in part, that people should "be safe from hostile intrusion or surveillance."[45] The jurors in these perverts' trials had no problem convicting them, but the jurists on the Washington State Supreme Court just couldn't determine right from wrong.

The court found—get this—that the law doesn't apply to filming people in a public place, even if it's *underneath their clothes.* "It is the physical location of the person that is ultimately at issue, not the part of the person's body,"[46] Judge Bobbe Bridge wrote. Really? What part of "safe from hostile intrusion or surveillance" doesn't Judge Bridge understand? Actually, the very act of wearing clothes implies some expectation of privacy when it comes to our bodies.

The judges' primary reasoning was that since the locations where these men were photographing—a mall and a festival— were public places, the law doesn't apply. Somehow, these judges were unable to grasp the concept, as two juries did, that under your clothing is still a private place regardless of your physical location.

Make no mistake here—I believe the morality it takes to interpret a voyeurism law correctly was missing in these judges. It's safe to say that the people who drafted the voyeurism law did not intend for it to be interpreted so narrowly. But that's what happens when standards, and the ability to make judgments based on decency, become clouded or are erased completely.

The outrageousness of this case isn't limited to the Washington State Supreme Court. One of the more revolting things I found when researching this story on the Internet was the way ABC News covered it. On ABCnews.com, the network's Web site for its news programming, the page for the morning show *Good Morning America* included the segment itself as it aired on the program.[47]

Does the teaser picture focus on the face of the victim ABC interviewed? No. Does it show the reporter walking with the victim? No. For the Real Player link to the video segment, ABC used what appears to be one of the "upskirt" shots. In fact, ABC appears to have used photography of unknowing victims throughout the story.[48] In other words, while the story focused on a victim, ABC apparently was giving airtime to material that breached the privacy of women in an extraordinary way. Now images originally destined for a Web site for perverts were being presented to the American people as a whole. And as with the promo for Paula Zahn that I discussed in chapter 8, this decision wasn't made by a couple of interns. Producers at ABC News, in this instance, decided that pandering to pornographic fetishists would be a good idea.

Legislating Every Move

One problem with not being able to trust judges to interpret the law as it was meant to be interpreted—with some decency and common sense—is that legislators start scrambling to write new laws specifically addressing the details of specific outrageous decisions. In this case, the Democratic state senator from Marysville, Washington, Jeri Costa, reacted by drafting a bill that would make it illegal to secretly film someone "under or through the clothing."[49]

You don't say! As you know by now, I'm a law-and-order type of gal, but I don't like the idea of being swamped with specific laws to deal with every single case, as opposed to making sure we have jurists who are good and decent people, and who can come to reasonable judgments. I like the idea that law has to be interpreted. This allows judges and juries to consider the totality of a case and apply justice accordingly. Absolutely ridiculous decisions, like the ones just discussed, completely undermine the value of such discretion.

> Getting people on the bench who are not morally confused or afraid to make judgments based in decency *is* the solution.

When we have such a void in the ability of jurists to determine right from wrong, the inevitable fallout is a reduction in the discretion of judges. That is *not* the solution. Getting people on the bench who are not morally confused or afraid to make judgments based in decency *is* the solution.

By the way, Sean Glas, one of our budding photographers who, according to the Washington State Supreme Court, committed no crime, is now serving a four-year sentence for statutory rape.[50] Surprise.

The Benefits of Being Depraved

While the importance of protecting innocent people from criminals cannot be overstated, there is another moral debacle in the justice system that is costing decent people their lives. Literally.

In January 2002 a California prison inmate received a new heart in a transplant operation that eventually cost the taxpayers nearly $1 million.[51] As a taxpayer, I am bothered by this, but as a citizen, I am enraged. Has our politically correct society gone so far as to guarantee convicts a level of health care superior to what the average law-abiding Joe can afford? The infuriating answer in our topsy-turvy world is yes.

Court decisions about health care for prisoners range from the reasonable to the absurd. Of course, the reasonable was over a quarter of a century ago. In 1976 the U.S. Supreme Court ruled that denying decent medical care to prisoners violates the constitutional prohibition against cruel and unusual punishment. Yes, I hope we can all agree that giving inmates "decent" medical care is more than appropriate.

Then in 1995, decades into the dramatic twisting of our culture by leftist ideology, a federal court ordered California to give a kidney transplant to an inmate whose request for one had been denied. That case set the precedent for the 2002 heart transplant.

Stephen Green, assistant secretary of California's Youth and Adult Correctional Agency, confirmed to Mitchell Landsburg of the *Los Angeles Times* that his agency believed the 1995 decision left them no choice but to give the prisoner the new heart. "This is all we can do under the law. . . . We must follow the court's mandate, and that's what we're doing."[52]

While the U.S. Supreme Court has effectively created a right to high-end health care for prisoners, the irony is that there is no equivalent right for law-abiding citizens. In fact, because of the absurd interpretation in 1995 that translated the 1976 Court's "decent" health care into extraordinary measures, you are more likely to get top-quality health care if you go out and rob a bank right now. Forget about working hard, respecting the law, supporting your family, raising your kids. Our justice system has determined that you—the decent, law-abiding citizen—count for less than a thief, rapist, or murderer.

In this instance, while state officials would not release the name of the prisoner who received the heart transplant, the *New York Times* reported that they did give some details about him. He was 31 and was serving his second prison term for robberies in Los Angeles. He had been paroled from his first term in 1996, and then was convicted of a second robbery and given a 14-year term in March 1997.[53]

By definition, robbery is not some quiet kind of pilfering. It includes the use or threat of physical force. So our transplant recipient was a man who risked other people's safety, and perhaps their lives, in order to take what was not his. He was a thug, and he relinquished his rights as a normal citizen when he decided on a life of crime.

While there have been numerous kidney and liver transplants for prisoners since 1976, this is believed to be the first heart transplant. And, ever since it was reported, doctors and other Big Thinkers from the medical community have been engaged in a debate about the ethics involved. The fact that there even has to be a debate is mind-boggling.

The Importance of Social Worth

One doctor writing in favor of transplants for prisoners argued that the U.S. Supreme Court "ruled in 1976 that the state could not bar prisoners from access to organ transplants and other support services without violating these Eighth Amendment rights."[54]

Now, just a minute. How did "decent" care translate into "access to organ transplants"? Transplants were hardly the focus of a decision made in 1976. The reality is that organ transplants did not become common until 1983 with the introduction of the immunosuppressant drug cyclosporine, the first medication to effectively block the body's effort to reject transplanted tissues.[55] Up until then transplants were considered highly experimental and certainly not a regular part of decent standards of care.

Now transplant surgery is readily available, but suitable organs still are not. There are more than 80,000 people on the waiting list for an organ transplant in the United States. Nearly 6,000 of them will die this year before a transplant becomes available.[56] That translates to 16 people dying *every day* in this country because they didn't get the organ they needed.

So, when the courts decide that murderers, rapists, and others who maliciously break our social contract deserve health care that most working Americans can't afford, they are condemning good people to death. In fact, according to the United Network for Organ Sharing, as quoted by the *Los Angeles Times*'s Landsburg, the day after our two-time

> When the courts decide that murderers, rapists, and others who maliciously break our social contract deserve health care that most working Americans can't afford, they are condemning good people to death.

felon received his new heart, there were 4,119 patients on the waiting list for a donor heart.[57]

Bizarrely, some have argued that *not* giving prisoners this type of extraordinary health care is somehow unethical. A Dr. David L. Perry declared in an opinion piece, "It would be morally repugnant for society to allocate organs based on estimates of persons' 'social worth.'"[58]

No it's not! The moral repugnancy lies in the fact that a decent person, who was not a robber, who followed the rules all his or her life, more than likely died because Two-Time Felon Prisoner Scum won the lottery by being a thug. That is a moral injustice like no other.

Not to a Dr. John Fung, who chimed in about the issue on ABCnews.com. "Some in the public have advanced the simplistic theory," opines Dr. Fung, "that prisoners are, on the whole, less deserving and contribute less to society than upstanding members of the community, and should therefore be passed over in allocating scarce organs."[59]

Dr. Fung, some theories are simple *and* right. Of course, Dr. Fung means to be derogatory in his reference, but the reality is that prisoners *do* contribute less to society (the fact that I even have to address this is nutty) and *are* less deserving of extraordinary health-care measures. They gave up some of their rights when they violated the rights of others. It's as simple as that.

Suddenly Clueless Doctors

If one or two doctors denied the importance of social worth, that would be disappointing. When an official publication of the American Medical Association (AMA) denies it, the unavoidable inference is that some of our best minds are clueless on issues of morality. Consider this comment from an Ethics Forum published by the AMA:

> The suggestion that prisoners should be excluded from consideration for transplantation is generally rooted in some notion of "social worth." This view is problematic for several reasons . . . physicians and other transplant

professionals have no special expertise in determining social worth.[60]

Really? Since when did physicians and transplant professionals become intellectual midgets? The problem here is that our society has to reconcile its understandings with court decisions that are simply nutty and morally void, and which lead to the conclusion that there's no real way to determine social worth.

Well, yes, there is.

Take that list of people who are waiting for organ transplants. Suppose a robber and rapist is now at the top of the list. Let's say he has spent half his adult life in prison. His victim is scarred for life, physically and mentally. Second on the list is a husband and father of two who works for a living, is a decent man, and is upset when he gets so much as a traffic ticket.

Gee, I wonder if a physician or other "transplant professional" (or, for that matter, a federal judge) could figure out which person has more social worth. I certainly can. You can, too. All of us should have the moral courage to admit that some people have more social worth than others. I'm talking about the most basic of considerations here. To allocate a rare organ to a prisoner instead of to someone who has followed society's rules is simply immoral and in my opinion criminal.

Ironically, with all this debate about not creating a hierarchy of worth, the court decision did exactly that. By making prisoners eligible to receive organ transplants at our expense, they automatically made the prisoners more socially worthy! Money is a big part of whether or not one gets a transplant. A person usually has to ante up $150,000 just to get on the list. With taxpayers being the guarantor for a prisoner, he will automatically be considered. You and I won't.

Renee C. Fox, a bioethicist at the University of Pennsylvania, terms the moral standing of a potential transplant recipient "ideally irrelevant." She told Landsburg that barring inmates from receiving heart transplants would create ethical problems. "Should merit be considered a criteria?" Fox asked. "Should organs go to people who are 'good,' who have lived good lives?"[61]

Here's a simple answer for the bioethicist: Yes.

Epilogue

In 1994 I was in my fourth year as president of the Los Angeles chapter of NOW. I had also served on the National NOW Board of Directors. It was a year I remember, for several reasons. It was the year O. J. Simpson killed Nicole Brown Simpson and her friend Ron Goldman, and the year my town was hit by the devastating Northridge earthquake. It was also the year Ronald Reagan announced to the nation that he had Alzheimer's.

I remember this especially not because I was saddened, but because I joined, albeit disingenuously, in the glee my friends and other feminist leaders expressed at the news that the former president had been struck with the devastating disease. He deserved it, we told ourselves. You see, he was one of the Great Oppressors. Among other things, he had blocked federal funding for fetal tissue research. We found that particularly ironic because there was a possibility that such research could help scientists find a cure for diseases like Alzheimer's.

Ronald Reagan was hated, and still is, in the feminist-establishment circles in which I grew up. That milieu subsists on enemies and hatred. I took my cues from the women around me, women I admired. They were strong and confident, and they *knew*. They knew who was out to get us. They knew who was determined to throw us back into the Dark Ages. They knew Reagan was evil.

I tell you this not as an excuse for my past actions but as a further illustration of what I've been discussing throughout this book—the way malignant narcissism is spread. You see, the seed of my politics, the politics I espouse now, were already manifested in my voting for President Reagan 10 years earlier. I liked him, and I believed he had the best interests of Americans in mind. During my involvement with NOW, however, what took over was my need to be accepted, the romanticization of my "victimhood," and the power I could achieve by following the models of the women at the top. Those women were happy that Reagan was sick, so I would be, too.

The conditioning of the Left Elite works so well partly because the people attracted to that camp are looking for family, they are looking to belong; consequently people like that—people like me—are easy pickings. My emptiness compelled me to cheer when a decent man who followed his principles was struck down by an unforgiving assailant. Alzheimer's had done what many feminist leaders fantasized about doing themselves, if only they could get away with it.

Today, I am still pro-choice, and I still support fetal tissue research. But I now realize that those who disagree with me also have good points. I hope they reflect on their position as often as I do on mine, because both camps are on the razor's edge. I have made my commitment to women and reproductive freedom, while my compatriots on the other side of the fence, mostly because of their religious faith, have made a pact with what they call "the unborn."

We will have to agree to disagree, but only now do I consider those on that other side decent people—as decent as I, but with a different focus. Ronald Reagan is one of those decent people, but in all the feminist establishment's mirth about his illness, never did they consider, never *would* they consider, the humanity of the man. Some may have made sympathetic public comments, but, like Madelyn Toogood, the woman who beat her little girl in a parking lot, they were simply looking around to make sure no one was watching before they returned to privately declaring that Reagan deserved to suffer.

Of course, this inhumanity wasn't confined to the feminist community—it was also quite the rage among the Gay Elite, and frankly even more so. There is no one as unforgiving as a queen scorned! AIDS took hold during Reagan's presidency, and, to say the least, gay activists were not happy that President Reagan didn't do what they thought best about the epidemic. As I also participated in one way and another in the Gay Elite, I am ashamed to say there was only a little tickle in the back of my mind that it was rather hypocritical for us to be condemning someone for not being compassionate enough.

By now, you may not be surprised to learn that in certain gay and feminist circles, bottles of champagne wait in refrigerators to be opened when President Reagan dies. I am ashamed that I contributed to this mentality, which has survived to this day, infecting young people with hate for a man they never even knew. They trust the older generations—including people of my age—to be telling them the truth about monsters in the closet, the Abominable Snowman, and how Ronald Reagan deserves to die a slow and awful death.

As I think about all of this, it is difficult not to cry. How is it that only now, at the age of 40, am I fully realizing how morally vacuous was my past—cloaked, of course, in the nobility of social activism and postmodern feminism? At that time, it seemed that wanting the best for women meant becoming callous and unkind toward a man who disagreed with us. Or so I was taught.

When Lives Collide

I write this on the night Nancy Reagan appeared on *60 Minutes II*. Mike Wallace interviewed her about the former president, their marriage, and their history. Watching the show, I remembered why I liked Reagan so much—old footage of an early interview with Wallace, at the time Reagan announced his first candidacy in 1976 (I was 14), deeply moved me and reminded me what great leadership was to come. Mrs. Reagan's humanity also reminded me how lacking in decency I had been. I know I'm basically a good person, but it was so easy for me to be otherwise in an environment that rewarded the unkind and the morally bankrupt. That is what I must remember, and what we all must fight to stop—the culture the Left Elite dream of, one that encourages and rewards the worst in us.

During the interview, Mrs. Reagan disclosed that she's not sure her husband recognizes her anymore. Long ago he had stopped recognizing his children, but he always knew her. Now, it seems, he doesn't. There was a deep sadness in the woman's face. It was the "long goodbye," as she called it. The Reagans, like so many other people, had probably approached their Golden Years trusting, assuming, that memories would be shared, and laughed and cried about. For Nancy Reagan that doesn't exist. She hasn't said goodbye to her husband because "he's still here," but the welling of tears in her eyes revealed a wounded, sad woman. I found it heartbreaking to see, as would any decent person of any political persuasion.

Part of my life, however, is still reflective of what I call my "old" life—my years of leadership in the feminist establishment and involvement in the gay-rights movement. This night, those two lives collided. As I cried after the interview because of the sadness of it and my own guilt and shame, I checked my phone messages. There was one from a gay male friend, whom I see infrequently these days but with whom I share some fun and important activist memories. He had been watching the same interview, but he was cheering. "Woo hoo! It looks like we might be opening up that champagne sooner than later! I hope you were watching the Dragon Lady on *60 Minutes* tonight. I suppose with Alzheimer's, he's not suffering anymore, but it sure looks like she is! There is a God after all."

I had never thought of my friend as an indecent person, just as I never thought of myself as one. But he really hates those two people and wishes them awful things. He believes he's in the right and they're wrong. He also believes that the questions that divide them are moral issues about life and death. The difference, however, is that I think it's safe to say neither Nancy nor Ronald Reagan ever had a bottle of champagne in the fridge waiting for a gay man or a feminist to die. The Reagans, I'll bet, don't hoot and holler at someone else's pain.

Mrs. Reagan's humanity illustrated by counterpoint the soullessness of the Left. We, the Feminist and Gay Elites, inflicted on society narcissists' biggest crime of all: We couldn't see beyond our own interests and desires. We became indecent in defending our principles.

Because Americans are compassionate and committed to individual liberty, we remain a pro-choice country. And because Ronald Reagan was in the White House at a critical time, the United States is great enough and strong enough to export democracy, freedom, and equality around the world, making untold millions of women in other countries safer and more powerful in their own lives.

Oh, sure, I'll always be on the front line when it comes to abortion rights. I'll probably meet some of you on the other side of that line, but I have learned a great lesson. The challenge for us is to be able to be true to our principles, while recognizing the humanity of those who disagree with us.

Then and now the Left Elite cannot comprehend how good, thoughtful people can come to critically different conclusions about serious social issues. Not *every* issue, of course: Decent people understand, as an example, that flying airplanes into buildings to kill unsuspecting people is evil, and not debatable on a moral scale. That is a given. There is a debate, however, among decent people about other issues, like fetal tissue research. I was heartened to learn that Mrs. Reagan, no doubt impelled by her personal experience, has quietly begun to lobby for such research, recognizing that perhaps it can eradicate this scourge that causes the slow, progressive disappearance of past and self.

Although it is too late for her husband, Mrs. Reagan has opted to try to make things better for others, because it is the right thing to do. Because she's decent.

Like her, we must be willing to change and grow. To become better people. While I don't hold out any hope for the damaged Left Elite I've exposed for you in this book, I know that we as *individuals* can overcome and reject what the Left demands of us—the abandonment of right and wrong, the banishment of decency and integrity, the rejection of what the Reagans, both of them, represent.

We can instead do our best to live honest lives, replete with the discomfort of shame, the difficulties of personal responsibility, and the joy, the genuine happiness, that only right and good can bring. We will, in the end, have the reward of being better people.

Notes

Chapter 1

1. Fred Kaplan, "Two Suspects Charged in N.Y. Teacher Death . . . ," *Boston Globe* (June 8, 1997), A25.

2. John Sullivan, "Last Moments of Levin Are Described by a Suspect," *New York Times* (June 27, 1997), Metropolitan Desk.

3. David Rohde, "Suspect Says Second Man Killed Teacher," *New York Times* (October 20, 1998), Metropolitan Desk.

4. "Two Suspects Arraigned in Levin Slaying," *Washington Post* (June 9, 1997), final ed., A9.

5. Laura Italiano, "Gory Details, Tears, as Levin Slay Trial Opens," *New York Post* (October 20, 1998).

6. David Rohde, "Jurors Faulted Police Work in Murder Case of a Teacher," *New York Times* (February 13, 1999).

7. New York Penal Code § 125.27.

8. Laura Italiano, "Acquittal Horrifies Jon Levin's Mother," *New York Post* (February 18, 1999).

9. Laura Italiano, Dereh Gregorian, and Neal Graves, "Levin Slay-Suspect's Booze and Pot Spree Sets Him Free," *New York Post* (February 12, 1999).

10. Italiano, "Acquittal."

11. For the most detailed and factual information about the murder of Daniel Faulkner, go to http://www.danielfaulkner.com.

12. Steve Lopez, "Wrong Guy, Good Cause," *Time* (July 31, 2000).

13. Marc Kaufman, "Abu-Jamal Said He Shot Officer, Two Tell Trial," *Philadelphia Inquirer* (June 25, 1982).

14. Lopez.

15. Francis X. Clines, "'81 Gunshots Still Reverberate in Philadelphia," *New York Times* (December 20, 2001).

16. Francis X. Clines, "The Nation: Killer or Victim? The Poster Boy for and Against the Death Penalty," *New York Times* (May 21, 2000).

17. Marc Kaufman, "Abu-Jamal, Sentenced to Die, Threatens the Judge," *Philadelphia Inquirer* (May 26, 1983).

18. Ibid.

19. Clines, "The Nation: Killer or Victim?"

20. "Philly and L.A. Cops Ready Battle Plans," *New York Post* (July 24, 2000).

21. Clines, "The Nation: Killer or Victim?"

22. Ibid.

23. Clines, "'81 Gunshots."

24. Ibid.

25. Don Terry, "The Democrats: 3,500 Rally to Condemn Death Penalty," *New York Times* (August 14, 2000).

26. Matt Smith, "Public Enema #2," *San Francisco Weekly* (February 23, 2000).

27. Ibid.

28. Ibid.

29. For complete discussions of malignant narcissism and its impact on society, see Otto F. Kernberg, M.D., "Aggression and Transference in Severe Personality Disorders," *Psychiatric Times,* vol. XII, no. 2 (2002), also available at http://www.psychiatrictimes.com/p950216.html, and M. Scott Peck, *People of the Lie: The Hope for Healing Human Evil* (New York: Simon & Schuster, 1997).

30. Dr. Sam Vaknin, *Malignant Self Love: Narcissism Revisited* (Prague: Narcissus Publication, 2001), 13.

31. Ibid., 10.

32. Aubrey Immelman, "Malignant Leadership," Unit for the Study of Personality in Politics (September 17, 2001), available at http://www.csbsju.edu/uspp/Research/Malignant Leadership.html.

33. Susan Bridle, "The Seeds of the Self: An Interview with Otto Kernberg," *What Is Enlightenment?*, issue 17, available at http://www.wie.org/j17/kern.asp. This is an outstanding discussion of spiritual and psychological issues—a must-read.

34. Aubrey Immelman, "Inside the Mind of Milosevic," Unit for the Study of Personality in Politics (May 21, 1999), available at http://www.csbsju.edu/uspp/Milosevic/Milosevic.html.

35. Dr. Judith Herman, *Trauma and Recovery: Aftermath of Violence—From Domestic Abuse to Political Terror.* (New York: Basic Books, 1997), 214.

36. Ibid., 28–29.

37. Ibid., 217.

38. Ibid., 29.

39. Immelman, "Malignant Leadership."

40. Theodore Millon, *Disorders of Personality: DSM IV and Beyond* (New York: Wiley-Interscience, 1995), 178. Also see http://www.csbsju.edu/uspp/Research/MalignantLeadership.html.

41. Peck, 297.

42. I discussed groupthink at length in *The New Thought Police* (Roseville, Calif.: Prima), 49–52.

43. Liza Mundy, "A World of Their Own," *Washington Post* (March 31, 2002).

44. Ibid.

45. Ibid.

46. Lloyd Grove, "The Reliable Source," *Washington Post* (April 11, 2002).

47. Ibid.

48. Ibid.

49. William Safire, "Moral Clarity," *New York Times* (May 12, 2002).

Chapter 2

1. Edward Rothstein, "Iconoclasm and Sacrilege," *New York Times* (June 9, 2001).

2. Cintra Wilson, "Giuliani's Sensation," Salon.com (September 29, 1999), available at http://www.salon.com/people/col/cintra/1999/09/29/rudy.

3. Ibid.

4. Rothstein.

5. C. S. Lewis, *Mere Christianity* (New York: HarperSanFrancisco, 2001), 77.

6. Ibid., 78.

7. Ibid., 79.

8. Ibid.

9. Bill Keller, "Is the Pope Catholic?," *New York Times* (May 4, 2002), Opinion Editorial Desk.

10. Ibid.

11. "ABC Catches Flak for Bleeping 'Jesus'," *Hollywood Reporter* (June 6, 2002).

12. Ibid.

13. Ibid.

14. "Actor Ordered to Jail," *New York Times* (December 10, 1997), National Desk.

15. Tamara Jones and John F. Harris, "Virginia's Election Blues: Voters See Little Response to Real Issues," *Washington Post* (October 30, 1993).

16. Mary McGrory, "Facing up to Failure," *Washington Post* (April 22, 1999), A3.

17. Jake Tapper, "Onward, Christian Soldiers," Salon.com (January 24, 2000), available at http://archive.salon.com/politics2000/feature/2000/01/24/evangelists.

18. "For the Record," *National Review* (February 21, 2000).

19. "Censoring Terrence McNally," *New York Times* (May 28, 1998), Editorial Desk.

20. John Leo, "Hello, Dung Lovers," *U.S. News & World Report* (October 11, 1999).

21. Martha Bayles, "The Perverse in the Popular," *Wilson Quarterly,* vol. 25, no. 3 (2001), 40. Available at: http://wwics.si

.edu/index.cfm?fuseaction=wq.index (a subscription is required to access archived files).

22. Margaret Carlson, "Whose Art Is It, Anyway?," *Time* (July 3, 1989).

23. Ariella Budick, "A Controversy Creates Undeserved Hype . . . ," *Los Angeles Times* (March 12, 2001), Commentary.

24. Pete Catapano, "Holy Art(!)," available at http://www.poppolitics.com/articles/2001-04-04-serrano.shtml.

25. "Christie's Auction 1999," available at http://www.thecityreview.com/f99ccon.html.

26. Caroline Krockow, "Art Market Watch," Artnet.com (October 27, 2000), available at http://www.artnet.com/Magazine/features/krockow/krockow10-27-00.asp.

27. Catapano.

28. http://www.connercontemporary.com/artists/serrano/bio.htm

29. T. R. Deckman, "Disputed Artist Explains Works," *Digital Collegian* (October 2, 1996), available at http://www.collegian.psu.edu/archive/1996_jan-dec/1996_oct/1996-10-02_the_daily_collegian/1996-10-02d01-001.htm.

30. Ibid.

31. Ibid.

32. Ibid.

33. http://www.catholicleague.org/2001report/summary2001.html

34. Ibid.

35. Ibid.

36. Vincent Carroll and David Shiflett, *Christianity on Trial* (San Francisco: Encounter Books, 2002), xii.

Chapter 3

1. Megan Hoyer, "Mother Adored Son, Friends Say . . . ," *Courier-Journal* (July 8, 2001).

2. Ibid.

3. U.S. National Institutes of Health, *Addison's Disease,* NIH Publication No. 90-3054 (Washington, D.C.: 1989). Also available at http://www.niddk.nih.gov/health/endo/pubs/addison/addison.htm.

4. "Tragedy Focuses Attention on Postpartum Psychosis," Statement of NOW President Kim Gandy, Press Release (September 6, 2001). Also available at http://www.now.org/press/04-01/09-06.html.

5. Evan Thomas, "Motherhood and Murder," *Newsweek* (July 2, 2001).

6. Announcement available at http://groups.yahoo.com/group/HoustonNOW/message/99. Joining the associated e-group will be necessary in order to view this link.

7. Anna Quindlen, "Playing God on No Sleep," *Newsweek* (July 2, 2001), 62.

8. Douglas Cruickshank, "The Andrea Yates Verdict Is Insane," Salon.com (March 14, 2002). Also available at http://www.salon.com/mwt/feature/2002/03/14/yates_verdict.

9. http://archive.salon.com/mwt/feature/2001/06/24/andrea_yates

10. Eleanor Clift, "Capitol Letter: A Problem with the Messenger," *Newsweek* (August 30, 2001), Web exclusive.

11. Tammy Bruce, *The New Thought Police* (Roseville, Calif.: Prima, 2001), 117–43.

12. Kris Axtman, "Texas Mom's New Defender: Feminists," *Christian Science Monitor* (August 31, 2001), available at - http://www.csmonitor.com/2001/0831/p1s3-usju.html.

13. Ibid.

14. "Births, Marriages, Divorces, and Deaths: Provisional Data for October 2001," *National Vital Statistics Reports* 50, no. 11 (2001), available at http://www.cdc.gov/nchs/data/nvsr/nvsr50/nvsr50_11.pdf. Adobe Acrobat reader is necessary to view the files.

15. Sally Satel, "The Newest Feminist Icon—A Killer Mom," *Wall Street Journal* (September 11, 2001), also available at http://www.sallysatelmd.com/html/a-wsj20.html.

16. "Yates Verdict Can Serve as a Warning to Prevent Future Tragedies," Statement of NOW President Kim Gandy, Press Release (March 13, 2002), available at http://www.now.org/press/03-02/03-13a.html.

17. Announcement available at http://groups.yahoo.com/group/HoustonNOW/message/244. Joining the associated e-group will be necessary in order to view this link.

18. http://www.now.org/history/purpos66.html

19. http://www.now.org/organiza/conferen/1998/vision98.html

20. John Stoltenberg, "Christianity, Feminism, and the Manhood Crisis," in *Standing on the Promises: The Promise Keepers and the Revival of Manhood,* ed. Dane S. Claussen (Cleveland, Ohio: The Pilgrim Press, 1999).

21. Ibid.

22. Patricia Ireland, "Beware of Feel-Good Male Supremacy," *Washington Post* (September 7, 1997), Opinion, C03. Also available at http://www.now.org/issues/right/promise/postoped.html.

23. Stoltenberg.

24. For the classic assessment of the harm pornography does to all our lives, read Andrea Dworkin, *Pornography: Men Possessing Women* (New York: EP Dutton, 1991), and John Stoltenberg, *What Makes Pornography "Sexy"?* (Minneapolis: Milkweed Editions, 1994).

25. http://www.now.org/eNews/june2001/060401bookstore.html

26. http://www.now.org/press/04-01/07-19.html

27. For the most extensive overview of the activities and intentions of the Falun Gong, visit http://www.gospelcom.net/apologeticsindex/f02.html

28. Ibid.

29. Julie Ching, "The Falun Gong: Religion and Political Implications," *American Asian Review* (January 1, 2001).

30. http://www.china-embassy.org/eng/7224.html and http://www.china-embassy.org/eng/24927.html

31. "Spiritual Society or Evil Cult?," *TIME Asia* (July 2, 2001).

32. For an extensive overview of the persecution of Christians in China, see http://www.persecution.org/humanrights/china.html.

33. http://www.time.com/time/asia/asia/magazine/1999/990510/interview1.html

34. Ibid.

35. The FBI's complete *Jonestown Summary* is now available online courtesy of the Freedom of Information Act. It can be accessed at http://foia.fbi.gov/jonestown.htm. Adobe Acrobat reader is necessary to view the files.

36. "Activists Vow to Defeat Federal Anti-Marriage Amendment," NOW Press Release (May 15, 2002).

37. Megan Peterson, "Marriage Movement Announces Itself," *National NOW Times* (fall 2000), available at http://www.now.org/nnt/fall-2000/family.html#marriage.

38. Ibid.

39. http://www.foxnews.com/story/0,2933,44908,00.html

40. Bruce, 123–4.

41. "Steinem Blames White Male Dominance for Church Sex Scandal, 9-11," *NewsMax Wires* (March 25, 2002), available at http://www.newsmax.com/archives/articles/2002/3/24/232249.shtml.

42. Ron Haynes, "Steinem: Inequality Breeds Violence," *Palm Beach Post* (March 23, 2002), 5B.

43. St. Cloud State University Women's Center, available at http://www.stcloudstate.edu/~womencnt/MentoMen/myth_facts.html. Also see the Montana Department of Justice's Web page on the issue of sexual assault at http://www.doj.state.mt.us/victims/talkinghelps.pdf. In fact, a simple search on any Web search engine with the words "rapists" and "married" will yield scores of documents confirming the fact that rapists and molesters are usually married or involved in a relationship at the time of their crimes.

44. Haynes.

45. Ibid.

Chapter 4

1. http://www.annelawrence.com/socrevisions.html

2. Ibid. Also, for more information about puberty in boys and girls, see the American Academy of Pediatrics at http://www.aap.org/family/puberty.htm.

3. http://www.annelawrence.com/socrevisions.html

4. http://www.annelawrence.com/presentations.html

5. http://www.espritgala.org

6. http://www.espritgala.org/be_a_little_sister.htm

7. http://www.espritgala.org/notes.htm

8. http://www.genderweb.org/~julie/medical/psych/dsmiv.html

9. David Horowitz, "The Plague Abettors," Salon.com (June 11, 2001), available at http://dir.salon.com/news/col/horo/2001/06/11/aids/index.html.

10. Ibid.

11. Marc Peyser, "A Deadly Dance," *Newsweek* (September 29, 1997).

12. Ibid.

13. Ibid.

14. Ibid.

15. Fred Dickey, "The Disaffection of Tammy Bruce," *Los Angeles Times Magazine* (June 2, 2002), 18.

16. Fleming, P.L., et al., *HIV Prevalence in the United States, 2000*. 9th Conference on Retroviruses and Opportunistic Infections, Seattle, Wash., Feb. 24-28, 2002. Abstract 11. Available at: http://63.126.3.84/2002/Abstract/13996.htm

    Also see: Centers for Disease Control and Prevention (CDC). *HIV and AIDS—United States, 1981-2001. MMWR* 2001;50:430-434. Available at: http://www.cdc.gov/mmwr/PDF/wk/mm5021.pdf

17. http://www.advocate.com/html/stories/869_70/869_70_bouley2.asp

18. http://www.advocate.com/html/poll/849_results.asp

19. Sara Russo, "Harvard Student Leader Urges Gays to Violate Red Cross Policy," http://www.academia.org/news/harvard_student.html.

20. http://www.gaymichiana.org/rainbowgazzette/October/national.html#3 -

21. http://www.cbsnews.com/stories/2000/07/12/eveningnews/main214626.shtml

22. http://www.advocate.com/html/poll/849_results.asp

23. Frank York, "Public Employees Teach Kids 'Gay' Sex," World-NetDaily.com, (May 9, 2000), available at http://www.worldnetdaily.com/news/article.asp?ARTICLE_ID=17490.

24. "Kids Get Graphic Instruction in Homosexual Sex," *Massachusetts News,* available at. http://www.massnews.com/past_issues/2000/5_May/maygsa.htm.

25. Rod Dreher, "Banned in Boston," *Weekly Standard,* July 3-10, 2000.

26. "Kids Get Graphic . . ."

27. Dreher.

28. http://www.glsen.org/templates/about/index.html?section=25

29. For a more extensive list of GLSEN's corporate sponsors, visit their Web site, http://www.glsen.org/templates/giving/record.html?section=23&record=423.

30. http://www.glsen.org/templates/news/record.html?section=13&record=1368

31. Brent Bozell, "Public TV's Elementary Gay Propaganda," NewsMax.com (June 9, 1999), available at http://www.newsmax.com/commentarchive.shtml?a=1999/6/9/024710.

32. Ibid.

33. For more information about the documentary and the filmmakers, visit their Web site, http://www.womedia.org/index.html.

34. http://www.womedia.org/our/elem.html

35. Bozell.

36. David Kupelian, "'Pedophile Priests' and Boy Scouts," World-NetDaily.com (May 8, 2002), available at http://www.worldnetdaily.com/news/article.asp?ARTICLE_ID=27539.

37. Ibid.

38. David M. Bresnahan, "Rape of a Sacred Trust," WorldNet Daily.com, available at http://www.worldnetdaily.com/news/article.asp?ARTICLE_ID=13210.

39. Kupelian.

40. "Health" Column, "Complications of Family Life," Advocate.com exclusive (June 27, 2002), available at http://www.advocate.com/html/goldstone/867_goldstone.asp.

41. Ibid.

42. Ibid.

43. Ibid.

44. Charles Ornstein, "Anti-Syphilis Campaign Toned Down," *Los Angeles Times* (June 26, 2002).

45. Ibid.

46. Ibid.

47. "HIV-Positive TV Muppet Worries U.S. Lawmakers," Reuters (July 15, 2002).

48. Peter Hawthorne, "Positively Sesame Street," *Time* (September 30, 2002), also available at http://www.time.com/time/europe/magazine/article/0,13005,901020930-353521,00.html.

49. "HIV-Positive TV."

50. Ibid.

51. http://www.info.usaid.gov

52. Elizabeth Jensen and Lisa Fackler, "HIV-Positive Muppet Not for U.S., PBS Says," *Los Angeles Times* (July 17, 2002), A12.

53. Ibid.

Chapter 5

1. *The Booker T. Washington Papers, Volume 1: The Autobiographical Writings*, extracts from *My Larger Education*

(1911), 430, available at http://stills.nap.edu/btw/Vol.1/html/ 430.html. (For complete Booker T. Washington papers, see http://stills.nap.edu/btw/Vol.1/html/index.html.)

2. Walter Williams, "Demoralizing Young Blacks," CNS Commentary (April 4, 2001), available at http://www.cnsnews .com/Commentary/Archive/200104/COM20010404a.html.

3. Ibid.

4. http://www.house.gov/waters/bio.htm

5. Michelle Malkin, "The Party of Maxine Waters," Capitalism Magazine.com (October 26, 2000), available at. http://www .capmag.com/article.asp?id=727.

6. Tammy Bruce, *The New Thought Police* (Roseville, Calif.: Prima, 2001), 102.

7. http://www.house.gov/waters/bio.htm

8. Bruce, 103.

9. Douglas P. Shuit, "Waters Focuses Her Rage at System Politics . . .," *Los Angeles Times,* May 10, 1992.

10. http://www.house.gov/waters/pr95ovs.htm

11. Ibid.

12. Bruce, 107–9.

13. David Horowitz, "No Reason to Glorify the Left's Legacy of Violence," Frontpagemag.com (March 26, 2000), available at http:// www.frontpagemag.com/Articles/Printable.asp?ID=1103.

14. Firestone, "60's Firebrand, Now Imam, Is Going on Trial in Killing," *New York Times* (January 6, 2002).

15. Brian Carnell, "H. Rap Brown Could Face Death Penalty for Atlanta Murder" (March 11, 2002), available at http://www .leftwatch.com/articles/2002/000031.html. See also David Firestone, "Ex-Black Militant Gets Life for Murdering Deputy," *New York Times* (March 14, 2002).

16. Ibid.

17. http://lightning.prohosting.com/~africa99/articles/jamil.shtml

18. http://www.adl.org/special_reports/farrakhan_own_words/on_ whites.asp

19. Ibid.

20. http://www.adl.org/special_reports/farrakhan_own_words/on_jews.asp

21. Ibid.

22. "Study Ties Hip-Hop, Rap Music to Drop in Test Scores," UPI (June 26, 2000).

23. Ibid.

24. Ibid.

25. Fahizah Alim, "A Presence Gone," *Sacramento Bee* (March 22, 1992), Metro Final, C1.

26. Ibid.

27. "Killer Enjoying Killer CD Career," NewsMax.com (November 23, 2000), http://www.newsmax.com/archives/articles/2000/11/23/104427.shtml.

28. David Barton, "Suspect's Rap Song Spoke of Killing," *Sacramento Bee* (May 14, 1992), Metro, D1.

29. X-Raided, "Shoot Cha in a Minute," *Psycho Active,* Black Market Records (1992).

30. Greg Braxton and Jerry Crowe, "Black Leaders Weighing In on Rap Debate," *Los Angeles Times* (June 14, 1995).

31. Ibid.

32. Ibid.

33. Barton.

34. Ibid.

35. Chris Macias, "Inmate's CD Sales Riles Victim's Family," *Sacramento Bee* (November 22, 2000), A1.

36. http://us.imdb.com/Name?Ice-T

37. Braxton and Crowe.

38. http://www.courttv.com/news/flashback/February.html

39. Chuck Phillips, "Man Named as Suspect in Death of Shakur Sues the Rapper's Estate . . ." *Los Angeles Times,* September 10, 1997.

40. http://www.nme.com/news/1224.htm

41. Chuck "Jigsaw" Creekmur, "Houston Rapper Sentenced to 45 Years in Jail" (June 3, 2002), available at http://www.bet.com/articles/0,,c3gb2931-3592,00.html.

42. Ibid.

43. Ibid.

44. Mark Allwood, "C-Murder Indicted for Murder" (March 5, 2002), available at http://www.bet.com/articles/0,,c3gb1961-2618,00.html.

45. http://www.bet.com/articles/1,,c2gb1996-2653-1,00.html# boardsAnchor

46. Augustin K. Sedgewick, "C-Murder Implicated in Killing," available at http://www.rollingstone.com/news/newsarticle .asp?nid=15275&cf=4423.

47. http://www.allmusic.com/cg/amg.dll?p=amg&sql=1C-MURDER

48. Sedgewick.

49. Allwood, "Snoop Dogg Crowned Stoner of the Year at 3rd Annual Stony Awards" (March 5, 2002), available at http:// www.bet.com/articles/0,,c3gb1964-2621,00.html.

50. Chuck "Jigsaw" Creekmur, "Rapper Charged with Murder After Human Flesh Found in Stomach," BET.com, (June 7, 2002), available at http://www.bet.com/articles/0,,c3gb2980-3641,00.html.

51. Jennifer Sinco Kelleher, "Aspiring Texas Rapper to Stand Trial in Death of L.A. Woman," *Los Angeles Times* (May 30, 2002).

52. Ibid.

53. Ibid.

54. John Pekkanen, "The Jesse Jackson Style, Militant but Nonviolent: Black Hope White Hope," *Life* (November 21, 1969), 69.

55. http://money.cnn.com/2000/01/10/deals/aol_warner/timeline.htm

56. http://www.pbs.org/wgbh/pages/frontline/shows/cool/tour/ tour3.html

57. Chuck Phillips, "Pop Eye: Billboard Backlash," *Los Angeles Times* (December 1, 1991). Also see Beth Kleid, "Morning Report," *Los Angeles Times* (December 22, 1993).

58. Chuck Phillips, "Gangsta Rappers' Arrests Spurs More Static over Genre," *Los Angeles Times* (November 7, 1993).

59. http://www.rainbowpush.org/founder

60. Ibid.

61. "3 Found Guilty of Defaming Prosecutor in Brawley case," CNN.com, (July 13, 1998), available at http://www.cnn.com/US/9807/13/brawley.verdict/.

62. Thomas J. Lueck, "Record Industry Is Attacked by a Top Star," *New York Times* (July 7, 2002).

63. "Mike Tyson: I'd Like to 'Stomp the Testicles' of Reporters' Children," NewsMax.com (May 4, 2002), available at http://www.newsmax.com/showinside.shtml?a=2002/5/4/92246.

64. Ibid.

65. Ibid.

66. Larry Elder, "Jesse and Black Illegitimacy," NewsMax.com (January 25, 2001), available at http://www.newsmax.com/commentmax/print.shtml?a=2001/1/25/212847.

67. Brookings Institution, "An Analysis of Out-of-Wedlock Births in the United States," Policy Brief #5 (August 1996), available at http://www.brook.edu/comm/policybriefs/pb05.htm.

68. National Center for Policy Analysis, "Out of Wedlock Births Soar," available at http://www.ncpa.org/pd/social/pd110999c.html.

69. Richard Johnson, Paula Froelich, and Chris Wilson, "Page Six," *New York Post* (August 10, 2002).

70. Janice Dickinson, *No Lifeguard on Duty: The Accidental Life of the World's First Supermodel* (New York: Regan Books/HarperCollins, 2002), 200–202.

71. John L. Mitchell, "Spousal Abuse Trial of Jim Brown Opens . . . ," *Los Angeles Times* (August 28, 1999).

72. Ibid.

73. http://www.amer-i-can.org

74. *Larry King Live,* Cable News Network (August 4, 1999).

75. Ibid.

76. Ibid.

77. Mike Freeman, "Jim Brown Is a Prisoner on His Own Terms," *New York Times* (March 28, 2002).

78. Jon Seraceno, "True Manhood and Perspective Elude Brown," *USA Today* (April 9, 2002), sidebar.

79. Monte Morin, "Judge Targets Men, Brown Motion Says . . . ," *Los Angeles Times* (October 22, 1999).

80. Ibid.

81. http://www.innsofcourt.org/contentviewer.asp?breadcrumb=6,9

82. Morin.

83. Seraceno.

84. Ibid.

85. Jamie Glazov, "bell hooks and the Politics of Hate," available at http://www.frontpagemag.com/Articles/ReadArticle.asp?ID=138.

86. Ibid.

87. Ibid.

88. Marc Levin, "hooks's Speech at Southwestern Divisive," *The Austin Review* (July 15, 2002), available at http://www.austin review.com/articles/2002_06/hooks.htm.

Chapter 6

1. Diana Jean Schemo, "A Nation Challenged: The Campuses . . . ," *New York Times* (November 25, 2001).

2. Jerry Martin and Anne D. Neal, *Defending Civilization: How Our Universities Are Failing America and What Can Be Done About It* (Washington, D.C.: American Council of Trustees and Alumni, 2002). For the complete report, go to http://www.goacta.org/Reports/defciv.pdf. Adobe Acrobat reader is necessary to view the files.

3. Ibid.
4. Ibid.
5. http://www.newsmax.com/showinside.shtml?a=2002/5/10/192731
6. Ibid.
7. Jay Ambrose, "Helping Students Fight Back," Scripps Howard News Service (September 10, 2002), also available at http://www.thefire.org/offsite/ambrose_091102.html. For more information about FIRE and their indispensable work, go to http://www.thefire.org.
8. Sun Staff, "Understanding and Remembrance," *Cornell Review* (September 11, 2002), also available at http://www.cornelldailysun.com/articles/5882.
9. Joseph J. Sabia, "How Not to Remember 9-11: Cornell's Day of Disgrace," *Cornell Review* (September 13, 2002).
10. Ibid.
11. http://www.frontpagemag.com/Content/read.asp?ID=10
12. Robert Stacy McCain, "Ivy Bias?" *Washington Times* (January 15, 2002).
13. Frank Luntz, "Inside the Mind of an Ivy League Professor," Frontpagemag.com (August 30, 2002), available at http://www.frontpagemag.com/Articles/ReadArticle.asp?ID=2642.
14. Ibid.
15. Steve Sexton, "School Sponsored 911 Remembrance Day to Exclude Patriotic Symbols and Religious References," *California Patriot,* 6 September 2002, available at http://www.frontpagemag.com/Articles/Printable.asp?ID=2783.
16. Ibid.
17. "Ethics, Enron, and American Higher Education: An NAS/Zogby Poll of College Seniors," National Association of Scholars (July 2002), available at http://www.nas.org/reports/zogethics_poll/zogby_ethics_report.htm.
18. http://www.nas.org/print/pressreleases/hqnas/releas_02jul02.htm
19. Sexton.

20. John Leo, "Professors Who See No Evil," *U.S. News & World Report* (July 22, 2002).

21. Jason Williams, "Student: Attack Praised," *Daily Aztec,* available at http://www.dailyaztec.com/Archive/Fall-2001/10-17-01/city/city01.html.

22. Ibid.

23. http://www.academia.org/news/san_diego.html

24. Williams.

25. Ibid.

26. Schemo.

27. http://www.academia.org/news/san_diego.html

28. Williams.

29. Schemo.

30. Ibid.

31. Gordon Dillow, "College's Reaction to Falsehoods Belies Justice," *Orange County Register* (December 13, 2001).

32. Schemo.

33. Dillow.

34. Ibid.

35. Ibid.

36. Schemo.

37. "A Double Standard," *Orange County Register* (April 19, 2002), Editorial.

38. Anne D. Neal, Jerry Martin, and Mashad Moses, *Losing America's Memory: Historical Illiteracy in the 21st Century* (Washington, D.C.: American Council of Trustees and Alumni, 2000), 2. To view the entire report, go to http://www.goacta.org/Reports/acta_american_memory.pdf. Adobe Acrobat reader is necessary to view the files.

39. Ellen Sorokin, "University to Replace Western Civilization Classes," *Washington Times* (April 19, 2002).

40. Ibid.

41. Ibid.

42. Diane Alden, "Occum's Razor at PCU," NewsMax.com (December 5, 2001), available at http://www.newsmax.com/commentarchive.shtml?a=2001/12/5/190432.

43. Neal, Martin, and Moses.

44. Young America's Foundation, "The Dirty Dozen: Twelve College Courses YOU Are Paying For," at http://www.yaf.org/press/08_30_02.html.

45. Regarding Italian and German internment, see:

http://www.foitimes.com/internment/FeingoldS1356.htm

http://www.internment.org/ja_faq.shtml

http://www.house.gov/apps/list/press/ny17_engel/pr010327.html

http://www.sfmuseum.org/hist8/evac.html

http://www.osia.org/public/newsroom/pr11_08_00.htm

http://www.villagevoice.com/issues/0015/goodyear.php

46. There are a number of sources that should be referred to for a complete view of Japanese atrocities and war crimes during World War II, including:

Iris Chang and William C. Kirby, *The Rape of Nanking: The Forgotten Holocaust of World War II* (New York: Penguin USA, 1998).

Gavan Daws, *Prisoners of the Japanese: POWS of World War II in the Pacific* (New York: Quill/William Morrow & Co., Inc., 1996).

George L. Hicks, *The Comfort Women: Japan's Brutal Regime of Enforced Prostitution in the Second World War* (New York: W. W. Norton & Co., 1997).

Timothy P. Maga, *Judgment at Tokyo: The Japanese War Crimes Trials* (Kentucky: University Press of Kentucky, 2001).

Yuki Tanaka, Toshiyuki Tanaka, and Yukiko Tanaka, *Hidden Horrors: Japanese War Crimes in World War II* (Boulder, Colo.: Westview Press, 1998).

47. "Abolish the White Race," *Harvard Magazine*, vol. 105, no. 1 (2002), 30. See http://www.harvard-magazine.com/on-line/0902135.html.

48. http://reason.com/0003/fe.ak.thought.shtml

49. Paul Craig Roberts, "Harvard Hates the White Race?" at http://www.vdare.com/roberts/harvard_genocide.htm.

50. http://www.harvard-magazine.com

51. Peter Berkowitz, "The Utilitarian Horrors of Peter Singer," *New Republic Online* (March 8, 2001), available at http://www.tnr.com/011000/coverstory011000.html.

52. Peter Singer, "Heavy Petting," available at http://www.nerve.com/opinions/singer/heavypetting/main.asp.

53. Ibid.

54. Berkowitz.

55. Ibid.

56. "The Appointment of Peter Singer," The President's Page, *Princeton Weekly Bulletin* (December 7, 1998), available at - http://www.princeton.edu/pr/pwb/98/1207/singer.htm.

57. Ibid.

58. "Group Honors PC Extremists," *CNSNews.com* (April 3, 2001).

Chapter 7

1. Judith Levine, *Harmful to Minors: The Perils of Protecting Children from Sex* (Minneapolis, Minn.: University of Minnesota Press, 2002), 225.

2. Anne Hendershott, *The Politics of Deviance* (San Francisco, Calif.: Encounter Books, 2002), 111.

3. For the most comprehensive data on child abuse and neglect, visit the National Clearinghouse on Child Abuse and Neglect at http://www.calib.com/nccanch/stats/index.cfm.

4. Michelle Burford, "Girls and Sex: You Won't Believe What's Going On," *O: The Oprah Magazine* (November 2002), 212–15.

5. "Suicide in the United States," Centers for Disease Control, available at http://www.cdc.gov/ncipc/factsheets/suifacts.htm.

6. Lynn Franey, "Many Criticize Professor's Writings on Pedophilia," *Kansas City Star* (April 1, 2002), also available at http://www.kansascity.com/mld/kansascity/news/local/2973524.htm.

7. Hendershott, 111.

8. Levine, xxxiv.

9. Meg Meeker, M.D., *Epidemic: How Teen Sex Is Killing Our Kids* (Washington, D.C.: Lifeline Press, 2002), 11–18. For complete up-to-date reporting on the epidemic, go to http://www.cdc.gov/nchstp/dstd/Stats_Trends/Trends2000.pdf and http://www.cdc.gov/nchstp/od/nchstp.html.

10. Ibid., 12.

11. Ibid., 12–16.

12. http://www.agi-usa.org

13. "Minors and the Right to Consent to Health Care," Alan Guttmacher Institute, available at http://www.agi-usa.org/pubs/ib_minors_00.html.

14. http://www.upress.umn.edu/HarmfultoMinorsQandA.html

15. Levine, cover flap.

16. Ibid., 89.

17. "Furor Over Youth Sex Book," Associated Press (April 4, 2002), also available at http://www.cbsnews.com/stories/2002/04/04/print/main505422.shtml.

18. Ibid.

19. http://www.msmagazine.com/oct01/dykes.html

20. http://www.worldnetdaily.com/news/article.asp?ARTICLE_ID=27104

21. There are two excellent resources regarding the impact of trauma on children and adults. Generally regarded as a classic in the field of psychology and the issue of trauma is a book I cited in chapter 1, Judith Herman's *Trauma and Recovery: The Aftermath of Violence—From Domestic Abuse to Political Terror.* See also Marta Cullberg Weston, *A Psychosocial Model of Healing from the Traumas of Ethnic Cleansing: The*

Case of Bosnia (Sweden: The Kvinna till Kvinna Foundation, 2001). Despite the specificity of the paper's title, the overview of the impact of trauma in general is excellent. This report can be accessed online at http://www.iktk.se/projekt/rapporter/Healingmodell.pdf. Adobe Acrobat reader is necessary to view the file.

22. http://www.time.com/time/magazine/notebook/0%2C9485%2C1101020415%2C00.html

23. http://www.thenation.com/doc.mhtml?i=20020520&s=wypijewski

24. For these and other comments, visit http://www.upress.umn.edu/HarmfultoMinorspraise.html

25. http://www.usatoday.com/news/nation/2002/04/17/adult-child-sex.htm

26. http://abcnews.go.com/sections/us/DailyNews/childsex_book020405.html

27. Dr. Laura Schlessinger, "Good Science Takes a Long Time," - http://www.worldnetdaily.com/news/printer-friendly.asp?ARTICLE_ID=27510 and http://www.usatoday.com/news/nation/2002/04/17/adult-child-sex.htm.

28. Joann Wypijewski, "The Wonder Years," *The Nation* (May 2, 2002), available at http://www.thenation.com/doc.mhtml?i=20020520&s=wypijewski.

29. Robert Stacy McCain, "Endorsement of Adult-Child Sex on Rise," *Washington Times* (April 19, 2002). Also see http://www.leadershipcouncil.org/Research/Rind/Rind-legal/rind-legal.html, and http://www.washtimes.com/culture/20020419-75530376.htm.

30. Ibid.

31. Franey.

32. Ibid.

33. McCain.

34. Ibid.

35. http://www.siecus.org

36. http://www.siecus.org/school/index.html

37. SIECUS, *Guidelines for Comprehensive Sexuality Education: Kindergarten-12th Grade*, 2nd ed. (New York: SIECUS), 3. You should personally review the entire set of guidelines at http://www.siecus.org/pubs/guidelines/guidelines.pdf.

38. Ibid.

39. http://www.siecus.org/pubs/srpt/srpt0020.html

40. Meeker, 28.

41. http://www.siecus.org/pubs/fact/fact0016.html

42. George Archibald, "Miss America Told to Zip It on Chastity Talk," *Washington Times* (October 9, 2002).

43. Ibid.

44. Ibid.

45. Lisa De Pasquale, "Miss America Chiefs Turn Politically Correct . . .," Clare Boothe Luce Policy Institute, available at - http://www.cblpolicyinstitute.org/missamerica2003.htm.

46. George Archibald, "Pageant Permits Promotion of Chastity," *Washington Times* (October 10, 2002).

47. Ibid.

48. http://www.plannedparenthood.org/library/facts/14anti-choice FS.html

49. http://www.plannedparenthood.org/politicalarena/From_Our_Perspective.html

50. http://www.plannedparenthood.org/about/president/020416_yale.html

51. http://www.plannedparenthood.org/centralok/edsafese.htm

52. http://www.plannedparenthood.org/library/sti/011120_hpv.html

53. Ibid.

54. http://www.teenwire.com/index.asp

55. Ibid.

56. Ibid.

57. http://www.courttv.com/trials/letourneau

58. Denise Noe, "Mary Kay Letourneau: The Romance That Was a Crime," available at http://www.crimelibrary.com/criminal_mind/psychology/mary kay_letourneau/5.htm.

59. http://www.courttv.com/trials/letourneau/background.html

60. David Kupelian, "'Pedophile Priests' and Boy Scouts," World NetDaily.com (May 8, 2002), available at http://www.world netdaily.com/news/article.asp?ARTICLE_ID=27539.

61. Ibid.

62. Ibid.

63. Hanna Rosin, "Priest Survey: Gay Cliques Exist," *Washington Post* (August 16, 2002), A6.

64. Ibid.

65. Michael S. Rose, *Goodbye, Good Men* (Washington, D.C.: Regnery Publishing, 2002).

66. Laurie Goodstein, "Trail of Pain in Church Crisis Leads to Nearly Every Diocese," *New York Times* (January 12, 2003).

67. Ibid.

68. Ibid.

69. Marco R. della Cava, "Church Calls Acts 'Disordered,' Gays Feel 'Blamed,'" *USA Today* (June 12, 2002). At http://www .usatoday.com/news/nation/2002/06/12/acov-usat.htm.

Chapter 8

1. Merriam-Webster's Collegiate Dictionary, 10th ed. (Springfield, Mass.: 1995).

2. Michael Medved, *Hollywood vs. America* (New York: HarperPerennial, 1992), 163.

3. Tammy Bruce, *The New Thought Police* (Roseville, Calif.: Prima, 2001), 173–206.

4. Karl Zinsmeister, "Growing Up Scared," *Atlantic Monthly* (June 1990), 53.

5. William J. Bennett, *The Index of Leading Cultural Indicators* (Washington, D.C.: Empower America, Heritage Foundation and Free Congress Foundation, 1993).

6. Douglas Smith and G. Roger Jarjoura, "Social Structure and Criminal Victimization," *Journal of Research in Crime and Delinquency,* vol. 25 (February 1988), 27–52. Also see Robert J. Sampson, "Urban Black Violence: The Effect of Male Joblessness and Family Disruption," *American Journal of Sociology,* vol. 93 (1987), 348–82. For an excellent overall analysis of the impact of single-parent households, see Barbara Dafoe Whitehead, "Dan Quayle Was Right," *Atlantic Monthly (Online)* (April 1993), available at http://www.theatlantic.com/politics/family/danquayl.htm.

7. Judith Michaelson, "Murphy: Off Deadline," *Los Angeles Times* (April 13, 1998).

8. Ibid.

9. http://www.worldnetdaily.com/news/article.asp?ARTICLE_ID=27597

10. http://www.cnn.com/2002/SHOWBIZ/TV/04/12/ozzy.star/index.html

11. Paul Bedard, "Washington Whispers," *U.S. News & World Report* (May 14, 2002).

12. http://www.mtv.com/onair/osbournes/law_kelly.jhtml

13. http://www.mtv.com/onair/osbournes/law_jack.jhtml?lNum=2

14. http://www.mtv.com/onair/osbournes/law_parents.jhtml

15. http://people.aol.com/people/special/0,11859,393462,00.html

16. James Poniewozik, "Ozzy, Not Ozzie," *Time* (March 4, 2002).

17. Jennifer Harper, "Ozzy & Harried," *Washington Times* (May 7, 2002).

18. For details about Viacom and all the elements of this global media megacompany, go to http://www.viacom.com.

19. http://www.cbsnews.com/stories/2002/05/10/print/main508651.shtml

20. Tammy Bruce, "Joe Liar," NewsMax.com, (January 13, 2003), available at http://www.newsmax.com/archives/articles/2003/1/13/123458.shtml.

21. http://media.guardian.co.uk/broadcast/story/0,7493,866514,00.html

22. Scott Collins, "Reality TV Leaves Bad Taste," *Hollywood Reporter* (January 17, 2003).

23. Bill O'Reilly, "Another Outrage by a Despicable Television Network," Talking Points Memo (November 12, 2002), available at http://www.foxnews.com/story/0,2933,70065,00.html.

24. Ibid. Also see http://www.vh1.com/shows/dyn/music_behind_bars/62206/episode_about.jhtml.

25. Lowell Ponte, "Rock Left, Rock Right," FrontPageMag.com (October 18, 2002), available at http://www.frontpagemag.com/Articles/ReadArticle.asp?ID=3990.

26. Ibid.

27. http://www.vh1.com/shows/dyn/music_behind_bars/61494/episode_notes.jhtml

28. Bruce, *The New Thought Police*, 59–82.

29. Richard Poe, "Why Cops and Firemen Hate Hillary," *NewsMax.com* (March 29, 2002), available at http://www.newsmax.com/commentarchive.shtml?a=2002/3/29/175614.

30. "Cyber Alert," Media Research Center, available at - http://www.mediaresearch.org/cyberalerts/2002/cyb20020830.asp#3.

31. Lisa de Moraes, "CNN Caught in Zipper Ad for Paula Zahn," *Washington Post* (January 8, 2002), The TV Column.

32. Jim Hu, "AOL Taps Studio Exec . . .," CNET News.com, available at http://news.com.com/2100-1023-253770.html?tag=bplst.

33. Moraes.

34. Bill Moyers, *NOW*, Public Broadcasting System, (November 8, 2002), Commentary. Available at: http://www.pbs.org/now/commentary/moyers15.html

35. http://www.emonline.com/topstorys/101402powerfullist.html

36. Adam Buckman, "PBS Yanks 9-11 Song," *New York Post* (June 22, 2002).

37. Ibid.

38. Brian Carnell, "The 'Good Rape': The Vagina Monologues Returns" (August 7, 2000), available at http://www.equity feminism.com/articles/2000/000029.html.

39. Eve Ensler, *The Vagina Monologues* (New York: Villard, 2001), 80–81.

40. Ibid.

41. Ensler, xxviii.

42. Bruce, *The New Thought Police*, 72–73.

43. http://www.donmega.com

44. http://www.fridayafternext.com/index_cast.html

45. Frank Rich, "Mr. Ambassador," *New York Times Magazine* (November 3, 2002).

46. Ibid.

47. For fun, as well as an excellent assessment of what has gone wrong with Dowd, see Josh Chavetz, "The Immutable Laws of Maureen Dowd, a Guide to Reading the New York Times Columnist," *The Weekly Standard* 8, no. 5 (October 14, 2002), also available at http://www.weeklystandard.com/Content/Public/Articles/000/000/001/741snfel.asp.

48. Maureen Dowd, "Rapture and Rupture," *New York Times* (October 6, 2002), Editorial Desk.

49. Maureen Dowd, "The Soufflé Doctrine," *New York Times* (October 20, 2002), Editorial Desk.

50. Maureen Dowd, "The Boomers' Crooner," *New York Times* (November 24, 2002), Editorial Desk.

51. Bernard Goldberg, "On Media Bias, Network Stars Are Rather Clueless," *Wall Street Journal* (May 24, 2001). Also see Bernard Goldberg, *Bias* (Washington, D.C.: Regnery Publishing, 2001), 223.

322 · NOTES

Chapter 9

1. Michael Browning, "The Day Nate Brazill Shot Barry Grunow," *Palm Beach Post* (June 11, 2000), available at http://www.gopbi.com/partners/pbpost/news/grunow6.html.

2. Dave Kopel, "Gunned Down: The Case for Prohibiting Abusive Lawsuits," *National Review* (November 15, 2002), available at http://www.nationalreview.com/kopel/kopel111502.asp.

3. http://www.handgunsmag.com/dynamic.asp?intSectionID=342&intArticleID=3338

4. http://www.click10.com/mia/news/stories/news-178688020021114-161135.html

5. Tammy Bruce, *The New Thought Police,* (Roseville, Calif.: Prima, 2001), 35–49.

6. "Defendant in Samantha Runnion Killing Waives Preliminary Hearing," Fox News (December 2, 2002), available at http://www.foxnews.com/story/0,2933,71968,00.html.

7. Christine Hanley and Evan Halper, "Kidnapping: As Events Unfold, Erin Runnion Calls Daughter a 'Fighter' and Hopes for Her Escape," *Los Angeles Times* (July 17, 2002).

8. Tina Dirmann, "Did System Fail to Protect Samantha? . . . ," *Los Angeles Times* (July 27, 2002).

9. Ibid.

10. Bill O'Reilly, "Blood Money," WorldNetDaily.com (July 25, 2002), available at http://www.worldnetdaily.com/news/article.asp?ARTICLE_ID=28404.

11. http://www.jpozzalaw.com

12. http://www.abanet.org/cpr/mrpc/rule_1_16.html

13. Kenneth V. Lanning, *Child Molesters: A Behavioral Analysis* (Washington, D.C.: National Center for Missing and Exploited Children, 2001), 143. For a comprehensive analysis of the subject, you can download the 160-page report at - http://www.missingkids.com/download/nc70.pdf.

NOTES • 323

14. Christine Hanley and Greg Krikorian, "FBI Says Slain Girl's Abductor Sent Message: 'Come Find Me' . . . ," *Los Angeles Times* (July 18, 2002).

15. Tony Perry, "Jurors Recommend Death for Westerfield . . . ," *Los Angeles Times* (September 17, 2002).

16. J. Harry Jones, "Plea Deal 'Minutes Away' When Body Found," *San Diego Union-Tribune* (September 17, 2002).

17. Kristen Green, "Jury Appears Weary of Bug Battle," *San Diego Union-Tribune* (August 2, 2002).

18. Kristen Green, "Jury Recommends Death | Jury Went About Work Slowly, Methodically," *San Diego Union-Tribune* (September 17, 2002).

19. Alex Roth, "Reduced Westerfield Sentence Sought . . ." *San Diego Union-Tribune* (December 17, 2002).

20. Alex Roth, "Feldman Discusses Trial in Magazine," *San Diego Union-Tribune* (December 1, 2002). You can view the *Trib*'s reporting of the interview at http://www.signonsandiego .com/news/metro/danielle/20021201-9999_1m1feldman.html.

21. Ibid.

22. "N.J. Teacher Who Had Sex with 13-Year-Old Student Gets Probation," Associated Press (May 23, 2002).

23. Associated Press, "Probation Sentence Appealed for Teacher Who Had Sex with Teen," *Asbury Park Press* (May 25, 2002).

24. Ibid.

25. "N.J. Teacher."

26. "Probation Sentence Appealed."

27. Philip Messing, "'Tryst' Rap for Teacher: She Bedded Male Catholic-School Teen: DA," *New York Post* (October 3, 2002).

28. Maria Panaritis, "For Some, Race Plays Role in Vet Rape Case . . . ," *Philadelphia Inquirer* (October 30, 2000), City and Region, PB01.

29. "Judge Reynolds' Bad Judgment; Jurist Mishandled Vet Rape Case," *Philadelphia Daily News* (August 23, 2001), Editorial, 15.

30. Panaritis.

31. "Judge Reynolds' Bad Judgment."

32. Jacqueline Soteropoulos, "Judge Properly Handled Rape Case, Board Finds . . . ," *Philadelphia Inquirer* (March 15, 2002), City, B1.

33. Ibid.

34. Ibid.

35. Dale Mezzacappa, "Harsher Sentence Sought in Rape Case," *Philadelphia Inquirer* (August 27, 2001), City, B1.

36. Phuong Ly, "Ruling Questions Accuser's Motivation," *Washington Post* (March 2, 2002).

37. Phuong Ly, "Judge Who Voided Rape Verdict Ready to 'Fight Back,'" *Washington Post* (March 27, 2002), B5.

38. "Injudicious," *Washington Post* (August 30, 2002), Editorial, A22.

39. Ibid.

40. Ibid.

41. Tracy Johnson, "Filming Up Women's Skirts Is Ruled Legal," *Seattle-Post Intelligencer* (September 20, 2002), also available at http://www.msnbc.com/local/PISEA/87863.asp?0dm=N238 N&cp1=1.

42. http://www.womensenews.org/article.cfm/dyn/aid/1054/context/outrage

43. Johnson.

44. ABCnews.com at http://abcnews.go.com/sections/GMA/Good MorningAmerica/GMA020923Upskirting_ruling.html. This quote is found in edited form in the text of the interview. For the full quote, see the video link on the page.

45. Johnson.

46. ABCnews.com.

47. Ibid.

48. Ibid.

49. Johnson.

50. Paul Queary, "Wash. Court: Voyeurism Law Doesn't Outlaw Upskirt Shots," Associated Press (September 19, 2002), available at http://www.saljournal.com/stories/092002/new_skirt .html.

51. Mitchell Landsburg, "Prisoner Received Heart Transplant . . . ," *Los Angeles Times* (January 26, 2002).

52. Ibid.

53. James Sterngold, "Inmate's Transplant Prompts Questions of Costs and Ethics," *New York Times* (January 31, 2002).

54. Dr. John Fung, "Transplants for Prisoners," Commentary, available at http://abcnews.go.com/sections/living/DailyNews/ oncall_transplant_prisoners_FUNG020303.html.

55. Landsburg.

56. American Medical Association, "Limited Organ Supply Raises Allocation Concerns," *American Medical News* (July 1, 2002), available at http://www.ama-assn.org/sci-pubs/am news/pick_02/prca0701.htm.

57. Landsburg.

58. David L. Perry, "Should Violent Felons Receive Organ Transplants?" available at http://www.scu.edu/ethics/publications/ submitted/Perry/transplant.html.

59. Fung.

60. American Medical Association, "Limited Organ Supply . . ."

61. Landsburg.

Index

Planned Parenthood, 198, 213–217
adolescents, Web site for, 217–220
Safer Sex fact sheet, 214–215
Plato, 178, 179
PMS (premenstrual syndrome), 152
Politics
gays and lesbians in, 89
puritanical compulsion and, 30
Pol Pot, 179
Pornography. *See also* Child pornography
NOW (National Organization for Women) and, 73
Postpartum depression, 18
NOW (National Organization for Women) and, 63–66, 67–70
Yates, Andrea and, 62
Postpartum psychosis, 66
Powell, Colin, 122
Poz magazine, 98
Pozza, John, 267–269
Premarriage counseling, 78
Presidential Rally for Family, Faith and Freedom, 51
Priest sexual abuse scandal, 19, 46–49, 222–228
Levine, Judith on, 201–202
seminaries, homosexuality in, 225–226
Steinem, Gloria on, 83–84
Princeton University, 190–191
Prisons and prisoners
music of prisoners, VH1 showcasing, 244–247
transplant operation for prisoner, 283–287
Pro-choice position, 199–200
Project Reality, 212
Promise Keepers, 70–74
Prostitution, 73
Prudence, 43
Prudishness, 235
Psycho Active (X-Raided), 137, 138
Psychological Bulletin, 203
Public Broadcasting System (PBS), 108
NOW (Moyers), 250–252
Pulitzer Prize, 257
Puritanical compulsion, 30

Q

Qigong, 77
Quayle, Dan, 236–237
Osbourne, Ozzy and, 238–239
Quindel, Jessica, 168, 170
Quindlen, Anna, 64

R

Race Traitor (Ignatiev), 188–189
Racism, 123
Jackson, Michael and, 148
Japanese internment, World War II, 185–188
as relic, 133
Rainbow/Pu$H Coalition Web site, 145
Rand, Ayn, 87
RAND Corporation, 126
Rangel, Charles, 123
Rape, 84
date rape, 71
leal system and, 276–278
in *The Vagina Monologues*, 252–254
Rap music, 134–139
crime and, 141–143
Interscope Records and, 145–146
Jackson, Jesse on, 140–141
Reagan, Nancy, 291–293
Reagan, Ronald, 86, 162
Alzheimer's Disease and, 289–293
Reality programming, 243
Reassignment surgery, 95
Red Cross blood donations, 101–103
Red flags, 23–24
Gender Identity Disorder (GID), 92–93
Redford, Robert, 251
Red Pope I-III (Serrano), 53
Religion. *See also* Christianity; Islam; Jews and Judaism
moral judgments and, 35
NOW (National Organization for Women) and, 74–77
Religion-neutral language, 56
Renna, Cathy, 227
Reproductive freedom, 217
Republican Party, black community and, 125

Respect, black youths and, 123
Respect, Inc., 211
Reynolds, Abram Frank, 276–278
Rhodes, Sacaree, 277
Rice, Condoleezza, 86, 122
Rich, Frank, 255–257
Richardson, Sidney R., 279
Ricketts, Glenn, 177
Rind Report, 203
Rios, Sandy, 213
Roberts, Paul Craig, 189
Robertson, Pat, 34
Roosevelt, Franklin D., 86
Roper Organization, 177
Rose, Michael, 224, 225, 226
Ross, Diana, 148
Rowan, Carl, 123
Rubino, Stephen, 223
Runnion, Eric, 266–267
Runnion, Samatha, 210, 266–269

S

Sabia, Joseph, 166
Sadomasochism, 89–90
Safe sex, 200, 213
Safire, William, 34
St. John the Divine Episcopal Cathedral Church, Manhattan, 53
Salon.com
  on Giuliani, Rudolph, 40
  on Presidential Rally for Family, Faith and Freedom, 50–51
  on White, Edmund, 97
  on Yates, Andrea, 64
San Diego Union-Tribune, 270, 271, 272–273
San Francisco Art Institute, 21–22
San Francisco Department of Health campaign, 115–117
Sarandon, Susan, 14
Satanism, 240
Satel, Sally, 66
Scaruzzi, John, 276, 278
Schlessinger, Laura, 1–2
  on Levine, Judith, 203
Schlessinger, Lew, 1–2
Schneider, Joel, 117, 119
Schools. *See also* Academic Elite; Sex education
  GLSEN in, 103–109
  rap music and, 134
Seale, Bobby, 130
Second Vatican Council, 225
Self-control, ,black youths and, 123
Self-indulgence, 12
September 11th attacks, 159–160
  Cornell University and, 165–166
  University of California, Berkeley and, 168–169
Seraceno, Jon, 155
Serial killers, 85
Serrano, Andres, 52–54
  Penn State talk, 54–55
Sesame Street, 117–119
Sex education, 200, 206–207
  organizations against, 211
  SIECUS guidelines, 207–210
Sex play, 213–214
Sex tourism, 112
Sexual abstinence
  abstinence-only education, 200–201
  campaign for, 212–213
  Planned Parenthood and, 214
  in priesthood, 224
Sexual abuse. *See also* Child abuse/molestation; Priest sexual abuse scandal
  gay men and, 99
Sexual discrimination, NOW and, 62–63
Sexual freedom, 195–196
Sexual harassment, Promise Keepers and, 71
Sexual issues in media, 232–233, 240
Sexuality Information and Education Council of the United States (SIECUS), 207–210
Sexualization of children, 193–228
  legal system and, 273–279
  Planned Parenthood and, 213–217
  SIECUS and, 211
  value-neutral language, 205
Sexual promiscuity, 18. *See also* AIDS; Priest sexual abuse scandal

Printed in the United States
by Baker & Taylor Publisher Services